Epistemic Angst

Soochow University Lectures in Philosophy

Chienkuo Mi, General Editor

The Soochow University Lectures in Philosophy are given annually at Soochow University in Taiwan by leading international figures in contemporary analytic philosophy.

Also in the series:

Robert Audi, *Moral Perception*
Scott Soames, *What Is Meaning?*
Ernest Sosa, *Knowing Full Well*

Epistemic Angst

RADICAL SKEPTICISM AND THE
GROUNDLESSNESS OF OUR BELIEVING

Duncan Pritchard

PRINCETON UNIVERSITY PRESS
PRINCETON AND OXFORD

Copyright © 2016 by Princeton University Press

Published in association with Soochow University (Taiwan)

Published by Princeton University Press, 41 William Street, Princeton, New Jersey 08540

In the United Kingdom: Princeton University Press, 6 Oxford Street, Woodstock, Oxfordshire OX20 1TR

press.princeton.edu

Cover art: *Ghetto Theatre* by David Bomberg. Courtesy of the Ben Uri Gallery and Museum, London.

All Rights Reserved

First paperback printing, 2019

Paper ISBN 978-0-691-18343-5

The Library of Congress has cataloged the cloth edition as follows:

Pritchard, Duncan.
Epistemic angst : radical skepticism and the groundlessness of our believing / Duncan Pritchard.
pages cm. — (Soochow University lectures in philosophy)
Includes bibliographical references and index.
ISBN 978-0-691-16723-7 (hardcover : alk. paper) 1. Skepticism. 2. Knowledge, Theory of. 3. Belief and doubt. I. Title.
B837.P75 2016
121—dc23
2015005925

British Library Cataloging-in-Publication Data is available

Clarke epigram appears courtesy of the *Journal of Philosophy* 1972.

Wittgenstein epigrams appear courtesy of Blackwell 1969.

This book has been composed in Sabon LT Std

For Mandi, Ethan, and Alexander

What is the skeptic examining: our most fundamental convictions, or the product of a large piece of philosophising about empirical knowledge done before he comes on stage?
—Thompson Clarke, "The Legacy of Skepticism," 754

Contents

Acknowledgments	xiii
Introduction	1
Part 1. Epistemic Angst	9
Chapter 1. Radical Skepticism and Closure	11
1. The Contemporary Radical Skeptical Paradox	11
2. Undercutting versus Overriding Anti-skeptical Strategies	16
3. An Overriding Anti-skeptical Strategy (I): Nonclosure	17
4. An Overriding Anti-skeptical Strategy (II): Epistemic Externalism	19
5. Radical Skepticism about Rationally Grounded Knowledge	22
6. An Overriding Anti-skeptical Strategy (III): Abductivism	25
7. Concluding Remarks	28
Chapter 2. Radical Skepticism and Underdetermination	29
0. Introductory Remarks	29
1. Radical Skepticism and the Underdetermination Principle	29
2. An Overriding Anti-skeptical Strategy: Epistemic Externalism	32
3. Attributer Contextualism as an Overriding Anti-skeptical Strategy	36
4. Attributer Contextualism as an Undercutting Anti-skeptical Strategy	40
5. Comparing the Two Forms of Radical Skepticism	46
6. The Source of Underdetermination-Based Radical Skepticism	49
7. Two Sources of Radical Skepticism	54
8. Anti-skeptical Desiderata	58

Part 2. Wittgenstein and the Groundlessness of Our Believing 61

Chapter 3. Wittgenstein on the Structure of Rational Evaluation 63
- 0. Introductory Remarks 63
- 1. Wittgenstein on the Structure of Rational Evaluation 63
- 2. Wittgenstein contra the Skeptical "Paradox" 66
- 3. A Core Problem for the Wittgensteinian Account of the Structure of Rational Evaluation 70
- 4. Epistemic Ways of Developing the Wittgensteinian Account of the Structure of Rational Evaluation (I): The Externalist Reading 73
- 5. Epistemic Ways of Developing the Wittgensteinian Account of the Structure of Rational Evaluation (II): The Entitlement Reading 77
- 6. A Nonepistemic Way of Developing the Wittgensteinian Account of the Structure of Rational Evaluation: The Nonpropositional Reading 84
- 7. Concluding Remarks 87

Chapter 4. Hinge Commitments 89
- 0. Introductory Remarks 89
- 1. The Nonbelief Reading 90
- 2. Hinge Commitments 94
- 3. Anti-skeptical Contrasts (I): Inferential Contextualism 103
- 4. Anti-skeptical Contrasts (II): Strawsonian Naturalism 110
- 5. Anti-skeptical Contrasts (III): Davidsonian Content Externalism 112
- 6. Wittgensteinian Anti-skepticism and Underdetermination-Based Radical Skepticism 113
- 7. Epistemic Priority and Underdetermination-Based Radical Skepticism 116
- 8. Concluding Remarks 118

Part 3. Epistemological Disjunctivism 121

Chapter 5. Epistemological Disjunctivism and the Factivity of Reasons 123
- 0. Introductory Remarks 123
- 1. Epistemological Disjunctivism in Outline 123

2. Three Core Problems for Epistemological Disjunctivism   127
　　3. Epistemological Disjunctivism qua Anti-skeptical
　　　　Strategy   132
　　4. Radical Skepticism and Favoring/Discriminating Epistemic
　　　　Support   136
　　5. Concluding Remarks   142

Chapter 6. Epistemological Disjunctivism and Closure-Based
　　Radical Skepticism   144

　　0. Introductory Remarks   144
　　1. Anti-skeptical Contrasts (I): Rational Support
　　　　Contextualism   144
　　2. Anti-skeptical Contrasts (II): Contrastivism   153
　　3. Anti-skeptical Contrasts (III): Dogmatism   157
　　4. A Weakness in Epistemological Disjunctivism   160
　　5. Epistemological Disjunctivism and Its Competitors   163
　　6. Concluding Remarks   166

Part 4. Farewell to Epistemic Angst   167

Chapter 7. Farewell to Epistemic Angst   169

　　0. Introductory Remarks   169
　　1. Recap: The Problem of Radical Skepticism   169
　　2. The Biscopic Proposal: Epistemic Angst Avoided   173
　　3. Some Anti-skeptical Contrasts   179
　　4. Concluding Postscript: Epistemic Vertigo   184

Notes   189

Bibliography   217

Index   237

Acknowledgments

THE PROBLEM OF RADICAL SKEPTICISM is a topic that I've worked on, intermittently, for about twenty years, and hence there are a lot of people I should acknowledge. To begin with, I'd like to mention those philosophers whose work has been such a big influence on my thinking in this regard. That the work of John McDowell falls into this category will be obvious to any reader of this book. Less obvious, but no less significant, is the work of Michael Williams and Barry Stroud, and in particular their (respective) groundbreaking books, *Unnatural Doubts* and *The Significance of Philosophical Scepticism*. Although I think that these works are in some fundamental ways mistaken, the careful reader will probably be aware they frame a good deal of my thinking about radical skepticism.

Although I would probably have written this book eventually, what stimulated me to write it when I did was the wonderful invitation to deliver the 2013 Soochow University Lectures in Philosophy, a lecture series that is held annually in Taipei. It was vital to these lectures that a Chinese translation of the lectures appeared above me as I spoke, which meant that there really was no alternative to writing each lecture out in full well in advance of its delivery (my normal practice is to "talk to the handout/PowerPoint" when giving research presentations, and only writing the piece up once I am satisfied that it has been sufficiently exposed to philosophical critique). Delivering these lectures was a fantastic experience. A great deal of the thanks for this goes to the magnificent hospitality of Chienkuo Mi, who runs this lecture series, and who I am now pleased to count as a good friend. But everyone in Taipei was wonderfully supportive and made my stay there a delight. I should especially thank the translators of my lectures: Chienkuo Mi, Hao-Cheng Fu, and Wen-Fang Wang. Thanks also go to Cheng-Hung Tsai, Christian Wenzel, Rita Lin, Wen-Fang Wang, and Wei-Ping Zheng. Finally, I am grateful to the National Science Council (NSC 102-2912-I-031-502) and Archie Hwang (chairman and CEO of Hermes-Epitek Corporation) who generously sponsor the Soochow University Lectures in Philosophy series.

Having drafting this book in preparation for the Soochow lectures, a second piece of good fortune came along, in that Thomas Grundmann asked me whether I would be willing to have my work the subject of the 2013 Summer School in Philosophy, an event that is held annually at the

University of Cologne. The timing could not have been better, since it meant that I had the chance to revise my Soochow lectures in response to their outing in Taipei and then subject them to another intensive grilling in Cologne. Thomas was a fantastic host, and he and the rest of the participants kept me on my toes throughout. Special thanks go to Tim Kraft, Andrew Kruse, and Michael Veber. Thanks also to Cameron Boult, Elke Brendel, Gerhard Heise, Dirk Koppelberg, Chris Ranalli, Stephen Wright, and to Kölner Gymnasial- und Stiftungsfonds, and its executive director Thomas Erdle, for funding the lectures.

My original intention was to finalize the book after the Cologne summer school, but while this did prompt me to produce a new version of the manuscript, further good reasons emerged to delay the final push. The first was that in early 2014 my manuscript was chosen as the subject of the Edinburgh Epistemology Reading Group, which gave me an opportunity to work through the material with colleagues and PhD students. Many thanks to Jie Gao, who was the organizer of this group, and also the participants: Natalie Ashton, J. Adam Carter, Mikkel Gerken, Sandy Goldberg, Orestis Palermos, Stephen Ryan, Dory Scaltsas, Ben Sworn, Kevin Wallbridge, and Ju Wang. In addition, I was fortunate in the spring semester of 2014 to be able to structure an advanced course on skepticism around this manuscript, and thereby put "research-led" teaching into action. I'm very grateful to the students in this course for their engagement with the text, particularly Matthew Bixby, Ewa Jonczyk, and William Kinzelman.

I wasn't expecting the material in this book to get another outing before it was finalized, but by good fortune it did, at the conference on "Skeptical Solutions: Provocations of Philosophy," which was held at the University of Bonn in November 2014. Special thanks to the organizers, G. Anthony Bruno and Abby Rutherford. Thanks also to Donald Ainslie, Jim Conant, Michael Forster, Markus Gabriel, Hannah Ginsborg, Andrea Kern, Sebastian Rödl, and Owen Ware.

I've been very lucky in receiving detailed comments on earlier drafts of the book from several people. These include Modesto Gómez Alonso, J. Adam Carter, Gregory Gaboardi, Changsheng Lai, Kevin McCain, Peter Murphy, Genia Schönbaumsfeld, Alan Thomas, and two anonymous referees from Princeton University Press. I've also had some very fruitful conversations about core elements of the book with Sandy Goldberg, John Greco, and Ram Neta. I'm particularly grateful in this regard to Ernie Sosa, who not only provided very detailed comments on an earlier draft of the book, but also has been supportive of the project throughout.

Indeed, in general (i.e., and not just with regard to this book), I owe a great debt of thanks to Ernie (as I'm sure many epistemologists of my generation do). His work has been a tremendous influence upon my development, to the extent that I think it is fair to say that I view much of the epistemological literature through the lens that he has provided with his own stimulating and game-changing contributions to the field. But, more than that, Ernie has been a constant source of encouragement, and I feel very fortunate to have benefited from his wise counsel.

Inevitably, in a project that has been ongoing for this long, I've also profited from the input of many other people over the years, including (I fear this isn't an exhaustive list) Anna Baker, Manuel Bermudez, Sven Bernecker, (the sadly late, but very great) Tony Brueckner, Sam Carter, Quassim Cassam, Annalisa Coliva, Stefano Cossara, Dylan Dodd, Pascal Engel, Peter Fosl, Georgi Gardiner, Brian Garrett, Neil Gascoigne, Thomas Giourgas, Patrick Greenough, Adrian Haddock, Allan Hazlett, Jesper Kallestrup, Chris Kelp, Scot Kerzman, Martin Kusch, Clayton Littlejohn, Michael Lynch, Marie McGinn, Aidan McGlynn, Robin McKenna, Alan Millar, Daniele Moyal-Sharrock, Quee Nelson, Claudio Salvatore, Declan Smithies, Mark Sprevak, Claudine Tiercelin, Crispin Wright, and Elia Zardini. I'd also like to thank my old pal Michael Brady, who has been a great friend to me and my family over the years, and also an excellent person to talk to about epistemology. Thanks also to my cousin, the artist Paul Hodgson, for his advice in thinking about the cover design of the book.

Thanks to everyone at Princeton University Press for their support for this project, especially Rob Tempio and Ryan Mulligan. Thanks also to the copy editor, Joseph Dahm, for his absolutely sterling work in getting the final manuscript into shape.

Finally, on the personal front, I've dedicated this book—as I do all my books—to my wonderful wife Mandi and my boys, Ethan and Alexander. Collectively they constitute a very different kind of antidote to epistemic *angst*.

DHP
Edinburgh, 2015

Epistemic Angst

Introduction

THE PROBLEM OF RADICAL SKEPTICISM is both my first love, philosophically speaking, and my true love. It was this puzzle that got me hooked into philosophy, and it is this puzzle that I find myself returning to at regular intervals. Although I'm interested in all the main varieties of radical skepticism, the broadly Cartesian skeptical problem regarding our knowledge of the external world—at least as this problem is understood in the contemporary literature—was always the one that fascinated me the most, and it is this version of the problem that I focus on in the book (though increasingly I have become intrigued by Pyrrhonian and Kantian forms of skepticism, both of which are very different beasts).[1] I have always felt that there was something very profound about this particular philosophical problem—this putative *paradox*—and although I have attempted various responses to the puzzle over the years, I was never really convinced that any of them quite did justice to the problem.

In earlier work I tried to meet the difficulty head-on, by offering a form of neo-Mooreanism that was motivated by epistemic externalism and situated within a research program I referred to as *anti-luck epistemology*. My first monograph, *Epistemic Luck* (Oxford University Press, 2005), is a good example of this. The careful reader of this book will have spotted, however, that I was not fully persuaded, in that the anti-skeptical proposal on offer starts to look very much like a "skeptical solution" once the details are unpacked. Indeed, I found myself arguing in effect that a form of radical skepticism that is aimed specifically at the rational standing of our beliefs was pretty much correct.[2]

Over the years, my response to radical skepticism became increasingly bifurcated. On the one hand, I developed an anti-skeptical theory (the essentials of which were already present in *Epistemic Luck*) that was inspired by Wittgenstein's (1969) remarks on the structure of rational evaluation in *On Certainty*.[3] Simultaneously, I also advanced a separate proposal, inspired by John McDowell's (e.g., 1995) work, which was cast along epistemological disjunctivist lines.[4] On the face of it, these two proposals are radically different. Nonetheless, I was convinced that they belonged together, though at the outset I couldn't quite see how to connect them. Fortunately, since each of these theories is highly contentious in its own right, it was inevitable that I only ever presented work on one of the two positions at any given time, and so I could gloss over the issue of how these two parts of my overall anti-skeptical view related to one another. (Occasionally, however, someone who had heard a recent talk of mine on the other proposal would challenge me to explain myself.)

I'm not quite sure exactly when the epiphany occurred, but it was certainly while working on the book that would be published as *Epistemological Disjunctivism* (Oxford University Press, 2012) that I saw the light. Very roughly, epistemological disjunctivism is the view that when it comes to paradigm cases of knowledge, the rational support available to the subject is both reflectively accessible and factive. In particular, one's reflectively accessible rational basis for knowing that p can be that *one sees that p*, where seeing that p entails p. As far as epistemological orthodoxy goes, such a position is held to be straightforwardly incoherent.

The goal of *Epistemological Disjunctivism* was to explain why this position, far from being the utterly mad proposal that many in contemporary epistemology suppose it to be, is in fact perfectly defensible. This point is crucial because, as I also argued in this book, epistemological disjunctivism is a stance that is rooted in our ordinary epistemic practices, and would be highly desirable if true. Accordingly, if the philosophical reasons why we have rejected this natural position turn out to be dubious, such that it is a live theoretical option after all, then a powerful case can be made that we should embrace it.

Since epistemological disjunctivism is such a contentious position, one of the self-imposed constraints I operated under in that monograph was that I would defend the view by appealing only to further claims that ought to be acceptable to all epistemologists. This meant that when I got to the point in the book where I demonstrate the anti-skeptical potential of the view, it simply wasn't an option to bring in Wittgenstein's radical account of the structure of rational evaluation, as most epistemologists would regard such a view as highly contentious. Instead, epistemological disjunctivism was obliged to stand on its own two feet. The result was a new kind of neo-Mooreanism, this time set within a provocative form of nonclassical epistemic internalism rather than epistemic externalism. But I was acutely aware that the anti-skeptical story I was telling was incomplete in a fundamental way, and that the full solution lay in integrating epistemological disjunctivism with the Wittgensteinian proposal.

In order to understand why, we need to revisit a debate that occurred in the literature just over a decade ago, and which I was fortunate to play a (relatively minor) part in. This concerned the logical structure of radical skeptical arguments, and in particular whether the formulation of radical skepticism that turns on a closure-style principle is logically distinct from a superficially very similar formulation of radical skepticism that turns on what is known as an underdetermination principle. My own contribution to this debate, such as it was—see Pritchard (2005b, pt. 1; 2005f)—was to defend the claim that these epistemic principles are logically distinct, and that this may have important implications for the debate regarding radical skepticism. It was only when I was writing *Epistemological Disjunctivism*, however, that I came to the view that the logical difference between these two epistemic principles is in fact profoundly important for our understanding of the two formulations of the skeptical argument.

In particular, I came to realize that this logical difference reveals that these two formulations of radical skepticism, while superficially similar, are in fact arising out of different sources. Underdetermination-based radical skepticism is trading on a specific point about what I call the *insularity of reasons*—roughly, how the rational support our worldly beliefs enjoy, even in the best case, is compatible with their widespread falsity. In contrast, closure-based radical skepticism trades on a very different claim, which is what I call the *universality of rational evaluation*—roughly, that there are no in principle limits on the extent to which our beliefs can be rationally evaluated, such that universal rational evaluations are entirely possible. Once one understands how these two formulations of the skeptical argument arise out of different sources, then it becomes apparent why the logical differences between the two epistemic principles on which they turn are so important. In particular, what one discovers is that these two formulations of the skeptical argument really constitute distinct skeptical problems that require distinct solutions.

By recognizing this point, I was able to get a handle on just what is right and what is unsatisfying about epistemological disjunctivism from the perspective of radical skepticism. This proposal confronts the insularity of reasons thesis head-on, and demonstrates that such a thesis, far from being common sense, is in fact the product of dubious philosophical theory. As such, epistemological disjunctivism is the *antidote* to underdetermination-based radical skepticism. But if one applies this idea, ungarnished with Wittgenstein's insight about the structure of rational evaluation, to closure-based radical skepticism, then one gets an extremely epistemically immodest (and hence unpalatable) proposal, one that contends that we can have a factive rational basis for dismissing radical skeptical hypotheses.

How does the Wittgensteinian account of the structure of rational evaluation help on this score? Well, the core thought in this account is that the very idea of a fully general rational evaluation—whether of a negative (i.e., radically skeptical) or a positive (i.e., traditional anti-skeptical, such as Moorean) nature—is simply incoherent. Instead, Wittgenstein argues that it is in the very nature of a system of rational evaluation that it takes certain basic commitments—the "hinge" commitments, as he called them—as immune to rational evaluation. Surprisingly, these hinge commitments can be regarding such apparently mundane propositions as that one has two hands. According to Wittgenstein, it is only with these hinge commitments in the background that rational evaluation is even possible. The upshot is that rational evaluation is an essentially local phenomenon. Moreover, this is not because of some incidental lack on our part (e.g., a lack of imagination or consistency), but rather reflects the very nature of what is involved in rational evaluation. (As Wittgenstein expressed the matter, his point was about the "logic" of rational evaluation.)

The challenge posed by the Wittgensteinian account of the structure of rational evaluation is to explain what purchase, exactly, it offers us on the skeptical problem. On my reading of Wittgenstein, the thought is that it gains us a very good grip on closure-based radical skepticism by offering us principled grounds for rejecting the universality of rational evaluation thesis. Crucially, however, my reading of Wittgenstein enables us to reject the universality of rational evaluation thesis without thereby rejecting the closure principle, thereby ensuring that the view can retain all of our commonsense epistemological commitments. As I argue, our hinge commitments, properly understood, are simply not the kind of propositional attitude to which the closure principle (again, properly understood) is applicable. It follows that the Wittgensteinian rejection of the universality of rational evaluation is entirely consistent with the closure principle, since the latter simply does not apply to our hinge commitments.

This point is very important to the *undercutting* credentials of this form of anti-skepticism. Wittgenstein was certainly very keen to offer a response to the radical skeptical problem that demonstrated that it was a puzzle that was arising out of dubious philosophical claims that are masquerading as common sense. According to Wittgenstein, the radical skepticism problem is really a product of faulty philosophical theory, rather than representing a genuine paradoxical tension in our most fundamental epistemic commitments. The skeptical "paradox" is thus undercut, in that it is shown to not be a bona fide paradox at all (this is as opposed to the paradox being *overridden*, which is when a genuine paradox is resolved by offering a plausible form of philosophical revisionism). If the closure principle is a highly intuitive principle, then it is all to the good as far as an undercutting anti-skeptical proposal goes that it does not involve the denial of this principle.

We can now see how the Wittgensteinian proposal, when understood in the right way, can help epistemological disjunctivism with its response to radical skepticism. Whereas epistemological disjunctivism is focused on the underdetermination-based formulation of radical skepticism, which trades on the underlying insularity of reasons thesis, the Wittgensteinian proposal is instead aimed at the closure-based formulation of radical skepticism, which trades on the underlying universality of rational evaluation thesis. The crux of the matter is that if we can combine these proposals, then potentially we can offer a unified treatment of radical skepticism that deals with both formulations of the problem.

Can we combine these proposals? On the face of it, they look very different; indeed, they look antithetical, and competing. Whereas the one proposal emphasizes the locality of rational evaluation, and hence rational support, the other emphasizes the *strength* of the rational support available to us in paradigm conditions, in that it is factive. But these differences are superficial. In fact, these proposals work very well with each other, in that they are not only compatible, but also mutually supporting and philosophically in the same spirit.

The compatibility claim is just the idea that the supposed tension between these views is merely superficial. There is nothing in the idea of rational evaluation being essentially local that precludes the possibility of factive rational support in the perceptual case. And there is nothing in the idea of factive rational support that excludes the possibility that all rational evaluation is local. Once one recognizes the compatibility of these two theses, then one can see how they might be combined, and how, in particular, they might be employed to support each other. The basic idea is that each proposal is more plausible when combined with its sister view. So, it is easier to live with the essential locality of rational evaluation if one is also able to demonstrate that paradigm cases of perceptual rational support are factive. And it is easier to live with the idea that paradigm cases of perceptual rational support are factive if one embraces the essential locality of rational evaluation (i.e., because one is not thereby committed to the epistemic immodesty of supposing that one can have a factive rational basis for dismissing radical skeptical hypotheses).

Note too the extent to which these proposals are in the same spirit. We have already seen that the Wittgensteinian proposal is an undercutting treatment of the skeptical "paradox." But note that this also applies to epistemological disjunctivism, in that the guiding idea behind this view is that we have been seduced, on faulty theoretical grounds, into regarding a dubious theoretical claim (regarding the insularity of reasons) as an item of mere common sense. Both of the formulations of the skeptical problem in play, whether closure-based or underdetermination-based, are thus shown to be merely pseudo-problems.

I call the unified defense against radical skepticism the *biscopic* proposal. It is, admittedly, an ugly name—I have tried hard to find a better moniker but without success.[5] But, despite its ugliness, it does convey the bare essentials of the proposal. This is that we have, completely unbeknownst to us, been looking at this problem through, as it were, only one eye—only one eye at a time anyway—and that we need to use both of our philosophical "eyes" in order to see the problem aright. Only then can we gain the right perspective on the problem and thereby recognize what the correct solution to the problem must be.

A final comment is in order about the very notion of *epistemic angst*. The problem of radical skepticism has always been a very real existential issue for me, and so I do not use this terminology lightly. Discovering that the skeptical problem has no clear answer is something that should unsettle any responsible inquirer.[6] Note, though, that while I believe the solution I offer to the skeptical problem genuinely is a remedy for epistemic *angst*, this is not to say that the anxiety in question will be entirely removed. This is because I think there is an inevitable psychological vestige of skeptical doubt that remains even once the solution has been embraced (albeit not one that is now tracking a genuine epistemic *angst* about one's epistemic situation).

I call this psychological state *epistemic vertigo* (or *epistemic acrophobia*, if one wants to be pedantic), in order to capture the idea that it is essentially a kind of phobic reaction to one's epistemic predicament. Just as one can suffer from vertigo when high up, even while fully recognizing that one is not in any danger, so I think that even after the problem of radical skepticism has been resolved, and hence the epistemic risk posed by this problem is defused, it can nonetheless be the case that one feels a residual unease about one's epistemic situation. The reason for this disquiet is embedded in the Wittgensteinian account of the structure of rational evaluation itself. For what Wittgenstein alerts us to is how one's apparently very ordinary commitments—such as that one has two hands—can be playing a quite striking role in the system of rational evaluation. Wittgenstein wrote that our hinge commitments "lie apart from the route travelled by inquiry" (OC, §88). He means that the question of their rational standing simply never arises in normal conditions, and so we are unaware that these ordinary commitments play an extraordinary epistemic role. Once one has inquired into their rational standing, however—and the stimulus for this inquiry will almost certainly be philosophical in nature—then it is hard not to continue to be struck thereafter by their peculiarity.[7]

Another way of putting this point is that while in everyday life we do not take it as given that universal rational evaluations are possible—indeed, we don't consider the issue at all—neither do we recognize that they are impossible. That's not to say that we don't recognize that our everyday practices of giving reasons for and against particular claims is local, as we surely do recognize this. The crux of the matter is rather that our practices of rational evaluation, while local, also seem to be entirely open to indefinite broadenings of scope. That is, there seems no inherent limits to the scope of rational evaluation, even if in practice it is always local in nature. That there is such an inherent limit—that a fully general rational evaluation, one that encompassed even our hinge commitments, is impossible—is a philosophical discovery. Moreover, in discovering it, we also realize that our everyday epistemic practices disguise this fact. It is thus unsurprising, then, that even once epistemic *angst* has been removed, epistemic vertigo might well remain, for we now have a perspective on our practices of rational evaluation that is in a certain sense completely *unnatural*. We have, as it were, epistemically "ascended" and adopted a vantage point that we would not normally adopt. From this unnatural vantage point, epistemic vertigo is a natural response.

My point is that one can accept that there is a genuine phenomenon of epistemic vertigo without thereby conceding anything of substance to the radical skeptic. Epistemic *angst* is averted—this is no skeptical solution of radical skepticism. But as with any engagement with a deep philosophical problem, things are not left entirely as they were before.[8]

PART 1

Epistemic Angst

> That in order to seek truth, it is necessary once in the course of our life, to doubt, as far as possible, of all things.
> —Descartes, *The Principles of Philosophy*, Principle 1

> An admission of some question as to the mystery of existence, or the being, of the world is a serious bond between the teaching of Wittgenstein and that of Heidegger. The bond is one, in particular, which implies a shared view of what I have called the truth of skepticism, or what I might call the moral of skepticism, namely, that the human creature's basis in the world as a whole, its relation to the world as such, is not that of knowing, anyway not what we think of as knowing.
> —Stanley Cavell, *The Claim of Reason: Wittgenstein, Skepticism, Morality, and Tragedy*, 241

> For in much wisdom is much grief, and he that increaseth knowledge increaseth sorrow.
> —Ecclesiastes 1:18

CHAPTER 1

Radical Skepticism and Closure

1. The Contemporary Radical Skeptical Paradox

My focus will be on the broadly Cartesian understanding of the problem of radical skepticism that appears in the contemporary epistemological literature.[1] As we will see, we can find in this contemporary discussion of radical skepticism—at least with a little digging and reworking—the essential elements of a particular kind of skeptical challenge that is of profound philosophical importance, and which is thus a genuine source of epistemic *angst*.[2]

Radical skepticism of this form specifically concerns our knowledge of a world external to us, and it proceeds by attempting to undermine the possibility that we might have knowledge of this world. It pivots on the use of radical skeptical hypotheses, where these are scenarios that are subjectively indistinguishable from a paradigm case of perception, but where one is in fact massively deceived.[3] For our purposes, we can take the so-called brain-in-a-vat (BIV) radical skeptical scenario as representative, where this concerns an agent who from her point of view reasonably supposes herself to be in paradigm perceptual conditions, but who is in fact not perceiving a world around her at all, her beliefs being instead in response to fake "perceptual" stimuli offered by supercomputers wired up to her brain (which is floating, disembodied, in a vat of nutrients).[4]

The initial plank in the case for skepticism comes from the contention that one cannot know that one is not a BIV. Such a claim seems entirely compelling. After all, since the BIV scenario is ex hypothesi subjectively indistinguishable from normal perceptual conditions, it is hard to see how one might come to know such a thing. What kind of rational ground might one have for such a belief, given that there is no subjective basis on which one can discern that one is not in a radical skeptical scenario?

We thus have $(S_1 1)$:

$(S_1 1)$ One cannot know that one is not a BIV.[5]

The idea now is to demonstrate that this claim is in tension with our conception of ourselves as perceptually knowing a great deal about the external world. We can bring this out by considering a paradigmatic case of "everyday" perceptual knowledge, the kind of perceptual knowledge such that, if one knows anything about the external world, then one knows this. In my case, for example, this might be that I am presently sitting at my desk, typing on my computer. Call this proposition "E":

($S_1$3) One knows that E.

If I do not have the perceptual knowledge at issue in ($S_1$3), then it is hard to see how I could know anything much (at least perceptually), as my epistemic basis for this perceptual belief is rarely, if ever, bettered.

On the face of it, of course, there is no immediate tension between ($S_1$1) and ($S_1$3), in that there seems no obvious reason why it cannot be the case both that one lacks the knowledge at issue in ($S_1$1) and that one possesses the knowledge at issue in ($S_1$3). The task in hand for the skeptic is thus to motivate the following connecting claim that puts ($S_1$1) in direct conflict with ($S_1$3):

($S_1$2) If one cannot know that one is not a BIV, then one cannot know that E.[6]

If we grant ($S_1$1) and ($S_1$2) to the skeptic, then it will follow that we must reject ($S_1$3) and so embrace the skeptical implications of that move. We've already seen that there is a prima facie case for ($S_1$1), so the issue thus turns on the skeptical case for ($S_1$2). The problem the skeptic faces is that ($S_1$2) is not intuitive in the way that ($S_1$1) is, and since allowing it in conjunction with ($S_1$1) calls ($S_1$3) into question, which *is* intuitive, there is a strong prima facie case for rejecting it.

So how is the radical skeptic to motivate ($S_1$2)? The most common way of doing this in the contemporary literature is by appeal to some form of "closure" principle for knowledge. For example, the principle that knowledge is "closed" under entailments would suffice for our purposes. Here is an initial formulation:

THE CLOSURE PRINCIPLE: FIRST PASS

If S knows that p, and p entails q, then S knows that q.

So, given that being seated at one's desk entails that one is not a BIV (since this scenario concerns a disembodied brain that is floating in a vat of nutrients), it follows that if one did know the former then one would know the latter. Conversely, if one is unable to know the latter, as ($S_1$1) alleges, then one would be unable to know the former.

While this formulation of the closure principle will suffice to motivate ($S_1$2), it is not itself very convincing. There are all kinds of propositions that are entailed by propositions that, plausibly, one knows, but where it does not seem at all credible that one should know all these entailed propositions. Indeed, there are entailed propositions that one is completely unaware of, and so one cannot know because one is not even in a position to form a belief about them.

At the very least, then, we ought to restrict our attention to those propositions that one knows are entailed by what one knows, such that one is at least in a position to form beliefs about the entailed propositions and so be in the market to have knowledge of them. We thus get the following adapted formulation of the closure principle:

THE CLOSURE PRINCIPLE: SECOND PASS

If S knows that p, and S knows that p entails q, then S knows that q.

This formulation of the closure principle would equally suffice to motivate ($S_1 2$), at least insofar as we make the reasonable assumption that anyone considering this argument will know that the relevant entailment holds (henceforth we will treat this assumption as granted). But even this formulation has its problems. For example, there is nothing in this principle that demands that the subject believes the entailed proposition on the basis of the relevant entailment, and yet the idea that the subject has knowledge of the entailed proposition in such cases is surely dependent on it being so based. For instance, if a subject believed the entailed proposition on a completely independent basis, then there would be no inherent reason why her knowledge of the entailing proposition and of the entailment should incline us to regard this belief as amounting to knowledge. Instead, it would depend on the epistemic credentials of this independent basis for belief.

This highlights a deeper point about why we might find these closure-style principles compelling. This is that such principles attempt to codify how one might legitimately extend one's knowledge via competent deduction from what one already knows. That this ought to be possible looks undeniable, but we haven't quite captured this thought in either of the formulations of the closure principle just offered. This is why most commentators in the epistemological literature now tend to formulate the closure principle diachronically, as opposed to synchronically, along the following lines, such that the competent deduction element of the principle is made explicit:

THE CLOSURE PRINCIPLE

If S knows that p, and S competently deduces from p that q, thereby forming a belief that q on this basis while retaining her knowledge that p, then S knows that q.[7]

With the closure principle so formulated it is built into the principle that the subject is acquiring her belief in the entailed proposition on the basis of her undertaking a competent deduction from her existing knowledge. Moreover, since competent deductions are diachronic processes, it is also important to specify that the subject retains her knowledge in the entailing proposition throughout. For if the knowledge in the entailing proposition is lost during this process (perhaps as a result of the process itself), then clearly there is now no longer the same intuition that the entailed proposition should be known.

With the closure principle so formulated, it is hard to see how it could be denied. How could one draw a competent deduction from one's knowledge (*modulo* the caveats just noted) without thereby coming to know the deduced conclusion? As Keith DeRose (1995) has remarked, denying such a principle seems to commit one to endorsing the possibility of "abominable conjunctions"—for example, that one knows that one is presently seated at one's desk, but that one has no idea whether one is a bodiless BIV floating in a vat of nutrients (even though it is quite obvious the former entails the denial of the latter).[8] Accordingly, henceforth when we refer without qualification to the "closure principle" we will have this highly compelling articulation of the principle in mind.

With this formulation of the closure principle in play, it follows that if one did know that one is seated at a desk (E), then one could, via closure, come to know that one is not a BIV. Conversely, if one cannot know that one is not a BIV, it follows that one does not—indeed cannot—know that one is seated at a desk. So while ($S_1 2$) isn't in itself very compelling, it can be motivated via the incredibly plausible closure principle, and with ($S_1 2$) and ($S_1 1$) in play, the anti-skeptical ($S_1 3$) is under threat.

Of course, the negation of ($S_1 3$) is some logical distance away from a radical skeptical conclusion, since it directly concerns only a single proposition which has been shown to be unknown. Even so, it is not hard to see how one could derive the radical skeptical conclusion from this initial skeptical victory. For the general pattern of argument on display could be repeated any number of times to call specific propositions into play—there might be a need to vary the radical skeptical hypothesis employed on a case-by-case basis, but other than that the mechanics of the skeptical argument would stay the same. More generally, insofar as the skeptic can call into question our knowledge of something so straightforward as that one is currently seated at one's desk in (what appear to be) otherwise normal conditions, then the potentially devastating power of the skeptical argument is manifest.

What we have here is thus a putative *paradox*, in that we have a series of claims that have been shown either to be intuitive, or to be immediate consequences from intuitive claims (like the closure principle), but which are in fact in logical tension with one another, such that one of them must be denied:

THE RADICAL SKEPTICAL PARADOX (I)

($S_1$1) One cannot know that one is not a BIV.

($S_1$2) If one cannot know that one is not a BIV, then one cannot know that E.

($S_1$3) One knows that E.[9]

More generally, notice that while we have focused on a specific radical skeptical error possibility and a particular instance of everyday knowledge, the paradox in play does not trade on these details. What we have determined is that the following three claims appear to be inconsistent:

THE INCONSISTENT RADICAL SKEPTICAL TRIAD

(I) One is unable to know the denials of radical skeptical hypotheses.[10]

(II) The closure principle.

(III) One has widespread everyday knowledge.

We can usefully represent this inconsistent triad in terms of ($S_1$1–3), in that these three more specific claims present us with a concrete instance of the triad. In doing so, ($S_1$1–3) makes the inconsistency at issue in (I–III) manifest.

Granted that this is an inconsistent triad, it follows that at least one of the claims that make up this triad must be false, since they cannot all be true on pain of contradiction. But given the intuitiveness of each claim, this means that radical skepticism appears to call on us to claim something deeply counterintuitive. While we can think of radical skepticism as a philosophical *position*, such that it involves the denial of (III)—and all that this entails—it is in fact more interesting to conceive of it rather as a paradox, in the sense that we are confronted with a deep tension within our own folk epistemological concepts, one that does not appear to be amenable to any obvious solution (including the skeptical solution of denying (III), which is surely the least palatable option of those available).

In particular, if we conceive of the skeptical problem as a paradox, then we will not be tempted to try to deal with this problem by aiming to convict an actual skeptical *adversary* of some dialectical error, such as by claiming that they are being incoherent in explicitly advancing their position. For suppose it were true that there is something seriously amiss with someone trying to actively advance the radical skeptical conclusion, via a rejection of (III), that we lack widespread perceptual knowledge of the world around us. Why would this offer us any intellectual comfort? After all, we knew *already* that the denial of (III)—of ($S_1 3$), say—is implausible, so it's not as if finding out that its rejection leads to incoherence is unexpected. Moreover, the logical conflict among (I), (II), and (III) remains, even though these are three claims that we appear to be individually committed to. Far from resolving the skeptical problem (*qua* paradox), discovering that the skeptical position is incoherent seems to leave it entirely untouched.[11]

2. Undercutting versus Overriding Anti-skeptical Strategies

With the skeptical challenge so understood, how might one go about responding to it? Notice that by conceiving of the problem as a putative paradox we thereby impose some constraints on philosophically adequate responses to this problem. In particular, while denying one (or more) of the claims that make up the inconsistent triad is obviously a necessary ingredient in any adequate response to the problem, *merely* denying one of these claims will not suffice to resolve it, at least not in a philosophically satisfying way. In particular, what is further required is some diagnostic story to explain the intuitive appeal of the claim in question even despite its falsity.

We can think of these diagnostic responses to radical skepticism as being of two main varieties. The first, an *overriding anti-skeptical strategy*, will offer a revisionary diagnostic story, one on which we have an independent theoretical basis for disregarding the relevant intuition in play. On this way of dealing with the problem, the skeptical paradox is bona fide, in that there is indeed a deep tension in our epistemological concepts, pretheoretically understood, which is being exposed by this puzzle. But it is also resolvable, in that we recognize that there are independent theoretical grounds for revising our epistemological concepts in fundamental ways that avoid the puzzle.

Compare an overriding anti-skeptical strategy with an *undercutting anti-skeptical strategy*, which is a much more ambitious response to the problem. On this proposal the diagnostic story on offer is meant to demonstrate that the skeptical "paradox" in play is in fact illusory. More specifically, the aim of this approach is to show that although the skeptical problem seems to be arising out of a tension in our epistemological concepts, pretheoretically understood, in fact it is the product of specific theoretical commitments that are revealed to be dubious. The skeptical puzzle is thus shown to be the product of faulty philosophical theory and not the natural manifestation of prephilosophical common sense.[12]

While both undercutting and overriding anti-skeptical strategies can be adequate ways of dealing with the skeptical problem, undercutting anti-skeptical strategies are clearly to be preferred, all other things being equal. For if the skeptical paradox is bona fide, in that it arises out of an authentic tension within our pretheoretical epistemological concepts, then even if we can supply a sound theoretical basis for rejecting one of the claims that make up this paradox it will remain the case that the skeptical problem will generate intellectual unease. In contrast, if we can show that the skeptical "paradox" is in fact illusory, such that no theoretical revisionism is called for, then clearly there is likewise no need to regard this problem as generating any cause for genuine intellectual discomfort.[13]

Of course, one could turn this point on its head and argue that by the same token an undercutting anti-skeptical strategy is in danger of being a response to the skeptical problem that is *too* strong. For if the problem of radical skepticism is the product of illicit philosophical theory rather than ungarnished common sense, then why hasn't this fact made itself apparent long before now? It is thus crucial to undercutting anti-skeptical strategies that they incorporate some account of why the theoretical basis for radical skepticism has been so hard to discern.

We will be examining some undercutting anti-skeptical strategies in due course below. First, though, we will look at some overriding anti-skeptical strategies. Given that rejecting (S_13)/(III) is tantamount to endorsing skepticism, our focus will be on the status of (S_11)/(I) and (S_12)/(II). In this section, we will examine, and reject, two rather crude overriding anti-skeptical proposals that, respectively, target each of these two claims. As we will see, understanding why these particular overriding anti-skeptical strategies fail to be compelling will enable us to get a better sense of what is at issue in closure-based radical skepticism.

3. An Overriding Anti-skeptical Strategy (I): Nonclosure

Let's start with (S_12). The natural way to object to this claim is to challenge the closure principle that motivates it, and thus claim (II) in our radical skeptical inconsistent triad. Given the tremendous plausibility of the closure principle, as noted above, it is going to be a tough call to mount a compelling case for such an anti-skeptical proposal. Still, there is a story that can be told in this regard.

To begin with, notice that it seems right to say that someone can come to (perceptually) know that she is presently seated at her desk (E) without first having any thoughts about whether she is a BIV, or indeed the victim of any skeptical hypothesis. A fortiori, it seems right to say that someone can come to know that she is presently seated at her desk even though she does not know that she is not a BIV. We might well explain what is going on here by saying that our agent is effectively taking it as given that she is not radically and undetectably deceived about her environment, and that such an assumption (which may involve no relevant occurrent thoughts on the part of the subject) is entirely reasonable. In particular, given that our agent has been given no rational basis to take the BIV error possibility seriously, it seems entirely reasonable for her to form her beliefs as if such an error possibility were false, even though, of course, she has no obvious rational basis for dismissing this possibility.

If that's the right way to characterize what is going when one comes to perceptually knowing something mundane such as that one is seated at one's desk, then we should be suspicious of the closure principle. This principle effectively makes knowledge that one is not the victim of a radical skeptical hypothesis a requirement for mundane perceptual knowledge, when in practice it seems that one ought to be able to reasonably assume that such skeptical hypotheses do not obtain.

Moreover, one might well add, although rejecting the closure principle goes against our intuitions, given that we are faced with a paradox in this regard it is inevitable that we will have to deny *something* intuitive. Indeed, one might plausibly argue that although the closure principle is intuitive, it is *less* intuitive than the claim that we are unable to know the denials of radical skeptical hypotheses. Accordingly, if one is going to be obliged to deny something intuitive in this regard, it may as well be the closure principle.

We thus have the outlines of a fairly rudimentary overriding anti-skeptical strategy that involves the denial of the closure principle. It is an overriding anti-skeptical strategy since while it grants the intuitive force of the claims that make up the radical skeptical paradox, it nonetheless argues on independent grounds that the closure principle should be denied and thus that a particular element of this paradox—that is, the closure-based claim, ($S_1 2$)—ought to be rejected.

I doubt many would find such an approach to radical skepticism very persuasive. Indeed, it very quickly unravels on closer inspection. The appeal of this line of argument lies in how it seems to charge the closure principle with making extreme epistemic demands on our quotidian perceptual knowledge, such that if we are to have this knowledge then we must know the denials of radical skeptical hypotheses. But closure makes no such demand. In particular, it is quite compatible with the closure principle that an agent might have mundane perceptual knowledge and yet fail to know the denials of any relevant radical skeptical hypotheses.

In order to see this, we need to remember that the closure principle essentially concerns the extension of knowledge from competent deductions. It follows that a subject who has had no occurrent thoughts about radical skeptical hypotheses—and hence has not made inferences from what they know to the denials of radical skeptical hypotheses—would be completely unaffected by this principle. In particular, the closure principle makes epistemic demands only on those who, like us, have considered the problem of radical skepticism and so are fully aware of the tension between our everyday knowledge and our apparent inability to know the denials of radical skeptical hypotheses.

This anti-skeptical line thus misses its target, in that it doesn't engage with the particular nuances of the closure principle as we have formulated it in the setup of the skeptical paradox. The upshot is that the closure principle, when properly understood at any rate, is not susceptible to this critique, and so remains standing.[14]

It should also be noted at this juncture that any *anti*-skeptical comfort that is offered by the point that closure affects only those who have become aware of the skeptical threat is severely limited. After all, once the skeptical argument has been made explicit, the subject will no longer have any epistemic insulation against its threat. Moreover, as we will see below, we can motivate the skeptical conclusion without appeal to the closure principle, in which case the epistemic insulation apparently on offer to those who haven't seriously reflected on their epistemic position is arguably illusory anyway.

We will consider below a more sophisticated response to the skeptical problem which is closely related to the nonclosure strategy. First, though, we will examine an equally rudimentary anti-skeptical approach that targets the other main claim that makes up the skeptical paradox—namely, $(S_1 1)/(II)$.

4. An Overriding Anti-skeptical Strategy (II): Epistemic Externalism

Consider again the case that was made for $(S_1 1)$, such that we cannot know we are not BIVs because it concerns a scenario that is subjectively indistinguishable from normal perceptual conditions. One basis on which $(S_1 1)$—and thus claim (I) in the inconsistent radical skeptical triad—might be challenged is via appeal to *epistemic externalism*.

We will be exploring the epistemic externalism/internalism distinction in more detail at a later juncture. For our current purposes, however, we can take it that epistemic internalists demand that knowledge be grounded in a sound rational basis, where this sound rational basis consists of the possession of reasons in support of one's belief in the target known proposition that are reflectively accessible to one.[15] In contrast, epistemic externalists deny this claim, and so maintain that there can be bona fide knowledge that lacks a sound rational basis of this sort. That is, epistemic externalists hold, contra epistemic internalism, that not all knowledge is rationally grounded knowledge. Although this characterization of the epistemic externalism/internalism distinction is far from uncontentious, it ought to suffice for our immediate concerns.

So, for example, according to a crude process reliabilism about knowledge, knowledge is to be understood as true belief acquired via a reliable belief-forming process (i.e., one that generally generates true beliefs as opposed to false ones).[16] One could clearly satisfy such an epistemic condition, and hence on this view count as having knowledge, even though one lacked any rational basis in support of one's belief. Thus epistemic externalism can allow that knowledge is possessed in cases that fail to satisfy the rubric laid down by epistemic internalism, as we are understanding this view (since the latter denies that there can be genuine knowledge that is not rationally grounded). Indeed, it is often held to be part of the attraction of epistemic externalism that it has this consequence, such that it is consistent with small children and even some animals possessing knowledge.

How might an epistemic externalist motivate a case against $(S_1 1)$? Well, notice that the rationale offered for why we are unable to know that we are not the victims of radical skeptical hypotheses, such as the BIV hypothesis, seems to be explicitly epistemically internalist. In particular, the argument goes that since one is unable to introspectively distinguish between normal perceptual experiences and the corresponding experiences of the BIV, one can't know that one is not a BIV. That consideration might well suffice to demonstrate that one lacks a rational basis, internalistically construed, for believing that one is not a BIV, but why should it thereby follow, by epistemic externalist lights, that knowledge is lacking of this proposition as $(S_1 1)$ alleges?[17] In particular, couldn't it be the case that we can know that we are not BIVs—and, more generally, the denials of radical skeptical hypotheses, contra (I)—but only in virtue of satisfying an externalist epistemic condition, such as a reliability condition?

The thinking behind this proposal is to convict the skeptical puzzle of trading on a commitment to epistemic internalism that we have independent grounds to reject. In particular, epistemic externalists will, I take it, grant to the skeptic that epistemic internalism is much closer in spirit to our commonsense way of thinking about the epistemic realm, while nonetheless maintaining that there is a sound theoretical basis for rejecting such internalism in favor of epistemic externalism. So while it might well be true that our commonsense way of thinking about the epistemic realm would have knowledge requiring sufficient rational support for one's belief in the target proposition, with the consequence that such rational support is lacking in the case of $(S_1 1)$, the epistemic externalist will counter with their independently motivated revisionist proposal that there be can be bona fide knowledge even in the absence of the relevant rational support. The skeptical case for $(S_1 1)$ is thus undermined, and with it the skeptical paradox as a whole, as part of a wider overriding anti-skeptical strategy.

This general type of anti-skeptical proposal—according to which we can know the denials of skeptical hypotheses, in conflict with $(S_1 1)$—has been described in the literature as *neo-Mooreanism*.[18] This is because the commonsense response to radical skepticism offered by G. E. Moore (e.g., 1925; 1939) also proceeds by arguing, contrary to intuition, that we can know the denials of skepticism hypotheses. Thus, on this score at least, neo-Mooreanism has affinities with Mooreanism (though it should be noted that it is in other respects a very different view).[19] While the version of neo-Mooreanism we have just considered is explicitly allied to epistemic externalism, as we will see below we can also delineate plausible internalist renderings of this view.

In any case, while the general shape of such a response to radical skepticism is appealing, the devil (as so often in philosophy) lies in the detail. For although the epistemic externalist is keen to break the logical link between knowledge and rational support, such that one can have the former without the latter, they surely do not wish to disengage our everyday knowledge from rational support altogether. Or, at least, the skeptic can force a dilemma here. On the first horn of the dilemma is the charge that the epistemic externalist is ultimately offering no response at all to the skeptical problem. On the second horn is the charge that the epistemic externalist is presenting us with an epistemological proposal that is so revisionist, so discontinuous with our ordinary epistemic practices, that even the most ardent proponent of epistemic externalism would find it unpalatable.

5. Radical Skepticism about Rationally Grounded Knowledge

In order to appreciate this dilemma, imagine that the skeptic simply reformulates the skeptical paradox in terms of rationally grounded knowledge. We thus have the following:

THE RADICAL SKEPTICAL PARADOX (II)

(S_21) One cannot have rationally grounded knowledge that one is not a BIV.

(S_22) If one cannot have rationally grounded knowledge that one is not a BIV, then one cannot have rationally grounded knowledge that E.

(S_23) One has rationally grounded knowledge that E.

The epistemic externalist has effectively granted (S_21), since her denial of (S_11) turns on the claim that all the skeptic has in fact shown is that one's belief that one is not a BIV cannot be rationally grounded, and not that one cannot know that one is not a BIV. If one cannot have a belief that one is not a BIV that is rationally grounded, then, a fortiori, one cannot have rationally grounded knowledge of this proposition either.

So far so good for the epistemic externalist. The trouble arises, however, once we reflect that the epistemic externalist presumably *does* want to consider our normal everyday knowledge, such as one's knowledge that one is presently seated at a desk, to be rationally grounded, and hence ought to want to endorse (S_23). For it is one thing for the epistemic externalist to offer a form of revisionism which says that bona fide knowledge doesn't always require rational support, and quite another thing to suggest that even paradigm cases of normal mature human knowledge don't involve rational support. Indeed, can't I offer entirely adequate rational support for my belief that I am right now seated at a desk, and doesn't this belief also amount to knowledge?

With (S_21) and (S_23) in play, however, the underlying worry becomes manifest. For why can't skeptics marshal the same kind of resources that they employed to generate a contradiction between (S_11) and (S_13) in order to generate an analogous contradiction here? For consider the bridging principle, (S_22), in this reformulation of the skeptical argument. While we could not motivate this claim with the closure principle as it stands above, it is easy to see how we would need to adapt this principle so that it can serve the task in hand.

Consider the following "closure$_{RK}$" principle, where "RK" stands for "rationally grounded knowledge":

THE CLOSURE$_{RK}$ PRINCIPLE

If S has rationally grounded knowledge that p, and S competently deduces from p that q, thereby forming a belief that q on this basis while retaining her rationally grounded knowledge that p, then S has rationally grounded knowledge that q.

Although this principle is more specific, and to that extent more demanding, than its sister closure principle, it is no less plausible. Indeed, the rationale that motivates the closure principle also motivates the closure$_{RK}$ principle. For if we hold that competent deductions cannot undermine the epistemic standing of one's deduced beliefs, such that knowledge must be preserved by this process, then it is hard to see why that shouldn't apply with just as much potency to rationally grounded knowledge. Competent deduction is, after all, by its nature a well-conducted rational process—indeed, it is a paradigm case of a well-conducted rational process—so how can the knowledge that results from this process be any less rationally grounded than the knowledge from which it is inferentially derived?[20]

What we have in play is now an inconsistent triad that is slightly different from that set out above:

THE INCONSISTENT RADICAL SKEPTICAL TRIAD*

(I*) One is unable to have rationally grounded knowledge of the denials of radical skeptical hypotheses.

(II*) The closure$_{RK}$ principle.

(III*) One has widespread rationally grounded everyday knowledge.

Rather than the radical skepticism being focused on knowledge *simpliciter* (which would allow for an externalist construal of that knowledge), this version of the inconsistent radical skeptical triad is instead targeted specifically at rationally grounded knowledge, with the closure$_{RK}$ principle creating the required bridge between a lack of rationally grounded knowledge with regard to the denials of radical skeptical hypotheses and everyday knowledge. As before, just as we can think of ($S_1$1–3) as instantiating the inconsistent triad at issue in claims (I–III), and thereby making the inconsistency at issue in the latter manifest, so we can think of ($S_2$1–3) as instantiating (I*–III*). And just as we saw claims (I–III) to be highly intuitive above, the same can also be said of (I*–III*). Indeed, on the face of it at least they seem to be claims that even an epistemic externalist ought to find plausible.

With the closure$_{RK}$ principle in place skeptics are able to force their dilemma on epistemic externalist neo-Mooreanism. For the choice facing the proponent of such a view is now stark.

On the one hand, they could stick to a modest form of epistemic revisionism and so insist that our everyday knowledge is rationally grounded. But then the reformulated skeptical argument just set out is brought to bear to show that even this modest form of epistemic revisionism, and in particular (III*), is in question. That is, with the closure$_{RK}$ principle in play one can motivate ($S_2$2). And with ($S_2$1) and ($S_2$2) in hand, one can derive the negation of ($S_2$3). But that would be inconsistent with a moderate form of epistemic externalism of a kind that would be compatible with (III*). The upshot is that if this form of epistemic externalism wants to retain both (III*) and (I*), then the closure$_{RK}$ principle, and thus (II*), will have to go. But given the implausibility of rejecting this principle, the mooted combination of moderate epistemic externalism and anti-skepticism looks in jeopardy.

On the other hand, there is the option of endorsing a far more radical form of epistemic revisionism, one on which there is a wholesale disengagement between knowledge and rational support. This would involve the epistemic externalist allowing that even in paradigm cases of perceptual knowledge, such as that at issue in ($S_2$3), the knowledge in question lacks rational support. This form of epistemic externalism could thus retain the closure$_{RK}$ principle, and hence (II*), by rejecting (III*).

Perhaps such radical revisionism could be motivated, but we can determine in advance that it would be a hard sell. In particular, overriding anti-skeptical strategies require a solid diagnostic story to explain why we should dismiss the natural intuitions that give rise to the skeptical puzzle. This means that the more revisionary the proposal in play—that is, the greater the intellectual distance between the natural intuitions that give rise to the skeptical puzzle and the alternative revisionary account on offer, the harder it will be to mount a philosophically compelling case for why we should endorse the revisionary alternative.

Of course, this dilemma is not a knock-down argument against this brand of anti-skepticism. But it does mean that if, for example, there are ways of dealing with the skeptical problem that are less revisionary—which there are, as we will see in subsequent chapters—then we should explore them first.[21]

6. An Overriding Anti-skeptical Strategy (III): Abductivism

We began this chapter by noting the plausibility of the radical skeptical claim that we are unable to know the denials of radical skeptical hypotheses, such as the BIV hypothesis. As we observed, what motivated this claim was the fact that radical skeptical hypotheses are ex hypothesi indistinguishable from corresponding scenarios involving normal veridical experiences. It seems to follow that one cannot have a rational basis for believing that one is not the victim of a radical skeptical hypothesis, and hence that one cannot know that this is the case either. A fortiori, one cannot have rationally grounded knowledge that one is not the victim of a radical skeptical hypothesis.

In putting matters in this way, however, we are effectively presupposing that one's rational support for believing that one is not the victim of a radical skeptical hypothesis must exclusively arise out of one's perceptual experiences, such that if those experiences do not distinguish between normal veridical perception and radical skeptical hypotheses then one lacks a rational basis for believing that one is not the victim of a radical skeptical hypothesis. But couldn't one's rational support for believing such a proposition arise from other sources?

The obvious option in this regard is to appeal to some sort of *abductive* basis for this belief (i.e., an inference to the best explanation). For while it might seem undeniable that one's perceptual experience alone cannot supply one with a rational basis for believing that one is not the victim of a radical skeptical hypothesis, on the face of it there do seem to be abductive reasons for excluding this error possibility. After all, isn't the hypothesis that one's experiences are veridical in the manner that one standardly takes them to be a better explanation of those experiences than any competing radical skeptical hypothesis? And, if so, then doesn't this supply one with a rational basis for believing that one is not the victim of a radical skeptical hypothesis? Call any response to the problem of radical skepticism that appeals to such an abductive rational basis *abductivism*.

Note that on the face of it at least abductivism seems a plausible candidate to be an *undercutting* anti-skeptical strategy. That is, what first seems to be a radical skeptical paradox is in fact nothing of the sort, since one of the claims that makes up that paradox—that is, (I*)—is shown to depend for its plausibility on an unduly restrictive conception of rational support. In particular, once we allow for the possibility that the rational support available for one's beliefs in the denials of radical skeptical hypotheses can include abductive grounds, and further contend that there is an entirely intuitive route to establishing those abductive grounds, then (I*) no longer has the intuitive support that the radical skeptic claims. The radical skeptic has thus failed to present us with a bona fide paradox.

In order to concentrate our discussion of abductivism, we will focus specifically on the issue of whether such an appeal to abduction gives one a better rational basis for believing the target everyday proposition over the corresponding radical skeptical hypothesis. As we will see in chapter 2, it is further logical step to go from this claim to the contention that one has a rational basis for believing that one is not a victim of the relevant radical skeptical hypothesis. But for the sake of argument we will grant to the abductivist that this further step can be made. All they need to demonstrate, therefore, is the weaker claim. Furthermore, although abductive reasoning has itself been subject to critique, we will grant for the sake of argument that in general it is a legitimate source of rationally grounded belief, and thus, potentially, rationally grounded knowledge.[22] The issue thus rests on whether the particular kind of abductive inference employed by the abductivist is acceptable.

Even with the deck stacked in favor of abductivism in this fashion, the proposal still unravels on closer inspection. To begin with, notice that the most natural ways of developing abductivism will appeal to considerations that are of dubious epistemic pedigree. So, for example, one might regard the hypothesis that one is sitting at one's desk as opposed to being a BIV as abductively grounded in virtue of the former being more in keeping with one's existing network of beliefs than the latter. This would be to appeal to a kind of *principle of conservatism*. There may be a rationale for such a principle when it comes to scientific theory choice, but it is at best questionable when applied to the problem of radical skepticism.

After all, we are seeking an *epistemic* basis for preferring the everyday scenario over the radical skeptical hypothesis, and this means a basis for treating the former to be more likely to be true than the latter. But why should an appeal to a principle of conservatism supply such an epistemic basis? Perhaps the truth is surprising; perhaps our current stock of beliefs is radically in error. Moreover, there is the further point that the radical skeptical hypothesis incorporates an explanation of why we have (wrongly, if this hypothesis is true) ignored radical skeptical hypotheses thus far—namely, that they are indistinguishable from the everyday scenarios that we take to obtain. But this means that we cannot reasonably appeal to our background empirical beliefs in forming an abductive judgment about whether we can rationally dismiss a radical skeptical hypothesis.

A second dubious consideration that might be cited by the abductivist is to appeal to the relative *simplicity* of the everyday scenario relative to the corresponding radical skeptical hypothesis.[23] Ceteris paribus, simple explanations seem preferable to complex ones, after all, so such a *principle of simplicity* seems a good general constraint on one's choice of explanations. Although it is undeniable that from our perspective the everyday scenario does seem to be a simpler explanation, of what epistemic relevance is this fact? Simplicity, after all, is in the eye of the beholder—someone convinced by a radical skeptical hypothesis might well regard this skeptical hypothesis as offering a simpler explanation than the alternative everyday scenario.[24] Moreover, as with appeals to conservatism, there is the further concern that simplicity is relative to one's existing network of empirical beliefs, and yet the radical skeptical hypothesis is offering us an alternative explanation of one's experience according to which those beliefs are radically in error. How then can an appeal to simplicity provide one with an epistemic basis for preferring belief in the everyday scenario over the corresponding radical skeptical hypothesis?

The immediate upshot of the foregoing is that abductivism cannot employ normal abductive inferences in order to motivate its anti-skepticism, but must rather restrict itself to a specific kind of abductive inference that doesn't involve appeal to one's background empirical beliefs, and hence doesn't employ the principles of conservatism or simplicity. But that means that the kind of abductive inference in question will be very different from what we were originally envisaging, not least because it would be an entirely a priori approach to the radical skeptical problem. In particular, notice that the type of abductive inference that is being appealed to here is quite unlike the standard variety of abductive reasoning that, it is often claimed, is commonly found in everyday thinking, and which is not restricted in this fashion.[25] And it is certainly very different from the kind of abduction that is commonly employed in scientific inquiry.[26]

It is hard to see how such a purely a priori defense of abductivism would proceed.[27] At any rate, we can at least say this much: that any such development of abductivism along these lines would be an *overriding* rather than an undercutting anti-skeptical strategy. Rather than offering a demonstration that, properly understood, there is an intuitive rational basis for one's belief that one is not the victim of a radical skeptical hypothesis, the claim becomes instead explicitly *revisionist* in flavor. That is, the abductivist is arguing for a very specific way of construing the abductive support in question, and arguing on independent grounds that one should prefer this revisionist account of one's rational basis for believing that one is not the victim of a radical skeptical hypotheses over the alternative intuition that such a rational basis is unavailable. This is very different from the kind of anti-skeptical strategy that was originally advertised. It also means that if there are plausible undercutting anti-skeptical strategies available—and I will be claiming in later chapters that there are—then they are to be preferred over abductivism.[28]

7. Concluding Remarks

In this chapter we have articulated a version of radical skepticism which essentially trades on a closure-style principle for knowledge. We have argued that, properly construed, this type of radical skepticism presents us with a putative paradox. That means that prospective anti-skeptical strategies will fall into one of two camps—either they will be *undercutting* anti-skeptical strategies that demonstrate that this putative paradox is not in fact bona fide, or else they will be *overriding* anti-skeptical strategies that grant that the paradox is genuine but nonetheless offer independent grounds for rejecting at least one of the claims that makes up this paradox. We have noted that undercutting anti-skeptical strategies are to be preferred to overriding ones. As part of our exploration of the radical skeptical paradox, we have examined three specific overriding anti-skeptical proposals, and found all of them to be problematic to some degree. Along the way we have also identified a more nuanced conception of the radical skeptical paradox that focuses on rationally grounded knowledge. As we will see in the next chapter, there is yet a further more nuanced way to conceive of the radical skeptical paradox, one that makes no essential appeal to a closure-style principle for knowledge.

CHAPTER 2

Radical Skepticism and Underdetermination

0. Introductory Remarks

The two formulations of the skeptical paradox offered in chapter 1 essentially turn on an appeal to a closure-style principle for knowledge, since this is required in order to motivate the second "bridging" claim (i.e., either ($S_1$2) or ($S_2$2)) in the paradox. While the first formulation of the skeptical paradox turned on a version of the closure principle expressed in terms of knowledge *simpliciter*, the second formulation concerned a sister closure principle specifically expressed in terms of rationally grounded knowledge. As we saw, while more specific, the second closure principle was no less intuitive than its sibling (indeed, it is arguably even more intuitive). We have thus witnessed a compelling route to radical skepticism via appeal to the closure principle.

As we will see in this chapter, however, there is another way of articulating the skeptical paradox, an articulation that doesn't essentially depend on a closure-style principle.

1. Radical Skepticism and the Underdetermination Principle

In order to see how this form of radical skepticism proceeds, we need to focus, with one eye on radical skeptical scenarios, on the apparent paucity of the rational basis we have for our perceptual beliefs in external world propositions. In particular, we need to notice that the rational support provided by our perceptual experiences does not seem to epistemically favor our ordinary perceptual beliefs over the kind of scenarios depicted by radical skeptical hypotheses. So, for example, one's rational basis right now for believing that one is seated at one's desk, no matter how epistemically propitious the conditions for one's belief in this regard, is never such (or so it seems anyway) as to give one more reason to think that one is seated at one's desk than that one is a disembodied BIV who merely falsely supposes that one is seated at one's desk. In short, one's rational support for a perceptual belief is *underdetermined* with respect to radical skeptical scenarios.

We can express this point as follows, using the quotidian proposition ("E") that one is seated at one's desk as representative of an epistemically "best case" of perceptual belief:

($S_3$1) One cannot have rational support that favors one's belief that E over the BIV hypothesis.[1]

This claim seems undeniable. For given that the experiences had by the subject in the BIV case are subjectively indistinguishable from everyday experiences, then how is one to come by rational support for an everyday perceptual belief that epistemically favors this belief over an incompatible radical skeptical alternative?[2]

As with the closure-based formulation of the skeptical paradox, the challenge facing the radical skeptic is to show that a claim of this sort is in tension with our everyday knowledge. That is, the challenge is to show that ($S_3$1) is in tension with a relevant claim about one's paradigmatic perceptual knowledge:

($S_3$3) One knows that E.

In particular, the skeptic needs to motivate the following bridging claim:

($S_3$2) If one cannot have rational support that favors one's belief that E over the BIV hypothesis, then one does not know that E.[3]

With this bridging claim in play, the tension between ($S_3$1) and ($S_3$3) is manifest. But how is ($S_3$2) to be motivated?

As with the closure-based formulation of the radical skeptical paradox, the answer to this question lies in the skeptical appeal to a general epistemic principle which can underwrite ($S_3$2). Consider the following principle:

THE UNDERDETERMINATION PRINCIPLE

If S knows that p and q describe incompatible scenarios, and yet S lacks a rational basis that favors p over q, then S lacks knowledge that p.[4]

This principle requires some unpacking. First off, since we are interested in radical skepticism, which undermines our perceptual knowledge, we will read this principle as applying only to this form of knowledge. Perhaps the principle has general application, but so long as it applies to perceptual knowledge it will suffice for our purposes. Second, note that the "incompatibility" in play in this principle is not one of contradiction, but rather concerns contrariety. That is, p and q need not be incompatible in the sense that if one of them is false then the other must be true (i.e., such that they cannot both be false), but rather in the sense that they cannot both be true. Finally, third, what is meant here by a subject possessing a rational basis that "favors" p over q is that she has a stronger rational basis for regarding p as true than she does for regarding q as true.

With these points in mind, let us consider the plausibility of the underdetermination principle. Let's take a mundane example to illustrate the principle in action. Imagine an agent believes that she is seated at her desk and she also knows that she cannot both be seated at her desk and be standing by the window. According to the underdetermination principle, it follows that unless our agent has a rational basis that favors her being seated at her desk over the alternative scenario that she is standing by the window, then her belief that she is seated cannot amount to knowledge. This seems eminently plausible, since if it really were the case that the subject had no stronger reason for thinking that she is seated at her desk than that she is standing at the window—if, for example, the rational support she has is indifferent between these two scenarios—then it is hard to see how she could have a solid rational foundation for her belief that she is seated at her desk. And if she lacks a solid rational foundation for her belief in this proposition, then it is difficult to comprehend why we would regard that belief as amounting to knowledge.

The foregoing makes very clear that this principle effectively takes it as given that knowledge—perceptual knowledge anyway—demands a solid rational foundation, such that if this is lacking (as it is held to be if the target favoring rational support is absent), then the subject lacks knowledge. This is a plausible assumption to make. As one might put the point: if perceptual knowledge lacks a solid rational foundation, then in virtue of what does it count as bona fide knowledge? Even so, this is a claim that might be questioned (indeed, we will be scrutinizing it further below).

In any case, with the underdetermination principle in play we can see how the skeptic could go about motivating the bridging claim, ($S_3 2$). In particular, ($S_3 2$) is clearly a manifestation of the underdetermination principle, at least where we assume, as is reasonable, that the subject in question knows full well that being seated and being a disembodied BIV are incompatible scenarios (disembodied BIVs don't *sit* anywhere, after all). With ($S_3 2$) and ($S_3 1$) in play, however, the logical tension with ($S_3 3$) is clear:

THE RADICAL SKEPTICAL PARADOX (III)

($S_3$1) One cannot have rational support that favors one's belief that E over the BIV hypothesis.

($S_3$2) If one cannot have rational support that favors one's belief that E over the BIV hypothesis, then one does not know that E.

($S_3$3) One knows that E.[5]

As before, we have a putative paradox, in that we have three claims that are either directly highly intuitive or rest on further claims that are highly intuitive, but where not all of these three claims could be true together. The challenge is thus to demonstrate which of these three claims should be rejected.

Just as with the closure-based formulations of the skeptical paradox put forward in chapter 1, we can think of this formulation as being a specific instantiation of an inconsistent triad, as follows:

THE INCONSISTENT RADICAL SKEPTICAL TRIAD**

(I**) One cannot have rational support that favors one's belief in an everyday proposition over an incompatible radical skeptical hypothesis.[6]

(II**) The underdetermination principle.

(III**) One has widespread everyday knowledge.

As before, the instantiation at issue—in this case ($S_3$1–3)—makes the inconsistency between these three claims, (I**–III**), manifest. The denial of one of these three more specific claims thus goes hand in hand with the rejection of one of the members of this more generally formulated inconsistent triad.

2. An Overriding Anti-skeptical Strategy: Epistemic Externalism

As with the closure-based formulation of the radical skeptical paradox, an obvious response is to try to motivate the rejection of the epistemic principle that is underpinning the second "bridging" claim that makes up the paradox, in this case ($S_3$2), and thus (II**), which underlies this claim. Again, as before, a fairly crude way of doing this, which is cast along neo-Moorean overriding anti-skeptical lines, is to appeal to epistemic externalism. We noted above that the underdetermination principle as presently formulated effectively takes it as given that knowledge demands a solid rational foundation. While this is a highly plausible claim to make, we also registered the point that it is not above contention. In particular, epistemic externalists will dispute this claim, at least insofar as the rational basis in question is construed along the normal epistemic internalist lines (such that the sound rational basis consists of reflectively accessible reasons in support of the belief in the known proposition). Accordingly, epistemic externalists could argue that a lack of favoring rational support for one's belief need not preclude that belief from amounting to knowledge.

In terms of the formulation of the skeptical paradox that we are considering, this response would amount to granting ($S_3$1) and ($S_3$3) while rejecting ($S_3$2), and thus (II**). That is, it can both be true that one lacks a rational basis that favors one's belief that one is presently seated at one's desk over the known to be incompatible alternative that one is a BIV *and* that one knows that one is presently seated at one's desk. In particular, the proponents of this anti-skeptical line will contend that all the skeptic has demonstrated is that one lacks a sound rational basis for one's knowledge that one is presently seated, and not that one thereby lacks knowledge (externalistically conceived) of this proposition. Moreover, in the spirit of an overriding anti-skeptical strategy they will further contend that while the idea that knowledge demands a sound rational basis is intuitive, there are nonetheless good independent grounds for rejecting the epistemic internalism that is being presupposed in this claim and endorsing instead an epistemic externalism that rejects it.

As with the crude overriding epistemic externalist response to the closure-based skeptical paradox above, however, the skeptic can undermine this proposal by forcing a dilemma. For while epistemic externalists characteristically allow that knowledge can be possessed in the absence of a sound rational basis in support of the target belief, such that the logical connection between knowledge and rational support is broken, they typically do not wish to contend that most of our knowledge lacks a rational basis. This latter claim, after all, is far more radical, in that it involves a much more extensive form of epistemic revisionism. Herein lies the source of the dilemma for the epistemic externalist who takes this anti-skeptical line, for we can easily reframe the radical skeptical paradox such that it commits the proponent of this line to endorsing the more radical revisionary position. The choice they face is thus to either stick to a modestly revisionary form of epistemic externalism but then have to contend with the newly formulated version of the paradox, or else revert to a more radical form of epistemic externalism, but thereby weaken the dialectical effectiveness of their overriding anti-skeptical strategy.

In order to see this dilemma in action, consider this revised version of the underdetermination principle, which makes explicit that it concerns only rationally grounded knowledge and not knowledge *simpliciter*:

THE UNDERDETERMINATION$_{RK}$ PRINCIPLE

If S knows that p and q describe incompatible scenarios, and yet S lacks a rational basis that favors p over q, then S lacks rationally grounded knowledge that p.

For an epistemic internalist, at least as we characterized the view in chapter 1 anyway, this formulation of the underdetermination principle will be equivalent to the previous formulation. For the epistemic internalist, after all, knowledge *just is* rationally grounded knowledge. For the epistemic externalist, in contrast, the difference between these two principles will be significant, for while they will presumably grant the truth of the underdetermination$_{RK}$ principle, they ought to be highly suspicious, as we have seen, of the sister underdetermination principle.

Crucially, however, one can develop a version of the skeptical paradox that trades only on the underdetermination$_{RK}$ principle. For consider this reformulation of the underdetermination-based skeptical paradox:

THE RADICAL SKEPTICAL PARADOX (IV)

($S_4 1$) One cannot have rational support that favors one's belief that E over the BIV hypothesis.

($S_4 2$) If one cannot have rational support that favors one's belief that E over the BIV hypothesis, then one does not have rationally grounded knowledge that E.

($S_4 3$) One has rationally grounded knowledge that E.

In keeping with the underdetermination$_{RK}$ principle, this formulation of the skeptical paradox makes explicit throughout that we are targeting specifically rationally grounded knowledge. Significantly, however, the skeptical implications of this formulation of the paradox seem almost as intellectually disturbing as the analogous formulation in terms of knowledge *simpliciter*. What goes for the knowledge at issue in ($S_4 3$) will apply to a wide class of one's everyday knowledge, and thus it will follow that one lacks rationally grounded knowledge of much, if not all, of what one takes oneself to know about the world. This is clearly radically in conflict with our how we conceive of our epistemic situation.

In moving to this new underdetermination-based formulation of the skeptical paradox, we have also shifted to a different way of thinking about the relevant inconsistent triad that is in play:

THE INCONSISTENT RADICAL SKEPTICAL TRIAD***

(I***) One cannot have rational support that favors one's belief in an everyday proposition over an incompatible radical skeptical hypothesis.

(II***) The underdetermination$_{RK}$ principle.

(III***) One has widespread rationally grounded everyday knowledge.

While the first claim is the same as before, the third claim makes clear that it is rationally grounded knowledge that is at issue, and accordingly the second claim now specifically concerns the underdetermination$_{RK}$ principle. As before, we are to think of ($S_4$1–3) as instantiating this inconsistent triad and thereby making the inconsistency that is at issue manifest.

What is the epistemic externalist to say about this reformulation of the underdetermination-based skeptical paradox? Well, one line of response might be to extend the overriding anti-skeptical strategy set out above so that it applies with as much force to this new formulation of the puzzle. That is, the epistemic externalist might contend that we have independent theoretical grounds not just for rejecting the necessity of a rational basis for knowledge, but also for discarding the idea that there is any significant correlation between knowing and possessing a rational basis for believing what is known. Consequently, the epistemic externalist will respond to the paradox just set out by taking the "skeptical" horn of dismissing ($S_4$3), with all that this entails. On this view, knowledge comes radically apart from the possession of reasons, such that our knowledge—our perceptual knowledge anyway—is generally, if not universally, lacking in rational support. (III***) thus has to go.

The difficulty facing this response is that it incorporates a far more revisionary story than the one initially advertised. As we noted in chapter 1 in our discussion of overriding anti-skeptical strategies, the more revisionary the diagnosis offered for why the relevant skeptical claim should be rejected, the less intellectually palatable this response to skepticism becomes. While we might be willing to live with an overriding epistemic externalist anti-skeptical strategy that proceeds by weakening the connection between knowledge and rational support, it is another thing entirely to embrace the more radical claim that our (perceptual) knowledge is in its nature lacking in rational support.

But if the epistemic externalist does not take this line, then their response to the skeptical problem simply loses application. For while they can offer a principled response to the underdetermination-based skeptical paradox, they are completely stumped when it comes to the underdetermination$_{RK}$-based skeptical paradox. After all, the underlying epistemic principle in play—that is, the underdetermination$_{RK}$ principle—does not conflict with their brand of epistemic externalism (since it makes clear that it is concerned only with rationally grounded knowledge), and with this principle in play the rest of the argument will follow. Accordingly, insofar as the epistemic externalist sticks to a modestly revisionary approach, such that our perceptual knowledge still generally enjoys rational support even if it does not entail it, then this formulation of the skeptical paradox poses a genuine problem for their view.

The foregoing should suffice to show that there is a genuine skeptical puzzle in play here, one that is not amenable to an obvious resolution. Moreover, it is a skeptical puzzle that, while generating the same kind of skeptical consequences as its closure-based counterpart, seems to constitute a very different way of arguing for radical skepticism.

3. Attributer Contextualism as an Overriding Anti-skeptical Strategy

One of the most influential treatments of the problem of radical skepticism in recent years has been that offered by attributer contextualism. According to this proposal, "knows" is a context-sensitive term, such that the truth value of an assertion of a sentence of the form "*S* knows that *p*"—call this a *knowledge ascription sentence*—can be dependent upon in which conversational context the sentence is uttered (i.e., the context of the *attributer*). More precisely, the kind of attributer contextualism that concerns us posits that "knows" can pick out more or less demanding epistemic standards in different conversational contexts. Thus, in a conversational context that incorporates a demanding epistemic standard for "knows," someone could assert a knowledge ascription sentence and thereby speak falsely, even though, in a different conversational context (i.e., one that incorporates a less demanding epistemic standard), the assertion of this very same ascription sentence could express a truth.[7]

The potential import of this way of thinking about "knows" to the problem of radical skepticism ought to be clear. Perhaps when the skeptic denies that we have knowledge she speaks truly, but only because her assertions of the negated form of the knowledge ascription sentences (i.e., "*S doesn't* know that *p*") are made relative to a conversational context that employs a very demanding epistemic standard. In contrast, in normal conversational contexts where radical skeptical considerations are not at issue, when subjects assert the corresponding (nonnegated) knowledge ascription sentences they also speak truly, because these assertions are made relative to a conversational context that employs an undemanding epistemic standard. In this way, we can contend that the two camps are in effect "talking past" one another.[8]

Arguably, at any rate, there are precedents for this kind of phenomenon in our ordinary language. Whether something counts as "tall," "short," "flat," "empty," and so on, can be determined by conversational context, such that a sentence ascribing this property to something can express a truth relative to one conversional context and a falsehood relative to another. So, for example, someone talking about John, who is over six feet tall, in a normal conversational context could assert "John is tall" and thereby speak truly, since the standards for tallness operative in this context are relatively undemanding. In contrast, in a conversational context that has more demanding standards for tallness—for example, where the coaches for the basketball team are discussing their options—someone could assert "John is tall" and speak falsely. If this is possible for predicates like "tall," then why not "knows"?[9]

Attributer contextualism can feel like a very natural response to the problem of radical skepticism, since when one first engages with this difficulty it does tend to strike one as trading on some sort of illicit raising of the epistemic standards. Moreover, on the face of it anyway, attributer contextualism offers an elegant response to the radical skeptical problem. Indeed, at first glance one might think that attributer contextualism is presenting us with an *undercutting* response to this problem, such that it offers us a philosophical basis on which we can plausibly maintain that this putative paradox is bogus. That is, attributer contextualists seem to be in a position to argue that radical skepticism looks like a bona fide paradox only because of a failure to appreciate the context sensitivity of "knows."

At least as applied to closure-based radical skepticism, this line of argument can appear very compelling. Consider, to begin with, the first formulation of the closure-based radical skeptical paradox that we offered in chapter 1:

THE RADICAL SKEPTICAL PARADOX (I)

($S_1$1) One cannot know that one is not a BIV.

($S_1$2) If one cannot know that one is not a BIV, then one cannot know that E.

($S_1$3) One knows that E.

Recall that this formulation instantiated the following radical skeptical inconsistent triad:

THE INCONSISTENT RADICAL SKEPTICAL TRIAD

(IV) One is unable to know the denials of radical skeptical hypotheses.

(V) The closure principle.

(VI) One has widespread everyday knowledge.

The appeal to context is meant to allow attributer contextualists to keep the closure principle, and thus (II) is retained.[10] And since this is an antiskeptical proposal, (III) is retained too, though this is where things get complicated. After all, the contextualist wants to argue that the skeptic's claims that we lack knowledge express truths relative to her skeptical context of epistemic appraisal. Relatedly, it is not obvious that the attributer contextualist wants to straightforwardly reject (I) either, given that she allows that knowledge ascription sentences tend to express truths in normal contexts of epistemic appraisal and that the closure principle holds.

If one opts for one of the crude renderings of the closure principle that we rejected in chapter 1, then this situation can look quite awkward for the attributer contextualist. Consider this formulation of the closure principle, for example, which we looked at in chapter 1, and let's call it a "weak" closure principle to indicate that it is not our favored formulation:

THE WEAK CLOSURE PRINCIPLE

If S knows that p, and S knows that p entails q, then S knows that q.

If this is the formulation of the closure principle at issue in (II), then it seems that the truth of knowledge ascription sentences in everyday contexts of epistemic appraisal (in conjunction with the closure principle, so formulated) will surely require agents in those contexts to also know the denials of radical skeptical hypotheses. But this looks puzzling, since in virtue of what is one able to know such propositions? In particular, notice that the claim at issue in (I) doesn't seem to at all trade on epistemic standards, since the point is not that we have a weak epistemic basis for belief in this respect, but not strong enough for knowledge, but rather that we have no epistemic basis at all.

We noted in the last chapter that one way of rejecting (I) is by endorsing a form of epistemic externalism, and so arguing that one has the contested knowledge in virtue of satisfying purely externalist epistemic conditions, such as a reliability condition. This neo-Moorean way of dealing with the problem of radical skepticism is an overriding anti-skeptical strategy, however, as we also explained in chapter 1. If attributer contextualism is allied to this way of rejecting (I), it therefore follows that it cannot offer the advertised undercutting anti-skeptical strategy. Worse, since the appeal to epistemic externalism to explain how we can reject (I) would itself suffice to block the radical skeptical paradox, it's now far from clear why we would need to in addition endorse attributer contextualism. Why not just be epistemic externalists and leave it at that?

We also noted in chapter 1 that this epistemic externalist response to the closure-based radical skeptical problem ran into further complications once we turned our attentions to a formulation of this problem that was explicitly cast in terms of rationally grounded knowledge. Here is that formulation again:

THE RADICAL SKEPTICAL PARADOX (II)

($S_2$1) One cannot have rationally grounded knowledge that one is not a BIV.

($S_2$2) If one cannot have rationally grounded knowledge that one is not a BIV, then one cannot have rationally grounded knowledge that E.

($S_3$3) One has rationally grounded knowledge that E.

Recall too that this version of the radical skeptical paradox was meant to instantiate the following inconsistent skeptical triad:

THE INCONSISTENT RADICAL SKEPTICAL TRIAD*

(I*) One is unable to have rationally grounded knowledge of the denials of radical skeptical hypotheses.

(II*) The closure$_{RK}$ principle.

(III*) One has widespread rationally grounded everyday knowledge.

Note though that currently we are not yet employing the competent deduction version of closure, but rather a much cruder rendering. In terms of rationally grounded knowledge, and keeping to the version of closure used above, this would be something like as follows:

THE WEAK CLOSURE$_{RK}$ PRINCIPLE

If S has rationally grounded knowledge that p, and S has rationally grounded knowledge that p entails q, then S has rationally grounded knowledge that q.

For our current purposes, we should regard the closure principle at issue in (II*) as being the weak closure$_{RK}$ principle.

With this closure principle in play, what should the attributer contextualist say about (I*)? It seems that she is committed to denying it, since knowledge ascription sentences will on this view tend to express truths in everyday contexts of epistemic appraisal, and presumably the knowledge at issue will be rationally grounded. Hence, via this closure principle, it seems she is committed to regarding agents as being able to possess rationally grounded knowledge of the denials of skeptical hypotheses. We thus get a form of neo-Mooreanism that is cast along epistemic internalist lines. But that is highly dubious, in that while we can at least make sense of the idea of an agent's beliefs in this regard satisfying externalist epistemic conditions, there doesn't seem to be any plausible sense in which those beliefs might enjoy rational support (which recall means *reflectively accessible* rational support). After all, the rational support we have for our beliefs seems to be completely indifferent to whether or not we are the victims of a radical skeptical scenario. Yet again, then, we find that filling out the details of the attributer contextualist response to radical skepticism requires us to commit that view to some counterintuitive claims, which of course undermines the plausibility of the idea that this could be an undercutting response to radical skepticism.[11]

4. Attributer Contextualism as an Undercutting Anti-skeptical Strategy

Attributer contextualism, qua anti-skeptical strategy, is on stronger ground insofar as it joins us in formulating the closure principle specifically along the lines we argued for in chapter 1. Here, for example, is the closure$_{RK}$ principle, so formulated:

THE CLOSURE$_{RK}$ PRINCIPLE

If S has rationally grounded knowledge that p, and S competently deduces from p that q, thereby forming a belief that q on this basis while retaining her rationally grounded knowledge that p, then S has rationally grounded knowledge that q.

As we saw in chapter 1, what is crucial to the intuitions that underlie the closure principle is the idea that competent deductions from our rationally grounded knowledge ought not to lead to beliefs that are any less rationally grounded. In particular, given that competent deduction is a paradigmatically rational process, if rationally grounded knowledge goes into such a deduction, then rationally grounded knowledge should be its output. As we saw, however, thinking of closure along these lines leads to a different kind of principle to the weak closure principles we just looked at. In particular, we are now to think of closure diachronically—that is, as a process that takes place over time—such that knowledge(/rationally grounded knowledge) of the antecedent proposition must be preserved throughout, and where the belief in the entailed proposition is formed on the basis of the competent deduction.

These differences are very important when it comes to evaluating attributer contextualism as an anti-skeptical strategy. This is because the problem we saw facing attributer contextualism above arises only because on the weak closure principles the attributer contextualist is committed, it seems, to treating agents as having knowledge(/rationally grounded knowledge) of the denials of radical skeptical hypotheses even when in normal (i.e., nonskeptical) contexts of epistemic appraisal. With the more nuanced formulation of the closure principle in play, attributer contextualists have grounds to resist this implication.

This is because in order for the closure$_{RK}$ principle to now apply one needs to actually undertake a competent deduction from one's everyday (rationally grounded) knowledge and on this basis form a belief in the denial of a radical skeptical hypothesis. But since one is now actively considering radical skeptical hypotheses, it is open to the attributer contextualist to argue that one is now in a skeptical context of epistemic appraisal, and hence that high epistemic standards apply. Accordingly, attributer contextualists are no longer committed to treating one as having (rationally grounded) knowledge of the denials of radical skeptical hypotheses, since they aren't now committed to treating one as having (rationally grounded) knowledge of the entailing everyday propositions either. That is, while it might have previously been the case that assertions of knowledge ascription sentences involving everyday propositions expressed truths, now that radical skeptical hypotheses are in play these same assertions will express falsehoods.[12]

So construed, attributer contextualism does look like a more plausible candidate to be an undercutting anti-skeptical strategy. Rather than denying (I) or (I*), in line with neo-Mooreanism, the attributer contextualist stance would instead be that whenever we consider radical skeptical hypotheses we are in a context of epistemic appraisal in which a claim to know these propositions would be false.[13] That can potentially suffice to ensure that their stance is consistent with the retention of (I) and (I*). Moreover, the relevant formulations of the closure principle, and in particular the closure$_{RK}$ principle, aren't being denied, and hence they can retain (II) and (II*). Finally, they are able to retain (III) and (III*) as well, at least to the extent that assertions of knowledge ascription sentences in everyday contexts of epistemic appraisal will tend to express truths. Thus it seems that what looked like a paradox was in fact nothing of the sort, in that there is a route through this problem that doesn't involve denying any of our deeply held claims.

Moreover, notice that this way of dealing with the radical skeptical problem at least concedes *something* to the skeptic, and hence can potentially explain why we were taken in by this puzzle in the first place. After all, on this view radical skepticism is correct in the context of epistemic appraisal in which the problem is posed. That is, the attributer contextualist "resolution" of the radical skeptical problem effectively involves conceding, in the philosophical context of epistemic appraisal in which one engages with this problem, that the sentences that the radical skeptic asserts regarding our epistemic position express truths. It is thus no wonder that we get taken in by this problem, since whenever we consider it we are thereby in a context of epistemic appraisal in which the skeptic's assertions are true. If the attributer contextualist is right, then the trick is simply to realize that this is only so relative to this specific context of epistemic appraisal. As Keith DeRose (1995, 42) has put the point, once "the conversational air has cleared" and one returns to a normal context of epistemic appraisal that employs quotidian epistemic standards, then assertions of knowledge ascription sentences will tend to express truths once more.[14]

Even so, one might be suspicious at the ease with which attributer contextualism disposes of the problem of radical skepticism. For example, if this difficulty simply trades on such a straightforward semantic point, then why has this philosophical problem gripped us for so long? Note that there is no parallel difficulty regarding the context sensitivity of supposedly analogous terms like "tall" and so forth. No one is remotely puzzled by the fact that someone can be considered tall in a normal conversational context and yet not be considered tall relative to a specialized conversational context in which higher standards for tallness are operative. So why has a radical skeptical problem arisen regarding our use of "knows"? Are we radically mistaken about the usage of this everyday term? As a number of commentators have noted, attributer contextualism seems to attribute a degree of semantic blindness to subjects that is independently suspect.[15]

A second problem that afflicts the attributer contextualist response to radical skepticism concerns how it endorses an epistemic hierarchy of contexts. That is, the attributer contextualist concedes that the radical skeptic is employing more demanding epistemic standards for "knows" than are operative in everyday contexts of epistemic appraisal. But doesn't this effectively cede the high ground to the radical skeptic? Recall that we saw in chapter 1 that the skeptical problem is best thought of as a putative paradox, in the sense that it arises out of a conflict in our fundamental epistemic commitments. The upshot of attributer contextualism seems to be that if we follow through on our basic epistemic commitments, then the paradox will disappear for the simple reason that radical skepticism, qua position, will be correct. Our only protection against this eventuality is to blinker ourselves to the radical skeptical context of epistemic appraisal. That is hardly a philosophically satisfying way of dealing with a paradox.[16]

I want to focus my critique of this proposal elsewhere, however. In particular, I want to suggest that any plausibility that attributer contextualism might possess as a response to radical skepticism completely disappears once we try to apply this proposal to underdetermination-based radical skepticism.

The roots of the problem I have in mind here are apparent even in the response that attributer contextualism offers to closure-based radical skepticism. Take the formulation of this problem specifically in terms of rationally grounded knowledge that we explored above. According to attributer contextualism, in everyday contexts of epistemic appraisal in which knowledge ascription sentences are asserted—sentences that presumably typically concern rationally grounded knowledge—these assertions express truths. Thus the attributer contextualist contends that she doesn't need to reject (III*), at least not in any way that would lend support to radical skepticism.

But of course the million-dollar question that one wants to ask at this juncture is what it is in virtue of that one possesses this rationally grounded knowledge of everyday propositions, given that one lacks a rational basis for ruling out radical skeptical hypotheses (something that attributer contextualists usually won't deny). Since attributer contextualism is first and foremost a theory about "knows," and thus knowledge ascriptions, rather than an epistemological proposal, it is perhaps inevitable that it tends to be silent on this question. And yet without a plausible story in this regard the entire anti-skeptical credentials of attributer contextualism are in doubt.

We can bring this point into sharper relief by applying the attributer contextualist anti-skeptical line to underdetermination-based radical skepticism. Consider again the inconsistent skeptical triad that we noted above underlay this form of radical skepticism:

THE INCONSISTENT RADICAL SKEPTICAL TRIAD***

(I***) One cannot have rational support that favors one's belief in an everyday proposition over an incompatible radical skeptical hypothesis.

(II***) The underdetermination$_{RK}$ principle.

(III***) One has widespread rationally grounded everyday knowledge.

Which of these claims are we to understand the attributer contextualist as denying? Well, clearly not (III***), at least where this concerns the truth of assertions of knowledge ascription sentences in everyday contexts of epistemic appraisal. But again, we might ask, in virtue of what are these assertions true, given that one lacks a rational basis for excluding radical skeptical hypotheses?

In particular, what is the attributer contextualist to say about claims (I***) and (II***)? There is certainly nothing in attributer contextualism that would suggest that it should reject one or both of these principles. This is hardly surprising, given that they are epistemological claims and attributer contextualism is primarily a semantic thesis. Even so, it is not as if there is a natural way of extending the attributer contextualist thesis into the epistemic realm so that it is able to offer a response to this problem. On what principled basis would the attributer contextualist deny either of these claims?

Presumably, the attributer contextualist line will be to focus on (I***). Since this claim explicitly mentions radical skeptical hypotheses, on this view even to consider such a claim is to put one into a skeptical context of epistemic appraisal in which high epistemic standards apply. So (I***) is inevitably true whenever one considers it. It is thus little wonder that we think that this claim is true.

For this line of response to gain some purchase on the underdetermination$_{RK}$-based skeptical paradox it would need to be supplemented with a further contention to the effect that relative to normal contexts of epistemic appraisal the rational support one has for one's beliefs is (for all the radical skeptic has shown anyway) entirely in order. But what would be the source of this claim? There seems nothing in the attributer contextualist approach to radical skepticism that would license such a thesis. And yet without it this particular formulation of the radical skeptical paradox is still standing.

The nub of the matter is that the underdetermination$_{RK}$-based skeptical paradox doesn't seem to trade on an appeal to epistemic standards at all, but rather turns on a perfectly general thesis about the inadequacy of the rational support available to us for our everyday beliefs. Since the attributer contextualist lacks the resources to counter this claim, it fails to effectively engage with this skeptical problem.[17]

Moreover, note that if the attributer contextualist could offer a basis for denying one of (I***) or (II***), then it is hard to see why we would need to appeal to attributer contextualism in order to deal with the skeptical problem. Notice that we made a similar contention above when we explored the combination of attributer contextualism and epistemic externalism in response to the closure-based skeptical problem. The more general point in play here is that once we start to supplement attributer contextualism with further epistemological claims in order to deal with the radical skeptical problem, then it seems that it is the epistemological claims that are carrying the anti-skeptical load, such that attributer contextualism becomes itself a superfluous element in the anti-skeptical strategy.

The upshot of the foregoing is that there is no substitute for an epistemological diagnosis of the radical skeptical paradox. For attributer contextualism to function as an anti-skeptical proposal—whether as an overriding or an undercutting anti-skeptical proposal—it needs to engage with the epistemological theses that generate the paradox. This is especially manifest when it comes to the underdetermination$_{RK}$-based radical skeptical paradox, in that attributer contextualism by itself has no story to tell at all about how our everyday knowledge can be rationally grounded given that we lack a rational basis that favors our everyday beliefs over radical skeptical alternatives.[18]

5. Comparing the Two Forms of Radical Skepticism

Our focus is now on two radical skeptical paradoxes, both formulated in terms of rationally grounded knowledge. At this juncture we might naturally ask how they relate to one another. In particular, is one way of thinking about radical skepticism more fundamental than the other, such that our attentions should properly be focused on dealing with this brand of radical skepticism? Or are they instead simply equivalent ways of formulating the target skeptical problem?

We can evaluate the relative logical strengths of the two epistemic principles in play by considering, in a simplified and analogous fashion, what each principle demands. Sticking to the mundane belief that one is presently seated at one's desk ("E") and the skeptical error possibility that one is a BIV, and taking it as given that one has knowledge of the relevant entailments and has, where applicable, undertaken the relevant competent deductions, we can summarize the epistemic consequences of each epistemic principle as follows:

THE SIMPLIFIED CLOSURE$_{RK}$–BASED ENTAILMENT

If S has rationally grounded knowledge that E, then S has rationally grounded knowledge that she is not a BIV.

THE SIMPLIFIED UNDERDETERMINATION$_{RK}$–BASED ENTAILMENT

If S has rationally grounded knowledge that E, then S's rational support favors her belief that E over the BIV hypothesis.

I take it that the simplified closure$_{RK}$-based entailment is an obvious, and uncontentious, simplification of what the closure$_{RK}$ principle demands in this case. That the simplified underdetermination$_{RK}$-based entailment is a simplification of what the underdetermination$_{RK}$ principle demands is not so obvious, but that is because we are effectively working with a contraposed formulation of the latter principle in order to make it analogous in formulation to the closure$_{RK}$ principle. A simplified version of the underdetermination$_{RK}$-based entailment that was not contraposed would state that if one lacks a rational basis that favors E (that one seated at one's desk) over the alternative skeptical scenario that one is a BIV, then one lacks rationally grounded knowledge that E. What we have just formulated as the simplified underdetermination$_{RK}$-based entailment is just the contraposition of this claim.

With the relevant underdetermination$_{RK}$-based and closure$_{RK}$-based entailments simplified in this way, we can detect one obvious difference that at least appears logically important, which is that whereas the closure$_{RK}$ principle demands that one has rationally grounded knowledge that one is *not* a BIV, the simplified underdetermination$_{RK}$ principle merely demands that one has a rational basis that favors the target everyday proposition over the BIV alternative. On the face of it at least, the former claim is much more demanding than the latter claim, in that one can have better reasons for thinking that one is seated at one's desk rather than that one is a BIV without thereby possessing rationally grounded knowledge that one is *not* a BIV.

This suspicion is borne out by closer analysis. Having better reason to believe that one is seated at one's desk as opposed to being a disembodied BIV plausibly entails that one has *some* reason for believing that one is not a BIV, but it would be a stretch to maintain that this *by itself* entails that one has rationally grounded *knowledge* that one is not a BIV (even granted that the entailed belief in question will be true). There is thus a strong prima facie basis for arguing that the underdetermination$_{RK}$ principle is logically weaker than the closure$_{RK}$ principle, in the sense that from the same antecedent the former principle extracts a logically weaker consequent.

This point is confirmed once we reflect on the logical relationships in the other direction—namely, from the closure$_{RK}$ principle to the underdetermination$_{RK}$ principle. For notice that if one has rationally grounded knowledge that one is seated at one's desk, and one thereby has rationally grounded knowledge, via closure$_{RK}$, that one is not a BIV, then of course one inevitably has a rational basis for thinking that one is seated at one's desk that favors that scenario over the alternative skeptical scenario that is a BIV. One has, after all, rationally grounded knowledge that one is *not* a BIV.

Expressed a bit more formally, we can outline the reasoning in play here as follows. First, we assume the common antecedent of the simplified closure$_{RK}$-based and underdetermination$_{RK}$-based entailments:

(P1) *S* has rationally grounded knowledge that E. [Premise]

Given the simplified closure$_{RK}$-based entailment we can infer:

(P2) *S* has rationally grounded knowledge that she is not a BIV. [From (P1), Simplified Closure$_{RK}$-Based Entailment]

But if the subject has rationally grounded knowledge that she is seated at her desk, and she also has rationally grounded knowledge of the falsity of the (known to be incompatible) skeptical hypothesis that she is a BIV, then clearly she must have better rational support for her everyday belief over the skeptical alternative. We thus get (P3):

(P3) *S*'s rational support favors her belief that E over the BIV hypothesis. [From (P1), (P2)]

Crucially, however, (P3) is the consequent of the simplified underdetermination$_{RK}$-based entailment. And since we can derive this from the common antecedent of the simplified underdetermination$_{RK}$-based entailment and the closure$_{RK}$-based entailment by appealing only to the closure$_{RK}$ principle, it follows that the closure$_{RK}$ principle entails the underdetermination$_{RK}$ principle.[19] Moreover, since we have already noted that there is no obvious analogous entailment from the simplified underdetermination$_{RK}$-based entailment to the simplified closure$_{RK}$-based entailment, it also follows that the closure$_{RK}$ principle is logically stronger than the underdetermination$_{RK}$ principle, in the sense that the former entails, but is not entailed by, the latter.

One might be tempted to conclude from the foregoing that the underdetermination$_{RK}$-based skeptical paradox is thus more fundamental to the skeptical debate than the closure$_{RK}$-based skeptical argument, in that insofar as we can adequately deal with the former skeptical paradox then that will itself present us with a resolution of the latter skeptical paradox. But this would be too quick.

In particular, all that follows from the fact that the closure$_{RK}$ principle entails the underdetermination$_{RK}$ principle is that a rejection of the latter would entail a rejection of the former. Hence, any response to the underdetermination$_{RK}$-based skeptical paradox which involved a rejection of the underdetermination$_{RK}$ principle would thereby be a response to closure$_{RK}$-based skepticism.[20] But notice that this claim falls well short of the more general thesis that any adequate treatment of the underdetermination$_{RK}$-based skeptical paradox is thereby an adequate treatment of the closure$_{RK}$-based skeptical paradox. After all, one could respond to the former skeptical paradox in a way that keeps the underdetermination$_{RK}$ principle entirely intact—for example, by denying ($S_4$1)—and clearly this manner of dealing with the underdetermination$_{RK}$-based skeptical paradox might have no obvious ramifications for how one should respond to the closure$_{RK}$-based skeptical paradox. Accordingly, even despite the point just noted that of the two principles the closure$_{RK}$ principle is the logically stronger, it remains that we should be wary of thinking that we should therefore focus our attentions on the underdetermination$_{RK}$-based formulation of the skeptical paradox and take our eyes off its sister formulation.

6. The Source of Underdetermination-Based Radical Skepticism

Even granted what we have argued above, there is still more to say about underdetermination$_{RK}$-based radical skepticism. This is because there is a way of motivating this form of radical skepticism that appeals to a principle that is arguably even more epistemologically basic than the underdetermination$_{RK}$ principle.

Consider the following epistemic principle:

THE RATIONAL GROUND PRINCIPLE

If S has a rationally grounded belief that p, then S lacks a rational basis for believing that not-p.

The rational ground principle looks eminently plausible. Indeed, the demand it lays on rational belief is so weak that it is hard to see how anything that failed to satisfy it would constitute a rational basis for a belief. For how could one have a rational basis for a belief that was compatible with one possessing a rational basis for belief in the negation of the proposition believed? Put another way, insofar as one does have a rational basis to believe that a proposition is false, then how can one possibly have a rational basis for believing that this proposition is true?

Of course, we are not denying here the obvious point that one could have reasons to believe both a proposition and its negation. That this is possible is surely undeniable. Our concern is rather with the *overall* rational support one has for one's belief. The claim at issue in the rational ground principle is that insofar as one has an adequate overall rational support for belief in a proposition, then one lacks a rational basis for belief in its negation. Accordingly, where one has a rationally grounded belief in a proposition, this principle dictates that whatever reasons one might have had for believing the negation of this proposition are swamped by the superior reasons one has for one's belief.

At the very least, when we consider rationally grounded *knowledge* we surely have in mind knowledge that enjoys a rational basis that satisfies this principle. Thus, even though there may be a conception of what constitutes a rational basis for belief that is so weak that it doesn't even satisfy the rational ground principle, this would not be a species of rational support that interests us for our purposes.

Insofar as one finds the rational ground principle compelling, however, then one ought to be similarly persuaded by this related epistemic principle:

THE RATIONAL GROUND* PRINCIPLE

If S has a rationally grounded belief that p, and S knows that p entails q, then S lacks a rational basis for believing that not-q.

Whereas the rational ground principle concerns only contradictory propositions, the rational ground* principle extends the remit to concern any proposition that is known to be incompatible with the truth of the proposition believed by the subject. Even despite this extension of remit, what motivates the rational ground principle also motivates the rational ground* principle. After all, the incompatibility of p and not-p is so straightforward that we can take it as given that any rational agent ought to be aware of this incompatibility. Where it comes to nonobvious incompatible propositions, however, insofar as the agent knows about the incompatibility in play then that should suffice to entail that the rational basis for the believed proposition excludes a rational basis for belief in the incompatible proposition.

As before, this principle is consistent with the undeniable fact that one might have reasons in favor of one's belief and also reasons in support of the target known to be incompatible proposition. The point is just that the rational support for one's belief ought to be such that it is superior to the rational support one has in favor of the known to be incompatible proposition, where this means that one's overall rational position is one that favors the target belief and not belief in the known to be incompatible proposition.

Moreover, note that by insisting that the incompatibility in question must be known, we are ensuring that this principle is not unduly strong. Inevitably, there will be propositions that are incompatible with what one believes but where the incompatibility is unknown. The rational ground* principle is entirely consistent with one having a rationally grounded belief and also possessing a rational basis for belief in the incompatible proposition, just so long as one is unaware of the incompatibility between the two propositions.[21]

In order to compare this principle with the underdetermination$_{RK}$ and closure$_{RK}$ principles, it will be useful to consider an instance of it which concerns the same examples of quotidian and anti-skeptical propositions (which we will take for granted the subject knows are incompatible), and which also focuses specifically on rationally grounded knowledge (i.e., rather than just on rationally grounded belief). We thus get the following:

THE SIMPLIFIED RATIONAL GROUND*–BASED ENTAILMENT

If S has rationally grounded knowledge that E, then S lacks a rational basis for believing that she is a BIV.

Note that we are here understanding rationally grounded knowledge such that it conforms to the rational ground* principle. Thus, since the subject knows that being seated at her desk (E) is incompatible with being a BIV, so it follows from her possession of rationally grounded knowledge that E that she lacks a rational basis for belief in the BIV skeptical hypothesis.

We will begin exploring how these three principles relate to one another by considering the logical relationship between the simplified underdetermination$_{RK}$-based entailment and the simplified rational ground*–based entailment. Interestingly, it appears to be one of logical equivalence. Consider first the entailment from the simplified underdetermination$_{RK}$-based entailment to the simplified rational ground*–based entailment. So, we begin with the common antecedent:

(P1*) S has rationally grounded knowledge that E. [Premise]

Given the simplified underdetermination$_{RK}$-based entailment we can infer:

(P2*) S's rational support favors her belief that E over the BIV hypothesis. [From (P1*), Simplified Underdetermination$_{RK}$-Based Entailment]

Now assume, for *reductio*, that the subject has rational support for the belief that she is a BIV:

(P3*) S has rational support for believing that she is a BIV. [Assumption for *Reductio*]

Given (P3*), it follows that our subject does not have rational support that favors belief that E over the incompatible skeptical scenario that she is a BIV, since if she did possess such rational support then she wouldn't have rational support for the belief that she is a BIV. We thus get (P4*):

(P4*) S's rational support does not favor her belief that E over the BIV hypothesis. [From (P3*)]

But of course (P4*) is in direct conflict with (P2*), which is an immediate consequence of the simplified underdetermination$_{RK}$ principle. We can thus conclude, via *reductio ad absurdum*, that the negation of (P3*) must be true:

(P5*) S does not have rational support for believing that she is a BIV. [From (P2*), (P3*), (P4*), RAA][22]

(P5*) is, of course, the consequent of the simplified rational ground*–based entailment. We can thus derive, from the common antecedent of the simplified underdetermination$_{RK}$-based and simplified rational ground*–based entailments, and appealing only to the simplified underdetermination$_{RK}$ principle, the consequent of the simplified rational ground*–based entailment. We can therefore conclude that the underdetermination$_{RK}$ principle entails the rational ground* principle.

Now the reverse direction of fit, from the simplified rational ground*–based entailment to the simplified underdetermination$_{RK}$-based entailment. Again, we begin with the common antecedent of the simplified underdetermination$_{RK}$-based entailment and the simplified rational ground*–based entailment:

(P1**) S has rationally grounded knowledge that E. [Premise]

Via the simplified rational ground*–based entailment we can thus derive (P2**):

(P2**) S does not have rational support for believing that she is a BIV. [From (P1**), Simplified Rational Ground*–Based Entailment]

From (P1**) it obviously follows that (P3**):

(P3**) S has rational support for her belief that E. [From (P1**)]

And from (P2**) and (P3**) it follows that (P4**):

(P4**) S's rational support favors her belief that E over the BIV hypothesis. [From (P2**), (P3**)]

That is, if S has a rational basis for her belief that she is seated at her desk, and she lacks a rational basis for belief in the known to be incompatible skeptical alternative that she is a BIV, then her rational basis for believing that she is seated at her desk must favor this scenario over the incompatible scenario that she is a BIV.

(P4**), however, is the consequence of the simplified underdetermination$_{RK}$–based entailment. By appealing only to the common antecedent of the simplified rational ground*–based entailment and the simplified underdetermination$_{RK}$-based entailment, and to the simplified rational ground* principle, we have derived the consequent of the simplified underdetermination$_{RK}$-based entailment. The rational* ground principle thus entails the underdetermination$_{RK}$ principle. And since we have already seen that the underdetermination$_{RK}$ principle entails the rational ground* principle, it follows that these two principles are logically equivalent.[23]

What should we conclude from this? To begin with, notice that since the rational ground* and underdetermination$_{RK}$ principles are logically equivalent, it follows that the logical relationship we observed above between the closure$_{RK}$ and underdetermination$_{RK}$ principles will equally apply to the rational ground* and closure$_{RK}$ principles. In particular, it follows that the rational ground* principle is logically weaker than the closure$_{RK}$ principle, in that it is entailed by, but does not entail, this principle.

We can see this by looking at the consequents of the simplified rational ground*–based entailment and the simplified closure$_{RK}$-based entailment. Whereas the former states only that one *lacks* a rational basis for the belief that one *is* a BIV, the latter states that one *possesses* a rational basis for believing that one is *not* a BIV. Having a rational basis for believing that one is not a BIV clearly entails that one lacks a rational basis for believing that one is a BIV, but the converse does not hold. From common antecedents, these two entailments thus extract logically distinct consequents, such that the simplified closure$_{RK}$-based entailment is the logically stronger. It's a short step from this claim to the more general contention that the closure$_{RK}$ principle entails, but is not entailed by, the rational ground* principle.

Beyond this point, the ramifications of the logical equivalence of the rational ground* and underdetermination$_{RK}$ principles are not so clear. As we noted above, merely determining that the closure$_{RK}$ principle is logically stronger than the underdetermination$_{RK}$ principle does not thereby ensure that we should treat the formulation of the skeptical paradox in terms of the latter as more fundamental. In particular, there might be resolutions of the underdetermination$_{RK}$-based skeptical paradox that don't adequately philosophically engage with the closure$_{RK}$-based skeptical paradox. We should be equally wary about drawing quick conclusions about the logical equivalence that obtains between the rational ground* and underdetermination$_{RK}$ principles.

In particular, we should be cautious about concluding that since these two epistemic principles are logically equivalent it follows that they are of equal philosophical interest to our understanding of the skeptical problem. Indeed, we have already noted that the rational ground* principle seems to be in some sense more fundamental to the radical skeptical problem than the underdetermination$_{RK}$ principle, and this point is not necessarily undermined by the discovery that these two principles are logically equivalent. After all, the sense in which the rational ground* principle is more fundamental is arguably conceptual, in that it incorporates a more basic feature of our epistemic concepts than the underdetermination$_{RK}$ principle. Moreover, a principle can surely be conceptually fundamental relative to another principle while nonetheless being logically equivalent.

Indeed, the right conclusion to extract from this discussion of the logical relationship that holds between these two principles is that it highlights just how weak one's conception of rational support needs to be in order to motivate this particular form of radical skepticism. That is, the skeptical ramifications of the underdetermination$_{RK}$ principle might lead us to think that it is somehow, despite its intuitiveness, imposing unduly austere epistemic demands upon us. But once we discover that all we need to get this form of radical skepticism up and running is the extremely weak requirement on rational support that we have formulated as the rational ground* principle, we thereby also realize that the prospects for resolving this form of radical skepticism by rejecting the underdetermination$_{RK}$ principle are not very appealing.

7. Two Sources of Radical Skepticism

So where does all this leave us in terms of our understanding of the problem of radical skepticism? I want to close part 1 by drawing together some of the threads in our discussion and extracting some morals that will guide our deliberations in the ensuing chapters. To this end I will offer some general reflections on the kind of skeptical challenge presented by, on the one hand, underdetermination$_{RK}$/rational ground*–based radical skepticism and, on the other hand, closure$_{RK}$-based radical skepticism. Then, in light of these general reflections about these two forms of radical skeptical challenge, I will set out what, both minimally and ideally, we would want from an intellectually satisfying response to the problem of radical skepticism, where this is a response to this problem that deals with both kinds of skeptical challenge.

Consider first closure$_{RK}$-based radical skepticism. This form of skepticism exposes the apparent skeptical consequences of what we might naturally refer to as the "universality" of rational evaluation, where this concerns the manner in which there is no *in principle* constraints on the extent of one's rational evaluations (this is in contrast to *practical* constraints, of which there are usually many: time, imagination, opportunity cost, and so on). Call this the *universality of rational evaluation thesis*. Such an idea seems to underlie closure$_{RK}$-based radical skepticism in virtue of how there seems no inherent problem with the idea of extending the scope of a rational evaluation indefinitely by undertaking competent deductions from one's current stock of rationally grounded knowledge. In this way, one moves from rational evaluations of one's everyday rational beliefs to a rational evaluation of one's anti-skeptical commitments. In so doing, one is in effect shifting from a local rational evaluation to a global one, where the latter involves a wholesale rational assessment of one's epistemic situation. That such a shift in epistemic focus is thought harmless reflects an implicit commitment to the universality of rational evaluation thesis, since without this in play we would not be so inclined to allow such closure$_{RK}$-based inferences. In particular, if we antecedently held that there were in principle constraints on rational evaluation, then we would be inclined to limit such inferences so that they did not enable subjects to extend the scope of their rational evaluation beyond these limits.

In contrast, underdetermination$_{RK}$/rational ground*–based radical skepticism is concerned with how the rational support we have for our perceptual beliefs about the external world, even in the best case, is troublingly weak, in that it is compatible with widespread falsity in those beliefs. In this way, underdetermination$_{RK}$-based radical skepticism exposes the "insularity" of our rational support for these beliefs. Accordingly, we will call this claim the *insularity of reasons* thesis. Whereas the universality of rational evaluation thesis is concerned with the lack of in principle constraints on rational evaluation, the insularity of reasons thesis is concerned with a certain limitation on rational support itself, at least as regards the rational support enjoyed by our perceptual beliefs.[24]

That the rational support we have for our perceptual beliefs is insular in this way is often taken to be a core epistemological datum that requires explanation. Indeed, it is the backbone of the so-called new evil demon intuition.[25] This can be summarized as the claim that the rational support we have for our perceptual beliefs even in optimal perceptual conditions can be no better than the rational support our envatted counterpart (whose experiences are indistinguishable from our own) has for her equivalent beliefs, even though her beliefs are of course radically false.

As such, the new evil demon is effectively just a particular instance of the more general claim that is at issue in the insularity of reasons thesis.

It should be clear that underdetermination$_{RK}$/rational ground*–based radical skepticism buys into the insularity of reasons thesis without question. After all, the key element in this argument is the effective granting of the new evil demon intuition, for without this component one could not derive ($S_4$1) in the first place, and the appeal to the underdetermination$_{RK}$ principle in ($S_4$2) would be idle. This formulation of the radical skeptical paradox is thus essentially wedded to the insularity of reasons thesis.

Although the ultimate skeptical import of the universality of rational evaluation thesis and the insularity of reasons thesis is the same, it is important to note that they pose distinct epistemological challenges. Suppose, for example, that one rejected the universality of rational evaluation thesis and therefore argued that there are in principle limitations on the scope of rational evaluation. In this way, one could argue that closure$_{RK}$-based inferences need to be restricted in some way to prevent them from taking the subject from local to global rational evaluations. One could thus undermine the closure$_{RK}$-based radical skeptical paradox. In particular, one could hold that one's rationally grounded knowledge of everyday propositions—as far as this formulation of the skeptical paradox goes at any rate—is entirely compatible with a lack of rationally grounded knowledge of the denials of radical skeptical hypotheses (on account of the fact that one cannot employ a closure$_{RK}$-based inference in order to claim that one's rationally grounded knowledge of everyday propositions, if genuine, would entail the contested rationally grounded anti-skeptical knowledge).

It is far from obvious how that would help one resolve the problem posed by the insularity of reasons thesis, however. That one can have rationally grounded knowledge of mundane external world propositions while lacking rationally grounded knowledge of the denials of radical skeptical hypotheses is one thing; that one can have adequately rationally grounded knowledge of mundane external world propositions when that rational basis (one is aware) does not favor one's everyday beliefs over skeptical alternatives quite another. As one might put the point, if one's everyday beliefs do not satisfy the underdetermination$_{RK}$ principle, then in virtue of what, exactly, do they amount to rationally grounded knowledge? Thus, even with the closure$_{RK}$ principle out of (skeptical) action, one can still employ the underdetermination$_{RK}$ principle—and, thereby, the insularity of reasons thesis—to motivate a radical skeptical conclusion.

The same is true in the other logical direction, in that merely denying the insularity of reasons thesis does not in itself deliver a satisfactory response to the skeptical problem posed by the universality of rational evaluation thesis. For suppose that one argues that one's rational support can, in optimal cases say, epistemically favor one's everyday beliefs over radical skeptical alternatives. The insularity of reasons thesis would thus be rejected, and the underdetermination$_{RK}$ principle—while still standing—would be deprived of its skeptical ramifications. But can one straightforwardly generate on this basis a response to the radical skeptical problem posed by the universality of rational evaluation thesis? Alas, no.

For notice that the claim that one's rational support favors one's everyday beliefs over radical skeptical alternatives is consistent with one nonetheless lacking rationally grounded knowledge of the denials of these radical skeptical alternatives. The extent to which one has better rational support for one's everyday beliefs over radical skeptical alternatives could, after all, be merely marginal, and not of a kind that could underpin rationally grounded knowledge of the denials of these skeptical alternatives. It follows that one could have better rational support for one's everyday beliefs over radical skeptical alternatives and yet nonetheless lack rationally grounded knowledge of the denials of these radical skeptical alternatives. And note that this could be so even if one further supposes that one has rationally grounded knowledge of these everyday propositions.

But insofar as the rejection of the insularity of reasons thesis is compatible with a lack of rationally grounded knowledge of the denials of skeptical hypotheses, then the radical skeptic can appeal to the closure$_{RK}$ principle—and, thereby, the universality of rational evaluation thesis—in order to call the possibility of rationally grounded everyday knowledge into question. Thus, the mere fact that one has a better rational basis for one's everyday beliefs over radical skeptical alternatives will not suffice to block the closure$_{RK}$-based radical skeptical argument.

The upshot of the foregoing is that a fully adequate response to the problem of radical skepticism may well need to be sensitive to the particular challenges posed by *both* of the articulations of this problem that we have examined. As we will see in later chapters, this conclusion is potentially important in terms of our understanding of two prominent styles of anti-skepticism which can appear to be in competition with one another. In particular, it invites the thought that these two responses to the problem of radical skepticism may well be responding to different versions of the radical skeptical challenge, such that on closer inspection they are not competing anti-skeptical proposals at all, but rather mutually supporting.

8. Anti-skeptical Desiderata

We are now better placed to understand what we should be looking for in an intellectually palatable response to radical skepticism. Obviously, a minimal requirement is that it should reject at least one of the claims that are generating the radical skeptical paradox. Moreover, since we have noted that there are two logically distinct formulations of the radical skeptical paradox, this means showing that there is at least one claim in each articulation of the paradox that is false. In particular, we should be wary of responses to radical skepticism that confront only one formulation of the radical skeptical paradox.

Merely denying a component claim in a radical skeptical paradox is easy, of course. The difficulty is motivating that denial in an intellectually plausible way, particularly given that the claims that make up the radical skeptical paradox, on either formulation, are highly intuitive. As noted in chapter 1, while overriding anti-skeptical strategies—that is, those strategies that respond to the problem by appealing to an independently motivated epistemic revisionism—can in principle offer compelling resolutions of the skeptical problem, it is important that the epistemic revisionism they offer is only as extreme as the independent support allows.

We saw both in this chapter and in the last that this problem afflicts a certain kind of ham-fisted epistemic externalist response to the problem of radical skepticism. In particular, we noted that while there is an independent basis for advancing a form of epistemic externalism that is incompatible with certain formulations of the radical skeptical paradox, in order for this response to adequately deal with all relevant formulations of the radical skeptical paradox the type of epistemic externalism in play would need to be so extreme that it went well beyond the view that was independently motivated. The appeal of this overriding anti-skeptical strategy is thus significantly diminished.

Ideally, however, what we would like is a response to the problem of radical skepticism that is undercutting rather than overriding. That is, what we would prefer is a response to the problem that demonstrated that it was not the paradox that it purported to be but rather rested on contentious theoretical claims that were being illicitly presented as ungarnished intuition. That's a tall order, though as we will see in later chapters it's one that we can plausibly satisfy.

But what kind of undercutting anti-skeptical strategy would we optimally seek? Given that we have seen how the underdetermination$_{RK}$-based skeptical paradox trades on an extremely weak conception of rational support, there doesn't appear much scope for trying to maintain that knowledge can be rationally grounded and yet enjoy *weaker* levels of rational support. It seems, then, that what we would preferably want from a resolution to this particular skeptical paradox is a demonstration that we have the favoring rational support for our knowledge that the underdetermination$_{RK}$ principle demands. That is, we would want to show that we are not rationally on par with our envatted counterparts as the insularity of reasons thesis—and hence the new evil demon intuition—would suggest, but in fact are in possession of better rational support for our beliefs, such that the insularity of reasons thesis is false. The trick here would be to show that the rejection of the insularity of reasons thesis is in keeping with our ordinary epistemic practices, and hence not in conflict with intuition after all, but merely reflects misguided philosophical theory. (That is, the trick would be to show that the new evil demon "intuition" is not a bona fide intuition at all.)

As we noted above, it doesn't follow from the fact that one has rationally grounded knowledge that satisfies the underdetermination$_{RK}$ principle that one is able to have rationally grounded knowledge of the denials of radical skeptical hypotheses. The import of this anti-skeptical line to the closure$_{RK}$-based skeptical paradox is thus moot. It is not as if, for example, one could straightforwardly infer from the fact that one has rationally grounded knowledge that satisfies the underdetermination$_{RK}$ principle, such that one has better reason for thinking that one is presently seated than for the alternative BIV skeptical hypothesis, that one thereby also satisfies the closure$_{RK}$ principle by having rationally grounded knowledge that one is not a BIV.

This logical gap is one that a good anti-skeptical strategy should aim to exploit. The idea that we have rationally grounded knowledge of the denials of skeptical hypotheses looks highly implausible after all. Accordingly, what we would ideally want from a response to the closure$_{RK}$-based skeptical paradox is a way of retaining the closure$_{RK}$ principle (along with the idea that rationally grounded knowledge is common) while not endorsing its apparent upshot that we are able to know the denials of skeptical hypotheses (even though, in line with our ideal response to the underdetermination$_{RK}$-based skeptical paradox, we do have better grounds for our everyday beliefs than for their skeptical alternatives). In effect, what we would be attempting is a principled rejection of the universality of rational evaluation thesis that somehow kept the truth of the closure$_{RK}$ principle intact.

As before, we would also want this demonstration of why the closure$_{RK}$ principle doesn't in fact generate this unwanted consequence to convict the skeptic of introducing some illicit faulty theoretical assumption that is contrary to intuition (such that our response to both skeptical paradoxes is of an undercutting variety).

Finally, what we would ideally want from a response to the problem of radical skepticism, in both its guises, is an *integrated* treatment, one on which the responses to the two distinct formulations of the skeptical paradox are not just compatible but mutually supporting.

On the face of it, to aspire to all of this seems sheer folly. The problem of radical skepticism has haunted us for a long time, and to suppose that we could offer such a dramatic and comprehensive resolution appears vainglorious. And yet, as I will try to show in the ensuing chapters of this book, just such a resolution of skepticism is indeed available to us.

PART 2

Wittgenstein and the Groundlessness of Our Believing

∼

> The difficulty is to realize the groundlessness of our believing.
> —Wittgenstein, *On Certainty*, §166

> None of us can think or act without the acceptance of truths, not intuitive, not demonstrated, yet sovereign.
> —John Henry Newman, *An Essay in Aid of a Grammar of Assent*, 150

CHAPTER 3

Wittgenstein on the Structure of Rational Evaluation

0. Introductory Remarks

We saw in part 1 that the contemporary radical skeptical problem has two main aspects, one that turns on a closure-style epistemic principle and one that turns on an underdetermination-style epistemic principle. In part 2 we will be considering the import of Wittgenstein's influential treatment of radical skepticism as found in his final notebooks, which are published as *On Certainty*. In particular, we will be examining how best to construe this treatment in light of the distinction between the two ways of thinking about radical skepticism that we explored in part 1. As we will see, what Wittgenstein is offering us is an *undercutting* anti-skeptical strategy, one that presents us with a direct response to the closure$_{RK}$-based radical skeptical paradox. In particular, what Wittgenstein is urging upon us is a principled rejection of the universality of rational evaluation thesis that we encountered in chapter 2 and that we saw is underpinning the skeptical employment of the closure$_{RK}$ principle. Interestingly, we will be arguing that, properly construed, Wittgenstein's anti-skepticism offers us a way of rejecting the universality of rational evaluation thesis that is entirely consistent with endorsing the closure$_{RK}$ principle.

Despite the appeal of this way of dealing with the radical skeptical problem, it is also in certain respects intellectually unsatisfying too. We will be offering a diagnosis of why this approach is unsatisfying in terms of its failure to properly engage with the underdetermination$_{RK}$-based formulation of the radical skeptical paradox, and thus with the insularity of reasons thesis, which (as we saw in chapter 2) underlies this particular formulation of the paradox.

1. Wittgenstein on the Structure of Rational Evaluation

The primary critical target of *On Certainty* is G. E. Moore's (1925; cf. Moore 1939) famous argument against skepticism. Moore responded to the skeptical challenge by enumerating some of the many things that he took himself to be most certain of, and thus that he took himself to know. These Moorean claims were meant to be such that if Moore knew anything, then he knew these propositions. Call these claims *Moorean certainties*. The most famous Moorean certainty is of course the claim that one has two hands. Such Moorean certainties are meant to play a kind of foundational epistemic role, in the sense that in virtue of being optimally certain they can be employed as the epistemic basis from which Moore can extract more controversial, and less certain, claims. As Moore points out, if one does know that one has two hands, then it surely follows that one can know that there is an external world (hands being, after all, physical items that occupy such an external world). Even Wittgenstein would grant Moore this conditional claim, since as he notes in the very opening line of *On Certainty*:

> If you do know that here is one hand, we'll grant you all the rest. (OC, §1)

That the structure of rational evaluation should be thought of along foundational lines is of course nothing new. Normally, though, the items that serve the foundational role—beliefs typically, though not exclusively—tended to be broadly philosophical in nature, in the sense that it took a certain kind of philosophical project—such as the Cartesian project of pure inquiry—to uncover them. What is distinctive about Moore's proposal, in contrast, is that he wanted to treat what he regarded as perfectly "everyday" certainties—that is, the kinds of claims that folk in normal circumstances are most certain of, such as that one has two hands, that one has parents, that the earth has existed for many years before one was born, and so on—as being able to perform this foundational role.[1]

Despite the superficial appeal of Moore's proposal, Wittgenstein argues in *On Certainty* that there is something profoundly problematic about it. Moore's idea is that the certainties he cites can play this foundational epistemic role because, due to their optimal certainty, they possess a kind of epistemic groundedness that less certain propositions lack. Wittgenstein contends, in contrast, that it is in the very nature of these Moorean certainties, in virtue of the fact that they are optimally certain, that they cannot be coherently thought of as rationally grounded. That is, Wittgenstein maintains that that which we are most certain of must be by its very nature rationally groundless.

Consider the Moorean certainty that (for most people, and in normal circumstances) one has two hands. Wittgenstein writes,

> My having two hands is, in normal circumstances, as certain as anything that I could produce in evidence for it.

> That is why I am not in a position to take the sight of my hand as evidence for it. (OC, §250)

Wittgenstein is suggesting that to conceive of this proposition as rationally grounded is to suppose that the rational grounds are more certain than the proposition itself, which of course is ex hypothesi impossible since the proposition at issue is held to be optimally certain. Wittgenstein brings this point into sharp relief by highlighting how odd it would be for one to treat one's conviction that one has two hands as being grounded in one's sight of one's hand. Consider this passage:

> If a blind man were to ask me "Have you got two hands?" I should not make sure by looking. If I were to have any doubt of it, then I don't know why I should trust my eyes. For why shouldn't I test my *eyes* by looking to find out whether I see my two hands? *What* is to be tested by *what*? (OC, §125)

In normal circumstances, one doesn't need to check by looking that one has two hands, and indeed to check by looking would make no sense anyway. If one doubts that one has two hands, then one ought not to believe what one's eyesight tells one, since this is no more certain than that one has two hands, which is in doubt.

A quite striking claim is emerging here. For not only are these Moorean certainties necessarily groundless, according to Wittgenstein, but it also seems they are by that same token immune to rational doubt. For any rational basis for doubting the Moorean certainty would be necessarily less certain than the optimally certain Moorean certainty, and hence one would have more reason to doubt the grounds offered for doubting the Moorean certainty than to doubt the Moorean certainty itself. At the very least, what Wittgenstein seems to be suggesting in this passage is that there could be no rational basis that would *mandate* doubt of a Moorean certainty, since one rational response to the presentation of this ground for doubt could simply be to doubt the ground itself. That claim falls short of the stronger thesis that rational doubt of a Moorean certainty is impossible, but it is even so a dramatic claim to make.

It soon becomes clear, however, that Wittgenstein wants to defend the stronger thesis. That is, that not only are Moorean certainties necessarily groundless, but that also rational doubt of a Moorean certainty is simply impossible (i.e., as opposed to being merely rationally unmandated). Wittgenstein claims that the very idea of a rational evaluation, whether positive or negative, presupposes a backdrop of Moorean certainties that are themselves exempt from rational evaluation. To attempt to rationally evaluate a Moorean certainty is thus an attempt to do something impossible. In particular, Wittgenstein repeatedly urges that the very idea of rationally doubting a Moorean certainty is incoherent. Such a doubt, he writes, would "drag everything with it and plunge it into chaos" (OC, §613). Doubt of a Moorean certainty is deemed akin to doubting everything, but Wittgenstein cautions that

> if you tried to doubt everything you would not get as far as doubting anything. The game of doubting itself presupposes certainty. (OC, §115)[2]

And elsewhere, "A doubt that doubted everything would not be a doubt" (OC, §450; cf. OC, §§370; 490; 613).[3]

The picture that emerges is thus one in which all rational evaluation is essentially local, in that it takes place relative to fundamental commitments that are themselves immune to rational evaluation, but that need to be in place in order for a rational evaluation to occur. In a memorable passage, Wittgenstein refers to these fundamental commitments—the Moorean certainties—as the "hinges" on which rational evaluations turn:

> The *questions* that we raise and our *doubts* depend upon the fact that some propositions are exempt from doubt, are as it were like hinges on which those turn.
>
> That is to say, it belongs to the logic of our scientific investigations that certain things are *in deed* not doubted.
>
> But it isn't that the situation is like this: We just *can't* investigate everything, and for that reason we are forced to rest content with assumption. If I want the door to turn, the hinges must stay put. (OC, §§341–43)[4]

Wittgenstein is thus offering a radically new conception of the structure of rational evaluation, one that has important implications for the extent to which one can coherently undertake rational evaluations. In particular, he is arguing that both the skeptical project of offering a wholesale *negative* rational evaluation of our beliefs and the traditional anti-skeptical (e.g., Moorean) project of offering a wholesale *positive* rational evaluation of our beliefs are simply incoherent. This is because, according to Wittgenstein, the very idea of a wholesale rational evaluation is itself unintelligible, for it is in the very nature of rational evaluations that they take place relative to hinge commitments that are both groundless and indubitable.

2. Wittgenstein contra the Skeptical "Paradox"

Before we begin spelling out the details of Wittgenstein's conception of the structure of rational evaluation—a task that, as we will see, is messy indeed—it will be useful to first reflect on the general kind of anti-skeptical approach that Wittgenstein is advocating. We noted in chapter 1 (§§1–2) that radical skepticism purports to be offering us a *paradox*, in the sense that it constitutes a fundamental tension in our folk epistemic concepts. We also noted that we could divide anti-skeptical responses into *undercutting* and *overriding* treatments of the problem. Responses of the first kind demonstrate that the skeptical "paradox" is in fact illusory, and arises instead out of faulty philosophical theory. Responses of the second kind concede that the skeptical problem trades on a genuine fundamental tension in our folk epistemic concepts, and so is to this extent a bona fide paradox, but nonetheless argues on independent grounds for a form of epistemic revisionism that evades the paradox. We noted that undercutting responses are to be preferred, all other things being equal, to overriding responses.

It ought to be clear that the kind of anti-skepticism that Wittgenstein is offering is of the undercutting variety. Wittgenstein is trying to get us to see that what looks like a puzzle that is arising out of entirely natural—that is, normal, unremarkable—epistemic moves, in fact trades on a philosophical picture that is very different from our normal epistemic practices and can be shown to be highly dubious. That is, while the shift from localized rational evaluations that occur in everyday epistemic contexts to the kind of global rational evaluations that the skeptic employs can look harmless—in that we are simply applying our normal system of rational evaluation in a more thoroughgoing fashion—there is in fact, argues Wittgenstein, a very real and fundamental difference between the two. For if Wittgenstein is right, the possibility of localized rational evaluations actually *precludes* the possibility of global rational evaluations. This is why Wittgenstein's anti-skepticism is of the undercutting variety, since he is treating the skeptical problem as arising out of a faulty philosophical picture that is masquerading as common sense.

Of course, we are still to be told exactly which of the claims that make up the skeptical paradox—more accurately, as we saw in part 1, the skeptical *paradoxes*—should be rejected, but as we will see this very much depends on how one spells out the details of the view. We will turn to this issue in due course. First, however, it will be useful at this juncture to distinguish Wittgenstein's anti-skepticism from a superficially similar anti-skeptical line, one that is also cast along undercutting lines but faces a fairly fundamental problem. In doing so, we will discern a bit more both about the conception of radical skepticism qua paradox, and also about Wittgenstein's distinctive response to this problem.

The alternative undercutting anti-skeptical line I have in mind is one that merely proceeds by emphasizing how very different our everyday practices of rational evaluation are from the kind of rational evaluation proposed by the radical skeptic. Such an anti-skeptical line is often credited, for example, to J. L. Austin (1961), who certainly offers us a vivid account of the difference between the kinds of doubts that arise in normal contexts and the very different doubts at issue in skeptical contexts. For example, in characterizing the kinds of legitimate doubts that might be raised about a claim to know in a normal context (e.g., about whether what one sees is a goldfinch), Austin famously opined,

> Enough is enough: it doesn't mean everything. Enough means enough to show that (within reason, and for present intents and purposes) it "can't" be anything else, there is no room for an alternative, competing description of it. It does not mean, for example, enough to show it isn't a *stuffed* goldfinch. (Austin 1961, 84)

That is, normal doubts (e.g., about whether what you see really is a goldfinch) are resolved by appeal to very normal supporting evidence (e.g., by appeal to one's expertise in this regard). In contrast, what the skeptic appears to be demanding is a very different, and much more demanding, kind of supporting evidence—namely, evidence for thinking that one is not the victim of skeptical hypotheses of some description.

The point of marking out this contrast between everyday and skeptical modes of epistemic evaluation is to try to demonstrate that what the skeptic is offering is not the natural employment of our folk epistemic concepts, but rather something very much opposed to those folk concepts. In doing so, the anti-skeptical thought runs, radical skepticism is deprived of much of its power. In terms of our formulation of radical skepticism as a putative paradox we can put our finger on the nub of the issue here, which is that what this way of dealing with the problem is attempting to do is offer us an undercutting response that demonstrates that the problem is not a bona fide paradox at all, but rather the product of faulty philosophical theory under the guise of folk intuition.[5]

The approach to radical skepticism that we have seen Wittgenstein offer can on the face of it look very similar to the Austinian anti-skeptical line just set out. Wittgenstein, after all, also emphasizes the differences between the everyday and the skeptical(/Moorean) systems of rational evaluation. Nonetheless, his view is different in a crucial respect, as we will see.

This is fortunate because the Austinian way of approaching the skeptical problem is inherently problematic, at least once we make clear exactly what is meant when we say that the skeptical problem is a paradox. In part 1 we expressed this point simply in terms of the idea that it is a problem that arises out of our folk epistemic concepts. While this is entirely correct, it is important to emphasize that this description is entirely compatible with skeptical doubts being such that they do not usually arise in normal contexts.

Indeed, as a number of commentators have pointed out—most notably Barry Stroud (1984)—the skeptic needn't claim that her wholesale doubts are ones that would naturally arise in day-to-day life. Rather, the skeptical thought is that if one *steps back* from everyday life and employs everyday epistemic principles in a thoroughgoing way, while setting aside the practical limitations of everyday contexts, then one is led to skeptical doubts. It is precisely in this sense that radical skepticism is held to "fall out" of our ordinary epistemic practices even while involving doubts that simply do not arise in quotidian situations. The thought is that the skeptic's wholesale rational evaluation of our beliefs is merely a "purified" version of our ordinary ways of rational evaluating beliefs, and hence ultimately trades on nothing more than our normal folk epistemological concepts.

With this point in mind, it ought to be clear that there is a crucial lacuna in the Austinian approach to radical skepticism just sketched that merely contrasts our everyday epistemic practices with the skeptic's mode of epistemic evaluation. For given that the claim that radical skepticism constitutes a paradox is entirely consistent with such a contrast between everyday and skeptical epistemic practices, it is hard to see what purchase merely marking this distinction has on the skeptical problem. In particular, the case offered by the Austinian approach for a genuine undercutting response to the skeptical paradox seems undercooked at best.

So why doesn't Wittgenstein's response to the problem of radical skepticism fall foul of the same problem? In order to understand why Wittgenstein's treatment of skepticism evades this difficulty we need to note that a crucial feature of his view is that it is an *inherent*, and thus nonnegotiable, feature of rational evaluation that it is local in the way that he describes. It is, he writes, part of the very "logic" of our system of rational evaluation that it is essentially local, to the extent that all doubt takes place relative to our arational hinge commitments, which are beyond doubt. This is what makes this type of undercutting anti-skeptical strategy so very different from the more modest undercutting anti-skeptical strategy just considered (i.e., one that merely emphasizes the contrast between everyday and skeptical methods of rational evaluation).

In particular, this feature of Wittgenstein's conception of the structure of rational evaluation, if tenable, excludes even the possibility that the radical skeptic's wholesale rational evaluations could constitute a "purified" version of our everyday local rational evaluations. On the Wittgensteinian picture, the wholesale rational evaluations at the heart of radical skepticism could not be our normal rational evaluations in their purified form, since the very idea of a wholesale rational evaluation is itself incoherent. There is thus an important difference of kind, and not merely degree, when it comes to our everyday practices of rational evaluation and the type of rational evaluation attempted by the radical skeptic (or, for that matter, attempted by the traditional anti-skeptic, like Moore).[6]

If this new conception of the structure of rational evaluation could be made defensible, then it would clearly have far-reaching ramifications for epistemology. The difficulty, however, is knowing how to turn Wittgenstein's sketchy remarks on this topic into a concrete proposal. In particular, part of the challenge is to develop this proposal in such a way that it doesn't end up looking like a form of radical skepticism in disguise. After all, to be told that all rational support takes place relative to a backdrop of ungroundable certainties does sound an awful lot like skepticism. Indeed, it invites the thought that the "rational support" in question, being inherently local in this way, is not really bona fide rational support at all, in virtue of being ultimately groundless.

Wittgenstein was certainly alert to this worry, writing that the "difficulty is to realise the groundlessness of our believing" (OC, §166). On his view the regress of reasons comes to an end, but it does not come to end with further reasons of a special foundational sort as we were expecting. Instead, when we reach bedrock we discover only a rationally groundless "animal" commitment (OC, §359), a kind of "primitive" trust (OC, §475). For Wittgenstein, understanding that this is so is meant to be the antidote to radical skepticism, and yet it must surely be admitted that, superficially at least, it looks very much like little more than a version of radical skepticism.

3. A Core Problem for the Wittgensteinian Account of the Structure of Rational Evaluation

We just noted that one general concern with the Wittgensteinian account of the structure of rational evaluation is that it might ultimately collapse into a variant of the very kind of radical skepticism that it was meant to evade. In particular, from a skeptical point of view it is hard to see just what is so *anti*-skeptical about the claim that the structure of rational evaluation has, at its core, arational commitments. Isn't that just what the radical skeptic claims? But if so, then how is this view to be distinguished from radical skepticism, exactly?

We can bring this general concern about the Wittgensteinian proposal into sharper relief by considering how one's hinge commitments are related to one's non–hinge commitments. The latter are, presumably, beliefs in the normal way, and for that matter are meant to be (ordinarily) supported by reasons. The former, however, are a more controversial class. They can't be supported by reasons if Wittgenstein is right (reasons for thinking the target proposition true, anyway—the point of this distinction will become clearer below). But now we face a puzzle. For is it not possible, at least in some cases, to reason one's way from rationally held belief in non–hinge propositions to beliefs in the propositions at issue in hinge commitments (i.e., reason one's way to belief in a hinge proposition)? But if that's correct, then why can't one's hinge commitments be thought of as rationally held beliefs after all (and thus, potentially anyway, rationally held knowledge)? Conversely, if we are unable to do this because Wittgenstein is right that such rational support for our hinge commitments is impossible, then doesn't that undermine the idea of even "local" rational support too, such that local rational support is ultimately no rational support at all?

In order to put some flesh onto the bones of the concern in play here, let's take a concrete example, based on one that Wittgenstein himself discusses (see OC, §183). One can surely know on a rational basis that Napoleon won the Battle of Austerlitz in 1805 (e.g., by reading this claim in an authoritative history text). But a relevant hinge commitment in the background here on the Wittgensteinian picture is presumably that the Earth has existed for a relatively long time, and didn't just spring into existence in the last five minutes replete with the traces of a distant ancestry.[7] Qua hinge commitment, this is not the kind of commitment that could be rationally supported. And that seems right, since what could rationally support such a commitment, given that it is in effect the denial of a radical skeptical scenario? Any reasonably reflective agent could presumably recognize, however, that their knowledge of the historical claim regarding Napoleon's victory entails the denial of the target "historical" radical skeptical hypothesis. But if the former is rationally supported, then what is stopping this agent from inferring, on this rational basis, that the latter anti-skeptical claim must obtain also? Moreover, once such an inference is made, doesn't our agent thereby have a rationally grounded belief in a hinge proposition (something that Wittgenstein claims is impossible)? And if they don't, then how can it be that they still have a bona fide rational basis for believing the more concrete historical claim that Napoleon won the Battle of Austerlitz in 1805?

It ought to be clear from our discussion in part 1 that the problem in play here essentially concerns the universality of rational evaluation thesis, and the related claim that one can harmlessly extend the scope of one's rational evaluations by making closure$_{RK}$-based inferences from one's current stock of rationally grounded knowledge. Consider again the closure$_{RK}$ principle as we formulated it in part 1:

THE CLOSURE$_{RK}$ PRINCIPLE

If S has rationally grounded knowledge that p, and S competently deduces from p that q, thereby forming a belief that q on this basis while retaining her rationally grounded knowledge that p, then S has rationally grounded knowledge that q.

Given the closure$_{RK}$ principle, if one has rationally grounded knowledge that Napoleon won the Battle of Austerlitz in 1805 (e.g., knowledge that is rationally grounded in the testimony of reliable historical records, and so on), and one competently deduces on this basis that the universe did not come into existence five minutes ago, then via this principle one ought to have rationally grounded knowledge of this hinge proposition. Conversely, according to this principle if one is unable to have rationally grounded knowledge that the universe did not come into existence five minutes ago, then the subject's putative rationally grounded knowledge that Napoleon won the Battle of Austerlitz in 1805 is under threat.

As we saw in part 1, the closure$_{RK}$ principle looks eminently plausible. In particular, it is hard to see how one would go about denying this principle. Given that competent deduction is by its nature a well-conducted rational process, how could it be that a belief gained via competent deduction, and which was derived from rationally supported knowledge, could be any less rationally supported than the belief from which it is derived? What could possibly prevent the deduced belief from being knowledge, and moreover from being any less rationally supported knowledge than the original belief?

But with this principle in play it ought to be possible for the rationally articulate subject to undertake competent deductions from their rationally supported knowledge of non–hinge propositions and in doing so gain rationally supported knowledge of hinge propositions. Since this would clearly be unacceptable on the Wittgensteinian account of the structure of rational evaluation, the upshot is that either this principle has to go or else one must deny that the nonhinge beliefs in these cases constitute genuine rationally supported knowledge. Neither claim is particularly appealing. Indeed, to take the latter route seems to be to straightforwardly concede that the Wittgensteinian account of the structure of rational evaluation cannot deal with the problem of radical skepticism, since it is tantamount to allowing that "local" rational support is ultimately no rational support at all.

We are thus faced with an apparent dilemma between, on the one hand, giving in to radical skepticism and, on the other hand, rejecting a highly intuitive epistemic principle. Call this dilemma the *closure problem* for the Wittgensteinian account of the structure of rational evaluation.[8]

4. Epistemic Ways of Developing the Wittgensteinian Account of the Structure of Rational Evaluation (I): The Externalist Reading

In the contemporary literature one can find several proposals which develop Wittgenstein's account of the structure of rational evaluation, though they often struggle to answer the closure problem. In this section and the next we will consider two of these proposals, which share as a common theme that while we lack a rational basis for thinking hinge propositions to be true, one's commitment to these propositions can nonetheless constitute knowledge (it is in this sense that they count as *epistemic* proposals).

The first proposal is to ally the Wittgensteinian account of the structure of rational evaluation to a form of epistemic externalism that allows that one can have knowledge even in the absence of supporting reasons. As we saw in part 1, epistemic externalists hold that knowledge can be sometimes "brute," at least from a rational point of view, in that one can possess it without having a rational basis for the target proposition. The merit of applying this proposal to the Wittgensteinian account of the structure of rational evaluation is that we needn't conclude from the fact that hinges lack rational support that they are thereby unknown. Call this the *externalist reading*.[9] It is effectively a form of neo-Mooreanism of the kind that we have encountered previously, in that it at least entails the key neo-Moorean claim that we can have knowledge of the denials of radical skeptical hypotheses.

Part of the attraction of developing Wittgenstein's account of the structure of rational evaluation along these lines is that it potentially gives one a principled basis for rejecting the closure$_{RK}$ principle, and hence avoiding the closure problem just set out. In particular, proponents of the externalist reading are in a position to claim that while Wittgenstein's conception of the structure of rational evaluation is incompatible with the closure$_{RK}$ principle, it is nonetheless entirely compatible with a related principle—namely, the closure principle for knowledge *simpliciter*, which we encountered in part 1:

THE CLOSURE PRINCIPLE

If S knows that p, and S competently deduces from p that q, thereby forming a belief that q on this basis while retaining her knowledge that p, then S knows that q.

As we saw in part 1, whereas the closure$_{RK}$ principle demands that one's rationally supported knowledge be preserved across competent deductions, the closure principle merely demands that one's knowledge be preserved across competent deductions. So, for example, the closure principle demands that if one knows that Napoleon won the Battle of Austerlitz in 1805, and one competently deduces on this basis that the universe did not come into existence five minutes ago, then one also knows the entailed proposition. What the closure principle for knowledge doesn't demand, however—unlike the closure$_{RK}$ principle—is that where the subject's knowledge of the antecedent proposition is rationally supported, it follows that the knowledge she gains of the consequent proposition via the competent deduction is rationally supported also.

As such, the closure principle is arguably more defensible than the closure$_{RK}$ principle, on account of the fact that it demands less. With that in mind, however, one might be tempted to hold that we can live with the rejection of the closure$_{RK}$ principle just so long as we can retain the closure principle. In particular, if one can appeal to epistemic externalism in order to make sense of the idea that hinge propositions can be known even despite their lack of rational support, then we can in principle allow agents to use competent deductions to acquire (mere) knowledge of a hinge proposition even while denying, contra the closure$_{RK}$ principle, that agents can use competent deductions to acquire *rationally supported* knowledge of a hinge proposition. One could then diagnose the appeal of the closure$_{RK}$ principle as arising out of a failure to recognize that it is a stronger epistemic principle than the closely related closure principle.

Indeed, as we saw in part 1, from an epistemically externalist perspective it is open to one to argue that the closure$_{RK}$ principle is independently dubious because it illicitly incorporates epistemic internalist commitments. If, as the epistemic externalist maintains, not all knowledge is rationally grounded, then why should we hold that the process of extending our knowledge via competent deduction should guarantee that where the agent's knowledge of the entailing proposition is rationally supported it follows that her knowledge of the consequent proposition is rationally supported also? The upshot would be that while it would indeed on this view be intellectually disastrous to deny the closure principle, so long as one can retain that principle one could live with the rejection of the closure$_{RK}$ principle.[10]

There are several problems with the externalist reading, but I will focus here on three key worries. We witnessed one of these problems in chapter 1 when we considered a crude epistemic externalist neo-Moorean response to the radical skeptical problem, which proceeded by denying, on epistemic externalist grounds, the closure$_{RK}$ principle. As we saw there, the problem facing this strategy is that the supposed epistemic externalist motivation for denying the closure$_{RK}$ principle is not very plausible on closer inspection. Epistemic externalists do not usually deny that there can be *any* rationally supported knowledge, and the thesis motivating the closure$_{RK}$ principle is only that when it comes to this specific type of knowledge the rational support should transfer across the relevant competent deduction. There therefore seems no inherent reason why this should be in conflict with epistemic externalism, specifically.

It is worth recalling in this regard the dilemma we posed for this style of anti-skepticism. An epistemic externalist response to skepticism of this sort is, remember, an overriding anti-skeptical strategy, in that it offers us independent theoretical grounds for rejecting an intuitive claim that makes up the skeptical paradox. As such, it is important that the epistemic revisionism on offer is proportionate to the independent motivation for this revisionism. This is where the dilemma crops up. For while there is indeed an independent theoretical basis for epistemic externalism, this only in itself motivates the contention that *some* knowledge lacks a rational foundation. But for epistemic externalism to offer the advertised response to the closure$_{RK}$-based skeptical paradox it is crucially important that *no* knowledge (or, in any case, hardly any knowledge) is rationally grounded. And yet there is no independent theoretical basis on offer for *that* claim. The dilemma facing this epistemic externalist rendering of the hinge proposition idea is thus that either it is appropriately grounded in an independent theoretical motivation, in which case it does not license a claim strong enough to rebut the skeptical problem by anyone's lights, or else it does rebut the skeptical problem by buttressing the required anti-skeptical claim, in which case it ceases to be a plausible overriding response to the skeptical problem (since it lacks the requisite independent motivation for epistemic revisionism of this kind).

A second worry with the externalist reading of hinge propositions is a general concern about the plausibility of denying the closure$_{RK}$ principle. For while one might agree that it would be even more problematic to deny the closure principle, it remains that rejecting even the closure$_{RK}$ principle has large prima facie costs. For example, as we noted in chapter 1, such a denial appears to commit us to (a variant of) what Keith DeRose (1995) has called "abominable conjunctions." That is, rejecting the closure$_{RK}$ principle in the way suggested seems to commit us to endorsing conjunctions such as "I have excellent reasons in support of my knowledge that Napoleon won the Battle of Austerlitz in 1805, but have no reason whatsoever for believing that the Universe was in existence at this time."[11] At the very least, in denying the closure$_{RK}$ principle one also needs to further show that these conjunctions are not as bizarre as they at first appear.

A third concern about this strategy is more specific to the details of the proposal. For notice that while epistemic externalism can open up the theoretical space within which we can make sense of an agent's possessing knowledge even in the absence of rational support for the target beliefs, it still remains to be shown that the target beliefs amount to knowledge by externalist lights. The problem, however, is that it is hard to see how such an account would go.

Consider, for example, the prospects of developing this account along process reliabilist lines.[12] The difficulty is that it doesn't seem at all plausible to suppose that we know hinge propositions in virtue of forming the target beliefs via a reliable belief-forming process. Indeed, our hinge commitments do not seem to be the product of *any* specific kind of belief-forming process, but rather are part of the tacit intellectual backdrop against which we acquire our beliefs in non–hinge propositions. For example, my hinge commitment to the universe having not come into existence five minutes ago was not acquired via a specific cognitive process, but is rather something that is presupposed in the specific cognitive processes by which I come to acquire particular historical beliefs, such as that Napoleon's victory at Austerlitz was in 1805. Or, to take another example that Wittgenstein (OC, §143) himself offers in this regard, while a child might be taught various facts about a mountain (e.g., that such and such was the first to climb it), she is not taught that the mountain has existed for a long time, and didn't simply pop into existence fairly recently. The latter is rather something that the child "swallows down" along with the things that she is explicitly taught. But if our hinge commitments aren't acquired via—or, for that matter, sustained by—a particular reliable belief-forming process, then they are not in the market for knowledge by the lights of this variety of epistemic externalism.

This problem is not specific to process reliabilist versions of epistemic externalism, since it is a common feature of epistemic externalist proposals that they evaluate a belief in terms of the manner in which it is formed. Consider, for example, virtue epistemologies that are cast along epistemic externalist lines, or the kind of modal conditions that are imposed by some forms of epistemic externalism, where the condition in question is almost always understood in a basis-relative manner.[13] It follows that it's going to be hard to tell even an epistemic externalist-friendly story about how one might have knowledge of hinge propositions, since whatever externalist epistemology one opts for will inevitably assess this putative knowledge by evaluating the epistemic credentials of the manner in which it was acquired, and yet our hinge commitments don't seem to have *any* epistemic pedigree in this regard.

5. Epistemic Ways of Developing the Wittgensteinian Account of the Structure of Rational Evaluation (II): The Entitlement Reading

A second epistemic way of developing Wittgenstein's account of the structure of rational evaluation is cast along broadly epistemic internalist lines. Like the epistemic externalist strategy, this proposal also argues that one can have knowledge of hinge propositions even while lacking a rational basis for thinking that these propositions are true. Accordingly, this stance also rejects the closure$_{RK}$ principle while retaining the closure principle. As such it is also a form of neo-Mooreanism, albeit not of an epistemic externalist variety. What is distinctive about this proposal is that rather than grounding our putative knowledge of hinge propositions in externalist epistemic support it instead appeals to a type of rational—and thus, in principle at least, internalistically respectable—epistemic support, albeit a special kind of rational support that does not consist in reasons for thinking the target propositions *to be true*. This special kind of rational support is known as *entitlement*. Accordingly, call this the *entitlement reading*.[14]

In essence, the idea is that where we are obliged, on pain of cognitive paralysis, to be committed to certain propositions that we have no reason for thinking are true, then, so long as there is no reason available for thinking those propositions to be false, one has a default rational basis—an *entitlement*—for these commitments. After all, or so the thinking goes anyway, one is surely rational in avoiding cognitive paralysis, and hence in cases where one has no reason to believe that not-*p*, and where a failure to believe that *p* would result in cognitive paralysis, it is arguably rational to believe that *p* even when one has no rational basis for believing that *p* is true.

Thus a lack of rational basis for the truth of a proposition is compatible, on this view, with there being a rational basis for believing it nonetheless. And hence there is an epistemic basis on which one can know this proposition too (even, potentially, by epistemic internalist lights, since the story told here is an entirely *rational* story, of a kind that ought to be in principle amenable to the spirit of epistemic internalism).

In this way the defender of the entitlement reading can motivate the claim that one can know hinge propositions. We noted above, for example, that one distinctive feature of hinge propositions is that to doubt them would lead to cognitive paralysis. Moreover, one can also plausibly argue that there are no grounds for believing the denials of hinge propositions too. Our beliefs in hinge propositions thus pass the "entitlement" test and hence can count as knowledge, even though we lack rational support for supposing these propositions true. And if we can know hinge propositions, then in principle at least we can retain the closure principle. That is, it will no longer follow that agents who undertake competent deductions from their rationally held beliefs in non–hinge propositions to form beliefs in hinge propositions will fall foul of this principle by failing to know the deduced propositions.

But the closure$_{RK}$ principle does have to go on this view, as it remains the case that one cannot have a rational basis for believing hinge propositions to be true, no matter what competent deductions one has made. It follows that one cannot have the rationally supported knowledge in hinge propositions that can be derived, via the closure$_{RK}$ principle, from one's other rationally grounded knowledge. Thus, insofar as the proponent of the entitlement reading wishes to maintain that we can have rationally grounded knowledge of non–hinge propositions, the closure$_{RK}$ principle must be denied.[15]

One might object to this line of argument by contending that there is now a distinction to be drawn between two kinds of rationally supported knowledge—namely, a "standard" kind that concerns reasons for believing the target proposition to be true, and an alternative "entitlement" kind that merely concerns an entitlement to believe the target proposition. Thus the proponent of the entitlement reading might contend that there is a perfectly legitimate sense—that is, in terms of entitlement—in which one's knowledge of hinge propositions can be rationally grounded, and hence that the conflict with the closure$_{RK}$ principle is illusory.

This line of response does not stand up to close scrutiny, however. For notice that the closure$_{RK}$ principle demands that one's belief in the entailed proposition is epistemically grounded in the competent deduction that one undertakes from one's rationally grounded knowledge (in the nonentitlement sense) of the entailing proposition. This means that the closure$_{RK}$ principle, when applied to competent deductions involving hinge commitments, makes explicit that one's hinge belief, if acquired in this fashion from one's other rationally grounded knowledge, is rationally supported in the standard, nonentitlement, sense. There is thus no room for maneuver on this score: the entitlement reading is incompatible with the closure$_{RK}$ principle.

It is important to note that the entitlement reading is explicitly cast as a kind of overriding anti-skeptical proposal, one that recognizes that there is a deep truth in skepticism. Here is the main proponent of this kind of anti-skeptical strategy, Crispin Wright:

> This strategy ... concedes that the best sceptical arguments have something to teach us—that the limits of justification they bring out are genuine and essential—but then replies that, just for that reason, cognitive achievement must be reckoned to take place *within such limits*. The attempt to surpass them would result not in an increase in rigour or solidity but merely in cognitive paralysis. (Wright 2004c, 191)

The idea is thus that given the specter of radical skepticism it is legitimate to reject certain intuitive claims—and in particular the closure$_{RK}$ principle—in order to resolve that problem, where the theoretical embedding provided by the entitlement strategy provides the rationale for this particular species of epistemic revisionism. As we saw in chapter 1, undercutting anti-skeptical strategies are to be preferred to overriding anti-skeptical strategies. Still, if it is only overriding anti-skeptical strategies that are available as philosophical options, then one can hardly turn one's nose up at them given the obvious intellectual undesirability of endorsing the radical skeptical conclusion.

There are a number of problems with the entitlement reading, but the overarching concern is that it does not ultimately offer us the kind of epistemic support that could suffice for knowledge of hinge propositions. This is important, since it is only if the entitlement reading can preserve knowledge of hinge propositions that it is able to retain the closure principle, and the retention of the closure principle is meant to be something that by the lights of this approach is nonnegotiable (unlike the retention of the closure$_{RK}$ principle).

One way of putting this worry is to say that the rational basis for believing hinge propositions provided by this strategy is of a *prudential* rather than *epistemic* nature, on the grounds that it is ultimately a rational basis rooted in the prudential value of believing these propositions rather than being a rational basis for thinking these propositions true.[16] But this is not quite right. For while it is true that an entitlement to believe does not on this view involve a reason for believing the target proposition to be true, such an entitlement is meant to be rooted in a rational perspective that is purely epistemic. The claim is that given that not believing hinge propositions would result in cognitive paralysis (and given also that there is no reason for thinking these propositions false), then from a *purely epistemic point of view* it is rational to believe hinge propositions (cognitive paralysis is, after all, something that it is *epistemically* rational to avoid). Accordingly, it is not at all clear that the rationality at issue in this proposal is ultimately prudential as opposed to being epistemic.

But the worry about epistemic versus prudential rationality in play here is indicative of a deeper problem, which is the very idea of a *belief* being explicitly rationally grounded in something like an entitlement. To believe a proposition, after all, is to believe that proposition *to be true*. But if that's right then there is something very puzzling about an entitlement being one's avowed epistemic reason to believe a proposition while at the same time conceding that one lacks a reason to believe that proposition to be true. Put another way, having a mere entitlement to believe a proposition seems to entail that one ought to be *agnostic* about whether p is true—since one is aware that one has no reason for thinking p to be true—but the problem is that belief that p seems incompatible with agnosticism about the truth of p.

At the very least, even if we can make sense of a notion of belief that is compatible with agnosticism about the target proposition, it is certainly the case that the variety of belief that is a component of knowledge is such that it excludes agnosticism of this sort.[17] In short, knowledge that p is incompatible with a propositional attitude toward p that is agnostic regarding the truth of p.[18] Accordingly, whatever kind of propositional attitude is involved when one's avowed reason for a belief is an entitlement, it cannot be *knowledge-apt* belief. And yet it is, of course, this specific kind of belief that we are interested in. (Accordingly, henceforth when we talk about belief we will, unless otherwise indicated, have knowledge-apt belief specifically in mind.)

It is for this reason that proponents of the entitlement strategy talk of the propositional commitment in play as being something distinct from belief, such as a *trusting* in or an *acceptance* of a proposition.[19] After all, one can make sense of one trusting or accepting a proposition that one is aware that one has no reason for thinking is true because one independently recognizes some epistemic benefit in doing so. This is because trusting in, or acceptance of, a proposition commits one to acting only *as if* the proposition in question is true, and does not commit one to actually regarding it as true (as belief does).

But this maneuver just trades in one problem for another, for the obvious worry now is that one needs to believe a proposition if one is to have knowledge of it; mere trust or acceptance of that proposition will not suffice. In particular, it will not suffice precisely because trusting or accepting that p is compatible—unlike believing that p, and especially knowing that p—with agnosticism about the truth of p. Given that point, however, anyone who takes this line is forced to grant that the hinge propositions are not known after all, and hence the strategy is undermined. In particular, the proponent of this strategy is now forced to deny not just the closure$_{RK}$ principle, but also the closure principle.

One might think that this is too quick, in that surely there must be a sufficiently belief-like propositional attitude available that could play the required belief-like role in a theory of knowledge—in particular, such that it excludes an attitude of agnosticism about the truth of the target proposition—while being nonetheless compatible with one self-consciously lacking any rational basis for holding the target proposition to be true. Wright, for example, has argued that there is a propositional attitude that can fit the bill. What we should focus on is not the propositional attitudes of acceptance or mere (blind) trust, but rather the attitude of "rational trust" (Wright 2004c, 194). Given the entitlement reading, after all, we are rational (even, plausibly, from a purely epistemic point of view) in trusting in the hinge propositions.

On the face of it, rational trust, so long as it is understood such that it explicitly excludes agnosticism about the truth of the target proposition anyway, looks like a plausible candidate in this regard. For, like mere (i.e., blind) trust and acceptance, but unlike belief, it is at least potentially compatible (qua a form of trusting) with the agent being aware that she has no rational basis for regarding the target proposition as true. Moreover, like acceptance, but unlike mere trust, it can be a rational stance to take with regard to the target proposition. Finally, like belief, but unlike acceptance or mere trust, it is—so we are told—incompatible with agnosticism about the truth of the target proposition. Rational trust thus seems to satisfy the relevant rubric.

The crux of the matter, however, is whether the rational trust in question really could legitimately exclude agnosticism about the truth of the target proposition. The reason why this is problematic is that it is hard to see how an agent who is fully aware that she has no rational basis for regarding the target proposition as true could be anything but agnostic about that proposition. After all, isn't the recognition that this rational basis is lacking simply tantamount to being agnostic about the truth of this proposition? How could it be otherwise?

In order to see this point, consider the following pair of cases. In the first, one is presented with two doors to choose from, and the only source of information about where the doors lead is an informant next to the doors (one can't open them oneself, say, and there is no one else who can open them for you). One knows nothing about the reliability of the informant. If the informant advises you to go through one of the doors rather than the other, and you act accordingly, then this will be a case of mere, or blind, trust in that you have no rational basis for making the choice that you have selected.

Now consider the second case. This is just like the first except that you are aware of two further salient features of the case that weren't available the first time around: (i) you recognize that if you don't select one of these two doors then cognitive paralysis will ensue; and (ii) you also recognize that while you have no rational basis on which to trust the word of your informant, you also have no rational basis to doubt him either. Given that cognitive paralysis is something that the epistemically rational person should avoid, it follows that trusting the informant is the epistemically rational thing to do, given the circumstances. We thus have a case of rational trust as opposed to blind trust that meets the precise conditions for the entitlement reading that Wright endorses.

Here is the crux: while there is something more rational (even from an epistemic point of view) about the agent opting to trust the informant in the second case (because cognitive paralysis is clearly something to be avoided), it remains the case that the agent's attitude toward the truth of the proposition she thereby endorses on this basis will (if she is epistemically rational anyway) be one of agnosticism. In short, being aware that cognitive paralysis will ensue if she doesn't trust this informant has no bearing on this issue at all.

Of course, Wright could respond to this by saying that insofar as the agent is agnostic about the truth of the target propositions then this would not be a case of rational trust in his sense *by definition*. But that would be to miss the point, which is that the kind of trust that is in play here should be exactly akin to the type of rational trust alleged to be available as a propositional attitude when it comes to the propositions that Wright is targeting with his entitlement strategy. That it is unavailable should tell us something troubling about Wright's notion of rational trust as it is meant to apply to these propositions. Basically, we have a dilemma in play. Either Wright sticks to his claim that rational trust excludes agnosticism about the truth of the relevant propositions, in which case one cannot coherently adopt a stance of rational trust toward the propositions in question. Or one can make sense of a notion of rational trust that can be applied to these propositions, but at the cost of conceding that such trust is compatible with agnosticism about the truth of these propositions, in which case the subject isn't in the market to have knowledge of these propositions. Either way, Wright's solution to the problem in hand is untenable.

I think we can diagnose where Wright went wrong in terms of an ambiguity in the very notion of rational trust. The natural way to understand this idea, I take it, is that one has *some* reason to believe the target proposition to be true, but that one at the same time is also to a significant extent trusting that this proposition is true. An analogy might be the testimonial case just given with the modification that one has some reason for believing what the informant says, but where this rational basis is rather weak (e.g., just a short track record of reliable testimony). One's trusting what one is told by this informant is epistemically rational to the extent that there is some reason available, however slender, for treating what she says as true. Depending on the degree of rational support in play, rational trusting of this sort may well exclude agnosticism about the truth of the target proposition.

84 • Chapter 3

But "rational trust" as it is used by Wright clearly does not mean this at all, since it remains that for him one's trust is supposed to be compatible with one being aware that one possesses *no* rational basis whatsoever for regarding the target proposition as true. Rather, the rational basis one has for engaging in this trust is entirely disconnected from being a rational basis for regarding the target proposition as true. But this is precisely why rational trust in Wright's sense doesn't exclude agnosticism (or at least, in view of the dilemma just posed for his view, it doesn't exclude agnosticism insofar as it is meant to be available as a propositional attitude that one can coherently adopt with regard to the presuppositional propositions in question). That there is a sense of rational trusting that might exclude agnosticism can explain why we might find Wright's appeal to rational trust superficially appealing. But once we make explicit what this notion actually involves, then it becomes clear that it cannot offer the advertised solution.

The problem, of course, is that any form of trust in the target proposition that is compatible with agnosticism about the truth of that proposition is not a plausible candidate for being a propositional attitude that could act as proxy for belief in an instance of knowledge, as Wright recognizes. We are thus back with the original problem that the appeal to rational trusting was supposed to help us avoid—namely, that the entitlement strategy is forced to deny the closure principle as well as the closure$_{RK}$ principle, on pain of endorsing radical skepticism.[20,21]

6. A Nonepistemic Way of Developing the Wittgensteinian Account of the Structure of Rational Evaluation: The Nonpropositional Reading

Given the problems facing the externalist and entitlement readings, one might be tempted to adopt a more radical proposal, one that is arguably closer in spirit to what Wittgenstein himself intended (to the extent that we can discern such a thing from these fragmentary notebooks). According to this proposal, we need to take very seriously how Wittgenstein talks of these commitments as being utterly visceral—or "animal" (e.g., OC, §359)—in nature, and conclude on this basis that such commitments simply are not in the market for knowledge (this is thus a *nonepistemic* reading of the Wittgensteinian account of the structure of rational evaluation). With this in mind, we are not to think of them as beliefs at all, or indeed as any other kind of propositional attitude either for that matter.

Rather, they represent ways of *acting* rather than a particular propositional attitude. Consider the following passage:

> Giving grounds . . . comes to an end;—but the end is not certain propositions' striking us immediately as true, i.e. it is not a kind of *seeing* on our part; it is our *acting*, which lies at the bottom of the language-game. (OC, §204; cf. OC, §§110; 148; 232; 342; 402)

On this view there is a very good reason why we do not have knowledge of hinge propositions—there simply isn't the corresponding propositional attitude that could put us in the market for knowledge of these propositions in the first place. Call this the *nonpropositional reading*.[22]

More generally, proponents of the nonpropositional reading point to a number of passages in *On Certainty* where Wittgenstein emphasizes that statements that putatively express our hinge commitments are, if not simply meaningless, then at the very least to be understood very differently from how they are normally understood. In particular, the claim is that what looks like a meaningful statement of an ordinary empirical propositions that purports to describe the world as being a certain way could in fact be anything but, such that conceiving of these statements as being on par with ordinary empirical statements reveals a fundamental mistake.

Take a statement like Moore's "I have two hands." Wittgenstein is not claiming that such a statement could never express an ordinary empirical proposition, since one could conceive of very unusual circumstances in which it is uttered as responding to an entirely normal (nonphilosophical) doubt. The crucial point is that such an assertion, in the context in which it is uttered, would not be playing the remarkable anti-skeptical role that Moore's assertion is trying to perform. So, for example, someone who had lost one of her hands, and who awakes from a transplant operation to discover that the operation is successful, such that she has two hands again, may well make this kind of declaration. But nothing of any anti-skeptical significance would follow from *this* assertion, as all it does is simply describe the world as being a certain way just as any normal empirical statement would. In particular, this assertion would not be of a proposition of which the asserter is optimally confident; indeed, it is precisely because this assertion concerns a proposition that is quite rationally dubitable for her that it makes sense as the assertion of a normal empirical proposition.

In contrast, when Moore asserts that he has two hands as a means of demonstrating an important anti-skeptical truth, he is, on the nonpropositional reading, trying to do what cannot be done. In particular, he is trying to express his absolute certainty regarding this proposition—his hinge commitment to this proposition—by asserting a meaningful empirical proposition. But according to the nonpropositional reading this is simply impossible. Although what Moore says looks like a normal empirical claim, and while we can (as just noted) imagine unusual circumstances in which it would be a normal empirical claim, in the philosophical context in which Moore utters this statement what he asserts is, ipso facto, precisely *not* a meaningful empirical proposition.[23]

For what it is worth, I think that the nonpropositional reading of *On Certainty* is the one that enjoys the greatest support from the text itself.[24] Time and again Wittgenstein makes clear that he views the attempt to express our hinge commitments in terms of normal assertions of empirical statements as revealing a fundamental mistake on our part, with the assertion itself being classed as meaningless, akin to saying (to use one of his most memorable examples), completely out of the blue, "good morning" in the middle of a conversation (OC, §464; cf. OC, §§10, 35–37, 461, 463, 500).[25] But while there is undoubtedly a philosophical interest in trying to determine what Wittgenstein's intentions in this work are, we should remember that our goals are not necessarily Wittgenstein's. In particular, while it may ultimately have been Wittgenstein's intent to motivate his anti-skepticism by appeal to a highly context-sensitive account of meaning, we should be wary of saddling ourselves with this philosophical baggage if we can avoid it.[26] For to take this kind of line with the radical skeptic is to make ourselves hostage to wider philosophical claims, extending well beyond epistemology, that may not be themselves plausible in the final analysis. And yet the promise of Wittgenstein's anti-skeptical strategy—the core idea, anyway, regarding the structure of rational evaluation—was that it offers us a way out of the skeptical problem that isn't encumbered in this way with such additional philosophical burdens.

This relates to a more general problem with the nonpropositional reading of *On Certainty*, which is the difficulty of making sense of the idea that a propositional attitude toward these hinge propositions is simply impossible. Recall that this is a key part of the strategy, and the move that is meant to extricate this proposal from the closure problem. This is because if it is impossible for one to adopt a propositional attitude toward hinge propositions, then of course one is not in the market for knowledge anyway, and hence we can thereby block any inference to knowledge of them. We can thus accept the closure(/closure$_{RK}$) principle and yet nonetheless resist the contentious inferences that this principle seems to license.

The trouble with this claim is that while we can surely make sense of the idea that these hinge commitments are simply ways of acting rather that propositional attitudes, it doesn't seem all that hard to convert such ways of acting into a corresponding propositional attitude in such a way as to generate the closure problem. What happens, on this view, when an agent reasons from her rationally grounded knowledge that Napoleon's victory at Austerlitz was in 1805 to the entailment that the universe must not have come into existence five minutes ago? Is not the result of this competent deduction a propositional attitude toward the entailed proposition, something very much akin to (if not identical to) a belief (at least to the extent that it excludes agnosticism about the truth of the target proposition)? But insofar as there is a propositional attitude in play here, then we can reasonably ask whether it amounts to rationally grounded knowledge (or, if we're epistemic externalists, knowledge that isn't rationally grounded for that matter), and a negative answer will lead to the closure problem.

Note that it is not being disputed here that for someone to assert her envisaged propositional commitment might result in a meaningless assertion. If the kind of model of meaningfulness being canvassed in support of the nonpropositional reading were feasible, then such an assertion would indeed be senseless. But would it follow that the subject didn't have the propositional attitude in question? While one could conceive of an argument that made the relevant bridging connection between these two claims, it is also clear that any such connecting thesis will inevitably be philosophically contentious.

With the foregoing in mind, before we endorse the nonpropositional reading we should first see if there are ways of developing Wittgenstein's account of the structure of rational evaluation available that don't trade on such contentious claims. Indeed, as we will see in the next chapter, there is a further nonepistemic reading of *On Certainty* available that can incorporate the main features of the nonpropositional reading but that isn't wedded to such further controversial claims.

7. Concluding Remarks

In this chapter we looked at Wittgenstein's iconoclastic account of the structure of rational evaluation, such that all rational evaluation takes place relative to essentially groundless hinge commitments and hence is inherently local. We noted that in principle this account presents us with an undercutting anti-skeptical strategy that undermines the radical skeptic's attempts to offer a universal negative assessment of our epistemic position. The difficulty, however, lies in finding a plausible way of developing the details of Wittgenstein's proposal. In particular, we saw that on the face of it Wittgenstein's account of the structure of rational evaluation seems to come into conflict with the kind of reasoning at issue in closure-style inferences, in that such inferences seem to license knowledge, perhaps even rationally grounded knowledge, of hinge propositions, in conflict with Wittgenstein's proposal.

With this in mind, we examined three ways of spelling out the Wittgensteinian account of the structure of rational evaluation. The first two proposals we looked at were epistemic in character, in that they allowed that one could have knowledge of hinge propositions, either in virtue of meeting epistemic externalist criteria or in virtue of exhibiting a form of epistemic standing known as entitlement. As we saw, neither proposal was appealing. The epistemic externalist reading of Wittgenstein encountered many of the problems that we saw facing epistemic externalist anti-skeptical strategies in earlier chapters. The entitlement reading unraveled on closure inspection due to a failure to ensure that epistemic entitlement was compatible with the subject having the kind of propositional attitude necessary to be in the market for knowledge of hinge propositions.

That leaves nonepistemic readings of *On Certainty*, ones on which subjects cannot have knowledge of hinge propositions. We looked at one version of the nonepistemic reading: the nonpropositional reading that claims that one's hinge commitments are not to be understood in terms of a propositional attitude—much less the kind of propositional attitude that would put them into the market for knowledge—but rather as a way of acting. We noted that while this reading enjoyed significant support from the text, it is also essentially wedded to further contentious philosophical theses, and hence is at a considerable disadvantage from an anti-skeptical point of view. The search thus continues for a nonepistemic reading of *On Certainty* that does not carry this additional philosophical baggage. The development of such a proposal will be the concern of chapter 4.

CHAPTER 4

Hinge Commitments

0. Introductory Remarks

In the last chapter we looked at Wittgenstein's innovative account of the structure of rational evaluation, which potentially offers us an undercutting anti-skeptical strategy. According to this proposal, all rational evaluation takes place relative to arational hinge commitments, with the consequence that there can be no such thing as a fully general rational evaluation, whether negative (i.e., radically skeptical) or positive (e.g., Moorean). We also noted that this account faces a difficulty that we labeled the *closure problem*. In short, this was that there seems to be a tension between the kind of reasoning licensed by closure-style inferences and the Wittgensteinian claim that our hinge commitments are not in the market for rationally grounded knowledge.

We examined three attempts at resolving this problem. The first two attempts—the externalist and entitlement readings—tried to deal with the problem by arguing that our hinge commitments were in the market for knowledge (and so not in tension with at least some closure-style inferences), albeit not in a way that was in conflict with the Wittgensteinian account of the structure of rational evaluation. Both of these "epistemic" accounts succumbed to serious problems. A third proposal—the nonpropositional reading—took the very different approach of arguing that our hinge commitments do not involve a propositional attitude at all but rather consist in a way of acting. This means that not only can these commitments not be in the market for knowledge, but neither are they of a kind that they can be the product of closure-style inferences either. Hence, the tension between the notion of a hinge commitment and closure-style principles disappears. As we noted in chapter 3, however, the difficulty with this "nonepistemic" proposal is that it is wedded to further philosophical theses that are independently controversial, which substantially lessens its appeal as part of an anti-skeptical strategy.

In this chapter we will be exploring a fourth way of casting the Wittgensteinian account of the structure of rational evaluation. Like the nonpropositional reading, this is a nonepistemic proposal in that it does not treat our hinge commitments as being in the market for rationally grounded knowledge. Unlike the nonpropositional reading, however, it is not allied to additional philosophical theses that are independently controversial. With this construal of our hinge commitments in place, we will then further explore the anti-skeptical ramifications of this proposal, including in contrast to superficially similar anti-skeptical stances.

1. The Nonbelief Reading

There is a middle ground available between the epistemic accounts of the structure of rational evaluation and the nonpropositional reading that we looked at in the last chapter. For regarding our hinge commitments as visceral in the way that Wittgenstein demands, while no doubt inconsistent with regarding them as akin to normal beliefs, could well be thought compatible with them being, at least sometimes, manifest in corresponding propositional attitudes. That is, given that our hinge commitments are ex hypothesi never the result of a rational process and are in their nature unresponsive to rational considerations, then they are not plausible candidates to be beliefs.[1] But perhaps there is a nonetheless a propositional attitude that we can take to our hinge commitments that is in sufficient respects belief-like.

Beliefs, after all, are propositional attitudes that by their nature are responsive to rational considerations. (At the very least, the notion of belief, which is of primary interest to epistemologists, and which is a component part of knowledge, has this feature, and recall from the last chapter that it is this *knowledge-apt* conception of belief that we are focusing upon.) This is not to say that beliefs are by their nature rational, of course, as this is manifestly false. It is rather to say that there are certain minimal, but constitutive nonetheless, connections between belief and truth such that a propositional attitude that didn't satisfy them simply would not count as a belief, but would be a different propositional attitude entirely.

In particular, it makes no sense, for example, for there to be an agent who believes that p while taking herself to have no reason whatsoever for thinking p to be true. A fortiori, it does not make sense for an agent to believe that p while taking herself to have overwhelming reasons for thinking that p is false. In such cases the propositional attitude in question would not be a belief but a different propositional attitude entirely, such as a wishful thinking. But if that's right, then if we take seriously Wittgenstein's suggestion that our hinge commitments are by their nature never the result of rational processes nor responsive to rational processes, then we are obliged to reject the idea that we could have hinge *beliefs* altogether.²

Call this the *nonbelief reading*. Like the nonpropositional reading, it precludes the possibility that we can have knowledge, much less rationally grounded knowledge, when it comes to our hinge commitments. If we are not even in the market for belief in this regard then we are, a fortiori, not in the market for knowledge either, rationally grounded or otherwise, particularly once we bear in mind that the notion of belief in play is precisely that notion that is meant to be a component part of knowledge (i.e., knowledge-apt belief). But unlike the nonpropositional reading, this proposal doesn't demand that we should think of our hinge commitments in inherently nonpropositional terms. For sure, such commitments can never coherently be thought of as beliefs, but that doesn't prevent them from being expressed via other propositional attitudes.

Now on the surface of things, one might be puzzled as to how this can possibly help matters. For insofar as one can conceive of one's hinge commitments in terms of a propositional attitude, albeit one that can never amount to knowledge, then why doesn't that simply exacerbate the closure problem? Notice, however, how the relevant closure principle is formulated, in particular the main closure principle of interest to us regarding rationally supported knowledge:

THE CLOSURE$_{RK}$ PRINCIPLE

If S has rationally grounded knowledge that p, and S competently deduces from p that q, thereby forming a belief that q on this basis while retaining her rationally grounded knowledge that p, then S has rationally grounded knowledge that q.

As we noted in part 1, it is key to this principle that it is describing the *acquisition* of a (knowledge-apt) belief via the *rational process* of competent deduction. These are not incidental features of this principle, since without these elements it would not capture the point that a rational process like competent deduction from rationally supported knowledge cannot lead one to form a belief in the entailed proposition that does not amount to rationally grounded knowledge.

With this point in mind, it follows that the proponent of the nonbelief reading can argue that they do not face the closure problem for the simple reason that one can never, via the kind of competent deduction at issue in the relevant closure principles, come to acquire a belief in a hinge commitment, much less acquire this belief as a result of the rational process of competent deduction at issue. It follows that on closer inspection that there is no tension between the unknowability of hinge propositions and the closure$_{RK}$ principle, in that the unknowability of hinge propositions, on this reading anyway, is entirely compatible with the closure$_{RK}$ principle. The closure problem is thus dealt with. Note too that there is nothing in the nonbelief reading that requires one to sign up to the further contentious theses that the nonpropositional reading is allied to, which lessens the dialectical burden that this proposal has to carry.

Of course, the proponent of the nonpropositional reading can make the point about the compatibility of their view with the closure$_{RK}$ principle too (although, as far as I am aware anyway, no proponent of this reading has done so). On their view, after all, agents do not have *any* propositional attitude that corresponds to the hinge commitment, and hence, a fortiori, they do not have any hinge beliefs either. But the nonpropositional reading faces the further mystery of accounting for the apparent propositional attitude that is generated by such competent deductions. In contrast, the nonbelief reading can grant that someone who undertakes the relevant competent deductions could be described as having a propositional attitude toward the entailed hinge commitment, without thereby having to face the question of why this propositional attitude doesn't amount to knowledge.

That is, it is compatible with the nonbelief reading that an agent who undertakes the relevant closure$_{RK}$-based competent deduction ends up adopting a propositional attitude of some sort toward the entailed hinge proposition. If she has never had any occurrent thoughts about the entailed proposition, then she might find herself in some sense *endorsing* that proposition, and may even conceive of herself as in this way coming to believe the hinge proposition. She will certainly not be agnostic about the truth of the target proposition, and here we have one important difference between the kind of propositional attitude at issue as regards the nonbelief reading and the kinds of propositional attitude that were offered by the entitlement reading. But thinking that you believe something does not entail that you do believe it (in the knowledge-apt sense at least), and endorsing a proposition, whatever that means—it seems right to you, you recognize that you are some sense committed to its truth, and so on—does not entail belief either. (We will return to explore this point further below.)

There is a very natural objection to the nonbelief reading. This is to argue that there must surely be a closure-type principle in the vicinity that can be utilized to resurrect the closure problem, such that even if one cannot generate this problem by appeal to the closure$_{RK}$ principle, the underlying difficulty is not thereby evaded entirely. In a nutshell, the worry is that this is little more than a subtle trick (or, expressed in a more Kantian spirit, a "wretched subterfuge"). The intuition underlying closure-style principles has been fleshed out in a very specific fashion and—what a surprise!—that way of formulating this intuition as a principle is entirely compatible with the nonbelief reading.

While I can see the temptation to view matters in this way, it should be clear on reflection that this is not a trick. I take it that any development of this critical response to the nonbelief proposal would involve weakening the epistemic standing at issue in the closure$_{RK}$ principle with regard to the subject's belief in the consequent proposition. So, for example, instead of rationally grounded knowledge in the consequent proposition, how about the competent deduction in play merely *putting one in a position* to acquire such knowledge?[3] We'd thus have something like the following variation on the closure$_{RK}$ principle:

THE CLOSURE$_{RK}$ PRINCIPLE*

If S has rationally grounded knowledge that p, and S competently deduces from p that q while retaining her rationally grounded knowledge that p, then S is in a position to acquire rationally grounded knowledge that q.

The closure$_{RK}$ principle* is weaker that the closure$_{RK}$ principle in that one can satisfy its antecedent even while not actually having rationally grounded knowledge of the entailed proposition. With this principle in play we can ostensibly reinstate our closure problem for the nonbelief reading. For even though our subject does not actually have rationally grounded knowledge of hinge propositions, in virtue of her rationally grounded knowledge in the entailing proposition and her undertaking the relevant competent deduction she at least has the *potential* to acquire such knowledge. Even this weaker claim seems to be in conflict with the idea that such propositions are not in the market for knowledge (rationally grounded or otherwise), and so the closure problem is apparently back on the table.

Now that we have a concrete proposal in play, however, the weakness in this critical line becomes obvious. For however we spell out the difference between rationally grounded knowledge and merely being in a position to gain rationally grounded knowledge, the point just raised about how our hinge commitments cannot be thought of as beliefs would gain a purchase. Suppose, for example, that being in a position to gain rationally grounded knowledge means roughly that if one were to form a belief on the basis of the competent deduction in play, then it would amount to rationally grounded knowledge. But so construed the closure$_{RK}$ principle* is no more threatened by the existence of hinge commitments than the closure$_{RK}$ principle, since we have already seen that one can't form a belief in a hinge proposition on *any* rational basis.

Alternatively, if being in a position to acquire rationally grounded knowledge is not to be understood in this way, then how is it to be understood? More generally, it ought to be clear that the difficulty in play here is not one of formulation, such that if only we got the formulation of the closure-style principle at issue right then we would be able to resurrect the closure problem. Either we have a formulation of a closure-style principle that demands rationally grounded knowledge, or the potential for rationally grounded knowledge at any rate, in the entailed proposition, or we have a formulation that doesn't demand this. On the former reading the principle will not be compatible with our hinge commitments; on the latter reading it will not capture the intuition that the target closure-style principle trades on. In either case, the principle won't be in conflict with the nonbelief reading.

There are other potential difficulties with the nonbelief proposal that we must explore, but the foregoing should at least demonstrate the prima facie plausibility of this approach. We will explore these potential difficulties as we go along, but before we do we need to say more about how the proposal should be understood. We will begin by further exploring the nature of hinge commitments.[4]

2. Hinge Commitments

On the surface of things, Wittgenstein's remarks on hinge propositions—and the very metaphor of the "hinge" itself—would seem to suggest that there is a great deal of variability in each person's hinge commitments, with these commitments changing—possibly quite dramatically—as we move from person to person, culture to culture, epoch to epoch, and so on. Wittgenstein writes, for example, about hinges concerning the fact that one has never been to the moon (e.g., OC, §106) or that one's name is such and such (e.g., OC, §425). But in each case the "hinge" in question seems very relative to the particular circumstances of the person in question: what age they live in, who they are, where they were raised, and so on. For example, someone in the future might not have a hinge commitment that she had never been to the moon (perhaps going to the moon as a child is so commonplace that it is the sort of thing that could well have happened without one being aware of it), and someone with a different name will presumably take it as a hinge commitment that her particular name is the name she thinks it is.

The foregoing suggests a highly context-sensitive account of hinge commitments, and one might be tempted on this basis to regard one's hinge commitments as being entirely context-bound. But this would be an unduly quick way of reading Wittgenstein's remarks on hinge propositions. For closer inspection of this apparently heterogeneous class of hinge commitments reveals that they all in effect codify, for that particular person, the entirely general hinge commitment that one is not radically and fundamentally mistaken in one's beliefs.[5] Call this commitment the *über hinge commitment*, and call the proposition endorsed by the über hinge commitment the *über hinge proposition*.

If one were to be completely mistaken about one's name, for example, then this would almost certainly mean that one's beliefs are radically and fundamentally in error. Imagine, for instance, that you go out into the world one morning and find that everyone you know is calling you by an unfamiliar name and telling you that you have had this name all along. Worse, everything you call upon to back up your story—bank statements, further testimony from friends, the electoral register, and so forth—in fact supports the opposing story. Although this commitment of yours is quite specific, its apparent falsity reveals a radical and fundamental error in your beliefs. Indeed, in all likelihood those around you in this case will think that you are losing(/have already lost?) your marbles.[6] The particular hinge commitment to this proposition is thus simply a reflection of the fact that, in your particular circumstances, to be wrong about something like this would reflect radical and fundamental error. In short, this particular hinge commitment is just a consequence of your more general über hinge commitment that you are not radically and fundamentally mistaken.

The importance of this observation is that it highlights that we shouldn't invest too much importance in the fact that people from different cultures, ages, and so forth have different overall hinge commitments, since these differences merely reflect the way in which different people will codify their über hinge commitment.[7] That is, we can distinguish, on the one hand, between the über hinge commitment that everyone holds and, on the other hand, the very different ways in which this über hinge commitment manifests itself in hinge commitments to specific propositions when it comes to particular people (within specific cultures, epochs, and so on). Call these latter commitments *personal hinge commitments*, and call the propositions endorsed by the personal hinge commitment the *personal hinge propositions*.

One advantage of this way of thinking about our hinge commitments is that it explains how they can change over time, something that would be puzzling if we thought that even these personal hinge commitments were on par with the über hinge commitment. The latter clearly is not something that can change over time, since to lose this commitment is to have no hinge commitments at all, and yet the former personal hinge commitments clearly *can* change over time, as the example of having never been to the moon illustrates. Once we see that they are simply codifying the über hinge commitment then there is no puzzle here. As one's personal circumstances change, so one's beliefs change with them and hence something that used to codify one's über hinge commitment now no longer plays this role.[8]

A further advantage of this way of thinking about our hinge commitments is that it demystifies them. If our hinge commitments really were a heterogeneous class, with no common core, then they would be very mysterious. Accordingly, by recognizing that our hinge commitments have this common core, the mystery evaporates. Moreover, notice that in the process we gain a way of distinguishing between a hinge commitment and a proposition about which we are merely very certain. There may, after all, be propositions that we find ourselves highly committed to, perhaps for pathological reasons, but that don't codify our über hinge commitment. If the only hallmark of a hinge commitment is the level of certainly involved, then these commitments would thereby qualify as hinge commitments. But that is surely not what we want to say about these particular certainties. By insisting that genuine hinge commitments codify the über hinge commitment, we have a way of excluding these certainties from the class of hinge commitments.

This way of thinking about Wittgenstein's account of hinge propositions also accords with a key metaphor that he uses to describe our hinge commitments. Consider the following passage:

> It might be imagined that some propositions, of the form of empirical propositions, were hardened and functioned as channels for such empirical propositions as were not hardened but fluid; and that this relation altered with time, in that fluid propositions hardened, and hard ones became fluid.
>
> The mythology may change back into a state of flux, the river-bed of thoughts may shift. But I distinguish between the movement of the waters

on the river-bed and the shift of the bed itself; though there is not a sharp division of the one from the other. . . .

And the bank of that river consists partly of hard rock, subject to no alteration or to only an imperceptible one, partly of sand, which now in one place now in another gets washed away, or deposited. (OC, §§96–99)

This manner of describing our hinge commitments dovetails with the idea that while such commitments might change over time, these changes are entirely at the periphery and the rate of change is inevitably slow. This is in keeping with the account of our hinge commitments just outlined, since on this view while the personal hinge commitments can change over time, they clearly can't change en masse without this endangering the über hinge commitment.

There is a third category of hinge commitment that we need to demarcate, between personal hinge commitments and über hinge commitments, which concerns our attitude to radical skeptical scenarios. Call these *anti-skeptical hinge commitments*, and call the propositions endorsed by the anti-skeptical hinge commitment the *anti-skeptical hinge propositions*. Clearly, in virtue of having the über hinge commitment one is thereby committed to regarding these scenarios as false. But these explicitly anti-skeptical hinge commitments are unlike the personal hinge commitments in that most people, prior to being introduced to skeptical scenarios anyway, will have no particular view about them (indeed, in all likelihood they won't even have ever considered them). But they are also unlike the über hinge commitment in that they are quite specific about the nature of the error in question.

I think we can explain what is going on here by noting that such scenarios are explicitly *designed* to call the über hinge commitment into question. Accordingly, such skeptical scenarios are simply very direct ways in which we could be radically and fundamentally in error, and hence our commitment to their denial is an immediate consequence of our commitment to the über hinge proposition. Indeed, we are able to straightforwardly recognize their connection. In contrast, because of their apparent logical distance from the über hinge commitment it comes as a surprise to discover that our personal hinge commitments in effect codify our über hinge commitment, and hence that they share similar epistemic properties, such as being rationally groundless.

By focusing on the über hinge commitment we can see why rational evaluation must be essentially local. For what possible reason could we have for holding the über hinge commitment? Whatever grounds we cited would already presuppose the truth of this commitment after all. Moreover, once we see that the other hinge commitments we have—to personal hinge propositions and to explicitly anti-skeptical hinge propositions—are simply a consequence of our über hinge commitment, then it becomes clear that the extent to which our system of rational support presupposes essentially groundless commitments is quite considerable.

Notice, too, that this way of thinking about our hinge commitments underlines Wittgenstein's point that there is nothing contingent about the limitation on rational evaluation that the existence of our hinge commitments reveals. It is not as though, for example, if we had been more careful or thorough in how we acquired rational support for our beliefs then we could have avoided this fate, since there simply is no rational process through which we could have gained rational support for belief in the über hinge proposition. And since we are unable to have a rationally supported belief in the über hinge proposition, it follows that we are unable to have rationally supported beliefs in the personal and anti-skeptical hinge propositions that codify our über hinge commitment. We thus get the Wittgensteinian conclusion: since all rational evaluation necessarily takes place relative to groundless hinge commitments, the very idea of a fully general rational evaluation—that is, one that does not presuppose any hinge commitments—is incoherent, whether that evaluation is positive (i.e., anti-skeptical) or negative (i.e., skeptical). The universality of rational evaluation thesis is thus rejected.[9]

By recognizing this threefold taxonomy of hinge commitments, we are in a better position to understand certain elements of the nonbelief reading. For example, I noted earlier, when discussing how the nonbelief reading deals with the closure problem, that there may well be a respectable sense in which the competent deduction at issue results in a type of propositional attitude toward the target hinge proposition (albeit not one of knowledge-apt belief). We now need to revisit this claim with this threefold distinction between different types of hinge proposition in play.

To begin with, notice that there isn't any closure-style inference in which the entailment is the über hinge proposition. This is because there isn't any particular proposition that I have rationally grounded knowledge of that *entails* that I am not radically and fundamentally mistaken in my beliefs. Take my putative rationally grounded knowledge that the car I drive is dark blue, for example. That this is so is entirely compatible with my being radically and fundamentally in error in my beliefs (just not about this particular proposition, and perhaps a sufficient number of related propositions in the vicinity of this proposition). And hence even if I do have rationally grounded knowledge of this proposition, I cannot via the closure$_{RK}$ principle undertake a competent deduction and thereby extract the über hinge proposition as a conclusion.

There are closure-style principles in the vicinity that would license such an inference, but they are independently implausible. Consider, for example, this variant of the closure principle:

THE CLOSURE$_{RK}$ PRINCIPLE*

If S has rationally grounded knowledge that p, and S competently deduces from the fact that she knows that p that q, thereby forming a belief that q on this basis while retaining her rationally grounded knowledge that p, then S has rationally grounded knowledge that q.

The difference between this version of the closure principle and the formulation we have been working with is that the entailment is not between the antecedent proposition and the consequent proposition, but rather between the subject's *knowledge* of the antecedent proposition and the consequent proposition. This is important, since while there isn't any particular proposition that I have rationally grounded knowledge of that entails the über hinge proposition, it is plausibly a consequence of one's knowing these particular propositions that the über hinge proposition is true. If the über hinge proposition were false, for example—that is, if it were true that I am radically and fundamentally mistaken in my beliefs—could I know that my car is dark blue? The point is that the über hinge proposition seems to be such that it must be true for one to even be in the market for knowledge of specific empirical propositions.

As a number of commentators have noted, however, this version of the closure principle is far too strong to be plausible. We can demonstrate this by noting how the closure$_{RK}$ principle* entails iterativity for rationally grounded knowledge, in the sense that if one has rationally grounded knowledge that p then one is in a position to have rationally grounded knowledge that one has rationally grounded knowledge that p (and so on, ad infinitum). After all, that one has rationally grounded knowledge that p trivially entails that one has rationally grounded knowledge that p, and hence one ought to be able to competently deduce the latter from the former. But that means that one's belief in the latter, so derived, will itself be an instance of rationally grounded knowledge, and so we have straightforwardly employed the closure$_{RK}$ principle* to epistemically ascend from first-order to second-order knowledge. Moreover, it ought to be clear that we can continue to epistemically ascend on this basis without restriction.[10]

That iterativity applies to rationally grounded knowledge is controversial, however, and so we should be wary of any formulation of a closure-style principle that entails it. More precisely, the point is that the difference between the closure$_{RK}$ principle and the closure$_{RK}$ principle*, while apparently small, is in fact philosophically significant. While the former is a principle that we would want to reject only as a last resort—indeed, that plausibly captures a deep insight about the nature of rational grounded knowledge—the latter is contentious and certainly apt for rejection if need be.[11]

If one doesn't appeal to the closure$_{RK}$ principle* in order to derive the über hinge proposition from a closure-style inference, then another alternative would be to employ a so-called multi-premise version of the closure$_{RK}$ principle. Rather than drawing an inference from a single instance of rationally grounded knowledge, this would instead draw an inference from a very large string of premises outlining one's rationally grounded knowledge in a wide range of specific propositions. After all, while it doesn't follow from any particular proposition that one knows that the über hinge proposition is true, the latter could plausibly follow from a large enough body of particular propositions that one knows.

Multi-premise closure-style principles are, however, generally acknowledged to be less compelling than their single-premise counterparts, so this would be again to appeal to closure-style reasoning that is some philosophical distance from the specific kind of closure-style reasoning that we want to try to preserve at all costs.[12] Even setting aside the general concerns about multi-premise versions of the closure principle, there are particular grounds to be suspicious of such reasoning according to the Wittgensteinian account of the structure of rational evaluation.

In particular, notice that at most one could use such reasoning to "aggregate" one's rational support for the propositions that one knows (and thus believes). If Wittgenstein is right, however, then (at least on our reading of him anyway) our core commitments are not in the market for knowledge and belief. Thus, there will be inherent limits on the extent that such an aggregation could take, since it couldn't cover one's commitments more generally. One simply couldn't undertake such a process in order to acquire a rational basis for belief in a hinge proposition, much less the über hinge proposition.

So there is no uncontentious deductive route, via a closure-style principle, from our rationally grounded knowledge of particular propositions to rationally grounded knowledge of the über hinge proposition. Interestingly, it is also far from clear that there are plausible instances of the closure$_{RK}$ principle where the entailed proposition concerns a personal hinge proposition. That is, while there are clearly propositions that I am committed to that entail, for example, that I have hands, it is hard to think of propositions that have this entailment that are instances of ordinary rationally grounded knowledge rather than also being personal hinge commitments. That I have two hands entails that I have hands, for example, but we have not here moved from a nonpersonal hinge commitment to a personal hinge commitment, but rather merely expressed two logically distinct personal hinge propositions. In general at least, personal hinge propositions are not of a kind that they are entailed by nonhinge beliefs that we hold.

This is in contrast, of course, to the denials of radical skeptical hypotheses, which clearly are entailed by lots of our everyday nonhinge beliefs. I think that it is here that we get to the interesting set of cases for our purposes. We do not normally encounter radical skeptical hypotheses in ordinary life, and yet we can be easily made aware of their incompatibility with our everyday beliefs. These hypotheses are thus ripe for the kind of competent deduction at issue in closure$_{RK}$-style inferences. The result of these inferences is plausibly a kind of propositional attitude toward the entailed proposition, whereby we recognize that we are committed to regarding it as false. But if this propositional attitude is not one of belief, as maintained above, then what kind of propositional attitude is it?

In order to answer this question, we obviously need to focus on someone who has undertaken this inference and finds the conclusion compelling, as opposed to someone for whom such an inference leads to doubt (even granted, if Wittgenstein is right, that such "doubt" is in an important sense fake, in that one does not—indeed cannot—really doubt one's hinge commitments). What is the propositional attitude in play as regards the anti-skeptical hinge commitment in such cases if it is not one of belief?

We should begin by noting that it is certainly a propositional attitude akin to belief in at least one important respect, in that it involves a commitment to the target proposition that is incompatible with an attitude of agnosticism about its truth. To that extent, this propositional attitude is belief-like in a way that a mere accepting that p or trusting that p is not. Crucially, however, insofar as we accept that such a commitment is merely codifying the prior über hinge commitment, a commitment that is not the result of a rational process or even in principle responsive to rational processes, then the anti-skeptical hinge commitment is also very different from belief in fundamental respects.

For sure, this commitment may feel like belief to the person concerned, in that its phenomenology may be identical to other, more mundane, beliefs that the subject holds. But the import of this point is moot once we remember that the phenomenology of a propositional attitude does not suffice to determine what propositional attitude is in play. The phenomenology of the propositional attitude of wishful thinking may be, in certain cases, subjectively indistinguishable from the phenomenology of the propositional attitude of believing, for example, but that does not make wishful thinking a kind of believing. The same goes for our hinge commitments, including our anti-skeptical hinge commitments, which, despite the potential for a shared phenomenology, are very different in fundamental respects to belief (at least in the sense of belief that interests us).[13]

Once we understand why closure$_{RK}$-style inferences can at most result in a commitment of this sort, we thereby understand why it can appear as if rationally grounded knowledge is not preserved across competent deductions. For the propositional attitude that results from such deductions in these cases, while superficially similar to belief, cannot be a genuine (knowledge-apt) believing, but is instead a mere codification of the prior über hinge commitment, a commitment that is not acquired via any rational process, much less the result of a specific rational process like a particular competent deduction. Rather than this being a counterexample to the closure$_{RK}$ principle, such cases of deductions involving one's hinge commitments are instead better characterized as instances where the closure$_{RK}$ principle is simply inapplicable.

On the nonbelief reading, then, we can reject the universality of rational evaluation thesis that we encountered in chapter 2 even while endorsing the idea, encapsulated in the closure$_{RK}$ principle, that rationally grounded knowledge is preserved across competent deductions. Wittgenstein's account of the structure of rational evaluation therefore exposes a hitherto unnoticed logical gap between these two theses. According to Wittgenstein, there are in principle constraints on rational evaluation, contra the universality of rational evaluation thesis. In particular, the kind of wholesale rational evaluation that is attempted when one considers the rational status of one's hinge commitments is simply incoherent. Rational evaluation is instead an essentially local activity, one that always takes place relative to arational hinge commitments.[14]

Nonetheless, this claim is not in tension with the idea that rationally grounded knowledge is preserved across competent deductions, as encapsulated in the closure$_{RK}$ principle, at least so long as we take seriously the idea that one simply could not form a belief in one of one's hinge commitments, much less form such a belief as a result of undertaking the kind of rational process at issue in closure$_{RK}$-based inferences. Such inferences are thus never applicable to one's hinge commitments.[15]

3. Anti-skeptical Contrasts (I): Inferential Contextualism

One of the most influential epistemological proposals in recent years, directly inspired by Wittgenstein's account of the structure of rational evaluation as set out in *On Certainty*, is due to Michael Williams.[16] Although there are a lot of superficial commonalities between the Wittgensteinian anti-skeptical proposal offered here and Williams's own position, there are also, as we will see, some fundamental divergences. Williams describes his view as a form of epistemic contextualism, though in order to keep his position distinct from the attributer contextualism we looked at in chapter 2 we will refer to it as *inferential contextualism*, for reasons that will soon become apparent.[17] Let's begin with the commonalities between inferential contextualism and the account of hinge commitments offered here.

Williams accepts the general Wittgensteinian point that all rational evaluation takes place relative to arational hinge commitments. In terms of Williams's own terminology, he rejects the "totality condition" (Williams 1991, 90) that is implicit in the traditional epistemological enterprise, such that it is possible to rationally evaluate all our beliefs at once, and he does so because he believes all rational evaluation takes place relative to "methodological necessities" (Williams 1991, 123) that are not themselves subject to rational evaluation. Thus he maintains that the very idea of a fully general rational evaluation is incoherent. Moreover, he also argues as a consequence of this claim that radical skepticism is not the paradox that it purports to be, but rather trades on dubious theoretical claims masquerading as common sense. Like us, then, Williams is proposing an undercutting anti-skeptical strategy that has hinge commitments/methodological necessities at its heart. Thus far there is hence little to separate the two views.

A possible source of divergence between our account and inferential contextualism comes with Williams's rejection of a metaphysical claim about the objects of epistemological study, which he refers to as *epistemological realism*. This is the view that a proposition can have an inherent epistemic status in virtue of its content. In particular, Williams is especially interested in the idea, which he refers to as *epistemic priority*, that propositions concerning the "inner" realm of one's own mind (e.g., regarding one's current mental states) have a privileged epistemic status relative to propositions concerning the "outer" realm of an empirical world (e.g., regarding one's immediate environment). Although Williams is never fully explicit about what he has in mind with regard to epistemic priority, we can get a good feel for his intentions from this passage:

> Beliefs to which no beliefs are epistemologically prior are epistemologically basic. Their credibility is naturally intrinsic, as that of all other beliefs is naturally inferential. (Williams 1991, 116)

Whether or not claims about the inner realm are epistemologically basic, they are at least typically thought to be epistemologically prior to claims about the outer realm in this sense: the rational basis for an instance of the latter kind of claim must involve an inference from an instance of the former kind of claim. So, for example, rationally grounded knowledge that there is chair in front of one must be based on an inference from one's beliefs about one's mental states (e.g., regarding one's experiences as of there being a chair before one).[18]

Williams rejects epistemic priority. For Williams, what can be legitimately inferred relative to what is determined by the methodological necessities in play, and these vary from context to context. Thus while there may be contexts in which, say, one can only rationally infer external world claims from propositions regarding one's mental states, there is no necessity in play here for there can be other contexts, no less legitimate, in which one can reasonably infer claims about one's mental states from claims regarding the external world. This is why Williams's view can be described as inferential contextualism.[19]

More generally, Williams wants to reject not just epistemic priority but also the more general thesis of epistemological realism. That is, not only is there not the kind of inherent epistemic status due to propositions of a certain type when it comes to the "inner/outer" dichotomy, but there is also no such thing as an inherent epistemic status *simpliciter*. For Williams, inferential contextualism is just the denial of epistemological realism. As he puts it, it is the view that

> the epistemic status of a given proposition is liable to shift with situational, disciplinary and other contextually variable factors: it is to hold that, independently of such influences, a proposition has no epistemic status whatsoever. (Williams 1991, 119)

So to reject epistemological realism is to endorse inferential contextualism, and to reject inferential contextualism is to endorse epistemological realism.

Although Williams clearly views his endorsement of the broad contours of the Wittgensteinian account of the structure of rational evaluation as going hand in hand with his rejection of epistemological realism, I think we should be cautious about allying the former with the latter. To begin with, we should note that while the rejection of the totality condition on rational evaluation does obviously follow from the Wittgensteinian account of the structure of rational evaluation alone, the same is not true of the rejection of epistemological realism. Perhaps all rational evaluation is essentially local but that within this constraint there are nonetheless invariant (i.e., context independent) epistemic categories? For example, perhaps it is both the case that all rational evaluation is local *and* that propositions regarding one's mental states have an epistemic priority relative to propositions concerning one's environment?

We will be exploring this point in more detail below when we consider how the Wittgensteinian account fails to properly engage with the underdetermination$_{RK}$-based radical skeptical paradox. This means that a fully adequate response to both forms of the skeptical paradox will require that we at least supplement this account with further claims. This reminds us of the importance of keeping these two logically distinct formulations of the skeptical paradox apart. It also highlights a key point on which our treatment of radical skepticism departs from Williams's, in that Williams clearly treats these two forms of skepticism as being a single kind, and hence amenable to a common solution.[20] But if our disentangling of these two paradoxes in part 1 is correct, then this can't be right, and hence Williams's diagnosis of radical skepticism must be flawed. We will return to this point below.

A more significant divergence between our Wittgensteinian proposal and inferential contextualism for our current purposes is the very different way in which Williams conceives of our hinge commitments as "methodological necessities." On our reading of Wittgenstein, all of our hinge commitments codify a general über hinge commitment. In this way, while there will be lots of divergence in a subject's hinge commitments as we move from person to person and culture to culture, there will also likely be a great deal of commonality. There will certainly be commonality as regards the overarching über hinge commitment, which applies regardless of an individual's personal circumstances.

Williams's conception of hinge propositions as methodological necessities is very different. For example, Williams regards methodological necessities as being dependent on the kind of inquiry one is engaging in. So, to take an example that Williams is fond of, consider the methodological necessities in play when we are conducting a historical inquiry:

> For a subject like history, there is more to method than abstract procedural rules. This is because the exclusion of certain questions (about the existence of the Earth, the complete and total unreliability of documentary evidence, etc.) amounts to the acceptance of substantial factual commitments. These commitments, which must be accepted, if what we understand by historical inquiry at all, have the status, relative to that form of inquiry, of *methodological necessities*. (Williams 1991, 123, italics in original)

The methodological necessities of historical inquiry will thus include claims about the reality of the past and about the reliability of documentary evidence, where these claims are not methodological necessities of some other kinds of inquiry. Hence, a change in one's inquiries can lead to a change in one's methodological necessities, and thus one's hinge commitments.

We should note straightaway one feature of this conception of hinge commitments that is very much in tension with the way Wittgenstein describes these commitments in *On Certainty*.[21] Which inquiries one undertakes is a matter of *choice*, after all, and hence on this view which methodological necessities one has at a particular point of time can be a matter of choice too, at least insofar as one is aware that certain inquiries demand certain methodological necessities. But can we really make sense of our hinge commitments as being *optional* in this way? Isn't the commitment in play meant to be visceral, an "animal" commitment? How could we square this way of thinking about hinge commitments with them being optional?

We can further bring out the odd nature of Williams's conception of hinge commitments by asking what sort of inquiry would lack any of the methodological necessities that Williams claims is distinctive of history. The way that Williams writes about methodological necessities suggests that there ought to be a range of inquiries that don't incorporate any of these commitments—they are particular to a specifically historical inquiry, after all. And yet once one reflects on the matter, it is hard to think of a specific inquiry that doesn't, for example, presuppose the reality of the past. Aren't commitments such as this simply consequences of the über hinge commitment? And if so, doesn't this mean that they are entirely general hinge commitments, and not relative to a particular kind of inquiry? Moreover, so conceived, shouldn't they have the same kind of properties as our other hinge commitments, such as being nonoptional (etc.)?[22]

Tellingly, the only inquiry that Williams offers as an example of an investigation which lacks any of the methodological necessities involved in doing history is that of the traditional epistemological enterprise, where by this he means the kind of fully general rational evaluation of our epistemic standing that is undertaken by the radical skeptic and the conventional (e.g., Cartesian, Moorean) anti-skeptic. A key part of Williams's diagnosis of radical skepticism is the observation that there is a sense in which skepticism is correct, albeit not (as it purports to be) as an acontextual thesis, but only relative to a particular set of methodological necessities. In particular, Williams argues that a hinge commitment to epistemological realism underlies traditional epistemology, and hence underlies the skeptical challenge too, such that it is only relative to this ungrounded methodological necessity that skeptical inquiry can take place. Here is Williams:

> The sceptic takes himself to have discovered, under the conditions of philosophical reflection, that knowledge of the world is impossible. But in fact, the most he has discovered is that knowledge of the world is *impossible under the conditions of philosophical reflection*. (Williams 1991, 130, italics in original)

We thus get another sense in which Williams is a contextualist, for not only are methodological necessities relative to contexts more generally, but also there is a specific context in which skepticism itself is legitimate. As we might put it, there is, on Williams's view, a truth in radical skepticism, although it is not quite the truth that the radical skeptic herself offers.

This is a general move that contextualist anti-skeptical strategies make of course—we witnessed a similar kind of claim with regard to the attributer contextualist treatment of radical skepticism in chapter 2. Notice the difference between the two claims, however. The attributer contextualist appeals to the idea that the context in which radical skepticism is presented involves higher epistemic standards with regards to knowledge ascriptions—indeed, in chapter 2 we noted that this was a problematic feature of the view, from an anti-skeptical point of view.[23] In contrast, for Williams there is no such anti-skeptical appeal to a raising of epistemic standards. In particular, contexts for Williams are not ordered in terms of a hierarchy of epistemic standards. Rather each context incorporates its own internal epistemic standards, as determined by the methodological necessities, and hence inferential structure, in play.

Indeed, since all epistemic evaluation is relative to some context or other (and thus to some particular set of methodological necessities), on Williams's view there is simply no sense in the idea that we can rank contexts in terms of how epistemically demanding they are, as the attributer contextualist supposes. For this would be to undertake the very kind of extracontextual epistemic evaluation that Williams claims is impossible.

There is something deeply suspect about allying the Wittgensteinian account of the structure of rational evaluation to contextualism of this variety. For although there are obviously no rational constraints on what can count as a methodological necessity—since they are by their nature immune to rational evaluation—even on Williams's view the methodological necessities must be true if that context is to yield rationally grounded knowledge. But if Williams has shown, on purely a priori grounds, that epistemological realism is false, then it follows that the skeptical context is simply defunct (i.e., relative to *any* inferential context). There is thus nothing for the skeptic to "discover" as part of her epistemological inquiry. Discovery implies knowledge, after all, and since the methodological necessities of this context are false, no knowledge can be produced by it (not even of a qualified context-dependent form).

Indeed, notice that we do not have to go so far as to accept Williams's rejection of epistemological realism in order to make this point. The rejection, on Wittgensteinian grounds, of the very idea of a fully general rational evaluation will suffice by itself to undermine the project of traditional epistemological inquiry as Williams understands it—that is, such that it essentially incorporates the totality condition. This means that the rejection of the totality condition is enough to ensure that the radical skeptic's context is epistemically illegitimate—such that radical skeptical reasoning cannot lead to rationally grounded knowledge—even if it turns out that epistemological realism is true. (Or, at least, this would be so if we were entitled to accept, with Williams, that there is just one kind of skeptical problem in play here, and therefore that only one diagnosis is needed—we will return to this point below.)

Once we reject the idea of there being a bona fide radical skeptical context—in the sense of potentially generating rationally grounded knowledge—what is left of the contextualist element of inferential contextualism? Everything now depends on whether methodological necessities really are variable across (nonskeptical) contexts in the way that Williams suggests, since without this claim there is nothing specifically contextualist about his proposal. But we have already seen that this is highly dubious. A conviction in the reality of the past is a hinge commitment not merely of historical inquiry, but of *any* inquiry. And we can explain this via our Wittgensteinian account in terms of how this commitment codifies the über hinge commitment. Hinge commitments on our view are never optional, nor are they, relatedly, the kind of commitment that comes and goes as one switches from one investigation to another.

This brings us to a final point of contrast between inferential contextualism and our Wittgensteinian proposal, which is that Williams's view seems completely unable to resist *epistemic relativism*. By epistemic relativism I have in mind the possibility of a specifically epistemic incommensurability, such that two agents have completely different hinge commitments and hence employ two completely distinct systems of rational evaluation. The upshot would be that where these two systems come into conflict, both agents could form their conflicting beliefs rationally and there is no way, even in principle, to rationally resolve their dispute.[24]

Far from being an undesirable possibility that Williams wishes to avoid, epistemic relativism seems instead to be a straightforward *consequence* of inferential contextualism as he understands this view. Here is Williams on just this point:

> As a rule, when people's beliefs differ profoundly, there is no guarantee that there will be neutral epistemic principles for determining who is right and who is wrong. (Williams 2007, 111)

Here we have a straightforward endorsement of what we are here calling epistemic incommensurability, and hence epistemic relativism.[25]

Note, however, that epistemic relativism, so conceived, is *not* a direct consequence of the Wittgensteinian account of the structure of rational evaluation, at least not as we have developed this view. That all rational evaluation takes place relative to hinge commitments is entirely compatible with there being a great deal of overlap in subjects' hinge commitments, even when they are from very different cultures. So the question we need to ask is whether there can be radical divergence in one's hinge commitments. Inferential contextualism seems committed to allowing this, at least to the extent that we can make sense of this proposal as a contextualist thesis at all, but insofar as we reject inferential contextualism, then the way is at least open to denying this possibility.

Interestingly, there are passages in *On Certainty* that suggest that Wittgenstein himself wanted to limit the extent to which there can be divergence of hinge commitments. In particular, he suggests that a divergence of hinge commitments that was too great would be incompatible with one's thoughts even being intelligible. Consider these passages:

> The truth of my statements is the test of my understanding of these statements. That is to say: if I make certain false statements, it becomes uncertain whether I understand them. (OC, §§80–81)

> In order to make a mistake, a man must already judge in conformity with mankind. (OC, §156)

If this is right, then we can at least count on a dispute between two agents who are intelligible to one another as involving a shared background of beliefs, and hence as having shared hinge commitments. There is thus no inherent reason why epistemic incommensurability should be possible on this view. That is, while there will be all the usual practical problems associated with resolving entrenched disagreements, it seems we can avoid the in principle problems posed by epistemic incommensurability, which lead to epistemic relativism.[26] (Note that we will return to the issue of there being an intelligibility constraint on divergence of hinge commitments below when we consider Donald Davidson's anti-skepticism.)

Again, then, we find that there are considerable advantages to taking the Wittgensteinian anti-skeptical line that we have set out over the inferential contextualist position offered by Williams.[27]

4. Anti-skeptical Contrasts (II): Strawsonian Naturalism

A second variety of Wittgensteinian anti-skepticism that is superficially similar to that set out here is the broadly Humean, or naturalistic, reading of Wittgenstein's *On Certainty* that gains its clearest expression in the work of P. F. Strawson (1985). According to Strawson, the anti-skeptical moral of *On Certainty* is to recognize that skeptical doubts should be "neglected" in virtue of the (Humean, naturalistic) fact that we are psychologically incapable of taking such doubts seriously. He writes,

> They [i.e., skeptical doubts] are to be neglected because they are idle; powerless against the force of nature, of our naturally implanted disposition to belief. (Strawson 1985, 13)

Strawson's point is that once we recognize that our anti-skeptical commitments are Humean in this very specific sense, such that we simply unable to properly entertain skeptical commitments, so we realize that the problem of radical skepticism can be legitimately ignored (i.e., treated as "idle").[28]

The Strawsonian naturalistic, or "Humean," reading of *On Certainty* has some support in the text. As Wittgenstein notes at one point, in a

Humean spirit, "It is always by favour of Nature that one knows something" (OC, §505). But by itself this anti-skeptical point seems somewhat blunt. Consider, for example, the philosophical project of engaging with radical skepticism. How is one to gain an intellectually satisfying resolution of that project by simply discovering that genuine anti-skeptical doubt is psychologically impossible and so in this sense idle? Given that, as noted above, we are faced with a putative paradox here: wouldn't this simply *accentuate* one's philosophical anxiety rather than relieve it?

This leads us to an important point, which is that while Strawson's naturalistic reading of *On Certainty* has at least one key feature in common with the Wittgensteinian anti-skeptical proposal outlined here, in that both views hold that our hinge commitments are not optional features of our doxastic architecture (indeed, on the view outlined here they are not part of our doxastic architecture at all, being merely belief-like rather than knowledge-apt beliefs per se), they are at a deeper level very different indeed. For the Wittgensteinian response to radical skepticism we have outlined (i.e., the nonbelief reading), while noting the psychological compulsion of anti-skeptical commitments, does not rest its case against radical skepticism on this point.

Indeed, this point is, I would argue, not load-bearing at all when it comes to the Wittgensteinian response to radical skepticism. Instead, a principled basis is offered, via the Wittgensteinian account of the structure of rational evaluation, for treating the putative radical skeptical paradox as being not a genuine paradox at all, but rather the product of dubious philosophical theory. It is *this* claim that bears the anti-skeptical weight, with the contention that radical skeptical doubts are psychologically implausible a mere dialectical stepping stone on the path toward this philosophical conclusion.

This point should be borne in mind when one reflects on the anti-skeptical move described above such that one holds that what results from closure$_{RK}$-style inferences is not belief in the denials of skeptical hypotheses but merely the realization that one has anti-skeptical hinge commitments, where these are contrasted with genuine (knowledge-apt) beliefs. That move can look like an appeal to mere naturalism in the manner of Strawson's reading of Wittgenstein, but in fact this point is simply a component part of a wider undercutting response to radical skepticism, one that demonstrates that what looks like a genuine paradox is not a real paradox at all, but merely the result of misplaced theory.

In contrast, Strawson's approach is effectively an overriding anti-skeptical strategy, in that it leaves the paradox entirely intact. Strawson's observation that skeptical doubt is psychologically unrealizable does nothing, after all, to undermine the intuitive force of the claims that make up the skeptical paradox. Instead, what Strawson is offering us is rather an independent theoretical basis for not engaging with the skeptical puzzle, on the grounds that whatever our stance on the skeptical problem we will continue to form our anti-skeptical beliefs regardless. Wittgenstein's undercutting anti-skeptical strategy is thus much to be preferred.[29]

5. Anti-skeptical Contrasts (III): Davidsonian Content Externalism

A third contemporary anti-skeptical proposal that has affinities with the nonbelief reading of *On Certainty* is the influential treatment of radical skepticism put forward by Davidson. Rather than get into the various twists and turns in the development of Davidson's view in this regard, we will instead jump straight to the concluding line of anti-skeptical thought that he offers.[30] This is that it follows from any plausible view about the nature of semantic content that we can make no sense of the idea that there could be a believer who has mostly false beliefs. As Davidson famously put it, we are entitled to hold that "belief is in its nature veridical" (Davidson 1983, 146).[31]

There are obvious affinities between this kind of anti-skepticism and the nonbelief reading of *On Certainty* outlined here (indeed, there are affinities between the Davidsonian proposal and most readings of *On Certainty*, though to keep things simple we will focus on the nonbelief reading in this regard). In particular, as we saw earlier, Wittgenstein was also keen to emphasize the point that belief presupposes certainty, to the extent that widespread doubt is simply incompatible with belief of any kind. As we saw in our discussion of Williams's inferential contextualism, Wittgenstein also emphasized semantic limitations on the potential divergence of our hinge commitments. One could thus see Wittgenstein as arguing for the same sort of anti-skeptical conclusion as Davidson.

But while the anti-skeptical upshot is, in this respect at least, very similar, the underlying style of anti-skepticism in play is very different. To begin with, notice that Davidson's anti-skepticism is both in one way significantly weaker and in another way significantly stronger than that offered by the nonbelief reading of *On Certainty*. It is weaker, in that Davidson's anti-skepticism makes no mention of the epistemic standing of our beliefs. In particular, widespread truth in one's beliefs is, at least on the face of it, compatible with a widespread lack of knowledge, as Davidson freely admits. As he puts the point, even though an agent's beliefs may be mostly true, it doesn't follow that they are all "justified enough, or in the right way, to constitute knowledge" (Davidson 1983, 319). In contrast, the account of the structure of rational evaluation that Wittgenstein offers is meant to be such that, insofar as our beliefs are broadly true in the manner that we suppose (i.e., and we are not in fact the victim of a radical skeptical scenario, something that is of course always possible and not in itself a license for radical skepticism), then in virtue of the kind of localized rational support that Wittgenstein delineates we do have bona fide rationally grounded knowledge.

But Davidson's anti-skepticism is also in another way significantly stronger than the nonbelief reading of *On Certainty*, in that the latter does *not* hold that one's beliefs cannot be both massively false and yet be, for all that, bona fide (i.e., knowledge-apt) beliefs. Wittgenstein takes issue with the idea that skeptical doubt could be consistent with belief, but *that* point is entirely compatible with one's beliefs being nonetheless massively false. That is, for Wittgenstein there is a tension between genuinely entertaining skeptical doubt and having beliefs, but that in itself doesn't entail that one's beliefs could not be massively false.

This highlights the point that the nonbelief reading of *On Certainty* offered here is not allied to any specific conception of the nature of semantic content. Davidson argues for the stronger conclusion on this score precisely because he holds on independent content externalist grounds that we can make no sense of an agent having mostly false beliefs. Davidson may be entirely correct this, and if he is then we might wish to supplement our account of Wittgenstein's response to radical skepticism with this claim. Crucially, however, Wittgenstein's response to radical skepticism does not require this claim in order to achieve its ends. Indeed, this makes it all the more plausible as a philosophical proposal, since it ensures that it is not hostage to the truth of further contentious philosophical theses.

6. Wittgensteinian Anti-skepticism and Underdetermination-Based Radical Skepticism

So Wittgenstein presents us with an undercutting response to the problem of skepticism, one that when cast in a particular way (i.e., along the lines of the nonbelief reading) offers us a compelling treatment of that problem. Moreover, this proposal is importantly different from some other leading, and superficially similar, contemporary anti-skeptical proposals. Can we rest content with this remedy for skepticism? I don't think so, despite its many attractions.

Here is the rub. While Wittgenstein's account of the structure of rational evaluation, suitably understood, offers us an innovative way of responding to the closure$_{RK}$-based formulation of skeptical problem, it barely touches the distinct underdetermination$_{RK}$-based aspect of the skeptical problem that we delineated in part 1. What is distinctive about Wittgenstein's proposal, at least on the reading that we have opted for, is that it gives one grounds to reject the universality of rational evaluation thesis (at least on an unrestricted interpretation of that thesis) that we saw underlay the closure-based skeptical problem, without thereby requiring one to give up on the highly compelling closure$_{RK}$ principle for knowledge. Rational support can be bona fide even though all rational evaluation, contra the universality of rational evaluation thesis, is essentially local. But so long as we properly characterize the nature of our hinge commitments, this claim is not in tension with the closure$_{RK}$ principle for knowledge. As regards the closure$_{RK}$-based skeptical problem, at least, we can thus have our cake and eat it too, in that we can reject the underlying thesis that is generating the skeptical problem without thereby losing the compelling epistemic principle that (we had wrongly supposed) was a mere manifestation of this underlying thesis.[32]

But what does this Wittgensteinian treatment of radical skepticism tell us about the underdetermination$_{RK}$-based skeptical problem, and hence the insularity of reasons thesis that we saw underlying this problem in part 1? In truth, the answer is "not very much" (indeed, it might well prove to be "nothing at all"). That all rational evaluation is essentially local is entirely compatible, after all, with it also being "insular" in the manner set out in part 1—namely, such that the rational support one's everyday beliefs enjoys is compatible, even in the best case, with those beliefs being radically in error. In short, rational support could be *both* local *and* insular. Is there anything in Wittgenstein's account of the structure of rational evaluation that could block this move?

Now one might be tempted to respond to this point by arguing that Wittgenstein's account has at least *indirect* relevance to the underdetermination$_{RK}$-based skeptical problem. For doesn't this view rule skeptical scenarios out of the epistemic court, in virtue of the fact that their denials aren't in the market for knowledge? If that's right, then while there is nothing in Wittgenstein's proposal that would suffice to show that we have the relevant favoring rational support for our beliefs, nonetheless there is enough to make the putative negative epistemic import of skeptical scenarios inherently suspect. Given that underdetermination$_{RK}$-based skepticism trades on these scenarios just as much as closure$_{RK}$-based skepticism, this would surely be bad news for both variants of the skeptical problem.

But a moment's reflection reveals that this train of reasoning, while superficially appealing, is far too quick. For while it is true that closure$_{RK}$-based skepticism and underdetermination$_{RK}$-based radical skepticism both appeal to radical skeptical hypotheses, we need to bear in mind that the manner in which they appeal to them is very different. The closure$_{RK}$-based skeptical argument demands that we must be able to have rationally grounded knowledge of the denials of radical skeptical hypotheses if we are to have widespread rationally grounded knowledge of everyday propositions. The Wittgensteinian proposal we have considered deals with this form of skepticism by showing that our everyday rationally grounded knowledge is compatible with a failure to have rationally grounded knowledge of the denials of skeptical hypotheses.

In contrast, the underdetermination$_{RK}$-based skeptical argument doesn't demand that we must be able to have rationally grounded knowledge of the denials of skeptical hypotheses at all, and hence the Wittgensteinian proposal doesn't gain purchase here. Instead, it makes the demand that we must have better rational support for our beliefs over skeptical alternatives if we are to have widespread rationally grounded knowledge of everyday propositions. As we saw in part 1, this is a logically weaker demand to make, in that one could have such favoring supporting for one's everyday beliefs over skeptical alternatives even while failing to have rationally grounded knowledge of the denials of skeptical alternatives. And therein lies the crux of the matter. The Wittgensteinian proposal is that our everyday knowledge is fine even despite our inability to have rationally grounded knowledge of the denials of radical skeptical hypotheses. But this is irrelevant to underdetermination$_{RK}$-based radical skepticism on account of the fact that this form of skepticism *never demanded* that we should have this kind of anti-skeptical knowledge if we are to have everyday rationally grounded knowledge.

The Wittgensteinian treatment of radical skepticism thus fails to engage with the underdetermination$_{RK}$-based formulation of this problem. The worry that the rational support for our beliefs might be both local and insular is thus very real indeed.

Worse, with the underdetermination-based formulation of the skeptical problem in play, it is surely even harder to be comfortable with the idea—which even Wittgenstein held took some getting used to (e.g., OC,

§166)—of essentially local rational support. For remember what this idea means in practice—namely, that the hinge commitments that underpin our system of rational evaluation are essentially unknown and lacking rational support. Wittgenstein offers us a compelling story as to why we should accept such a claim, despite it being in tension with a certain widely held philosophical picture (as encapsulated in the universality of rational evaluation thesis). But once we recognize the danger posed by underdetermination$_{RK}$-based skepticism, this story starts to look much less compelling. The idea that rational support is essentially local is acceptable only so long as we can retain our conviction that this rational support is bona fide. But with the underdetermination$_{RK}$-based skeptical problem in play, there is no assurance that such local rational support is genuine at all.

7. Epistemic Priority and Underdetermination-Based Radical Skepticism

Earlier we looked at Williams's inferential contextualism, and one of the points we raised there was that there seemed to be a significant logical gap between the Wittgensteinian rejection of the universality of rational evaluation and the further claim that Williams wanted to extract from the Wittgensteinian picture—namely, that epistemological realism, and with it, epistemic priority, needs to be abandoned also. As we noted, there seems to be no inherent reason why rational support couldn't be both essentially local as Wittgenstein demands and yet there also be invariant epistemic categories, such as the kind of epistemic categories that determine epistemic priority.

We are now in a better position to diagnose where Williams goes awry on this score. Unlike us, Williams does not distinguish between closure$_{RK}$-based and underdetermination$_{RK}$-based formulations of the radical skeptical paradox, and hence he runs these two problems together.[33] As such, he is seeking a version of the Wittgensteinian claim about the structure of rational evaluation that can deal with both kinds of skepticism simultaneously. But once we realize that these are logically distinct routes to radical skepticism that trade on very different underlying theses, then it becomes clear that this is a hopeless endeavor: while Wittgenstein offers us a way of resolving closure$_{RK}$-based radical skepticism, there is no direct way of extending this approach to underdetermination$_{RK}$-based radical skepticism.

The foregoing is of course consistent with the idea that if we only added a rejection of epistemological realism, and the epistemic priority thesis that (Williams claims) goes with it, to the Wittgensteinian account, then we would have an anti-skeptical response that dealt with both formulations of the skeptical paradox. If this were right, then Williams could at least salvage something from this anti-skeptical strategy. Unfortunately, even this redescribed version of Williams's anti-skeptical strategy, such that it consists of two distinct anti-skeptical theses, doesn't work.

We will focus on epistemic priority in this regard, since this is clearly the thesis that holds the whip hand in this regard as far as Williams is concerned. That is, he wants to renounce epistemological realism since it licenses epistemic priority, where epistemic priority leads to radical skepticism and so has to go. Would the rejection of epistemic priority suffice to block the underdetermination$_{RK}$-based radical skeptical paradox?

This might initially look quite plausible, in that one might think that if it is sometimes—as part of a particular context of inquiry—legitimate to rationally infer claims about one's mental states from claims about the external world, then this must be in conflict with the insularity of reasons thesis, and hence with underdetermination$_{RK}$-based radical skepticism. But this train of reasoning does not stand up to closer scrutiny. This is because it is in fact entirely consistent with the rejection of epistemic priority that the insularity of reasons thesis holds.

Suppose it is true, for example, that in certain psychological contexts of inquiry it may be legitimate to make inferences about one's mental states from claims about the external world. Why should it follow from this that the insularity of reasons thesis is false? For notice that the latter claim is specifically about whether the rational support we have for our beliefs is necessarily compatible with the possibility that one's beliefs are radically in error. Why should it follow from the fact that a particular belief about one's mental states can be rationally inferred from a particular belief about the external world that this latter possibility is excluded? In itself, all this shows is that some of our beliefs about our mental states might have a weaker epistemic pedigree than some of our beliefs about the external world, but there is nothing in this claim that is in conflict with the insularity of reasons thesis.

More generally, in rejecting the insularity of reasons thesis we are not thereby rejecting epistemic priority. Rejecting the insularity of reasons thesis means allowing that that the rational support enjoyed by our everyday beliefs can potentially exclude the possibility that we are in radical error, but this is entirely consistent with thinking of the direction of rational support in play as being from mind to world. Indeed, as we will see in part 3, there is a way of thinking about our reflectively accessible rational support such that it offers the favoring anti-skeptical support that we need to block the insularity of reasons thesis and thereby deal with underdetermination$_{RK}$-based radical skepticism, but which is nonetheless entirely compatible with epistemic priority.

It seems, then, that denying epistemic priority is neither necessary nor sufficient for blocking underdetermination$_{RK}$-based skepticism. It follows that Williams has not only misdiagnosed the source of skepticism in virtue of failing to distinguish between the closure$_{RK}$-based and underdetermination$_{RK}$-based versions of this problem, but also misunderstood the extent to which the skeptical problem (of either form) essentially trades upon epistemic priority, and thus epistemological realism.

8. Concluding Remarks

The upshot of the foregoing is that if we wish to retain the Wittgensteinian treatment of radical skepticism that we have set out here, then we will need to supplement it with additional anti-skeptical resources that can deal with the specific problem posed by underdetermination$_{RK}$-based radical skepticism. To this end, in part 3 we will be considering an influential response to radical skepticism—due at root to John McDowell—which, it will be argued, is best understood as primarily directed at the underdetermination$_{RK}$-based formulation of the problem. As with the Wittgensteinian response to radical skepticism outlined here, this proposal is compelling only insofar as it is directed at the specific variety of radical skepticism to which it is applicable. In particular, while this broadly McDowellian response to radical skepticism is effective when aimed at underdetermination$_{RK}$-based skepticism, it gains far less of a purchase on closure$_{RK}$-based radical skepticism.

The reader who suspects that a synthesis is in the offing would be right. For I shall also be arguing in part 4 that the solution to the general skeptical predicament lies in integrating these two—on the face of it very different—treatments of radical skepticism. The McDowellian response to radical skepticism can take up the dialectical slack that we saw present in the Wittgensteinian anti-skeptical proposal, and the Wittgensteinian response to radical skepticism can return the favor in the other direction.

Moreover—and this is crucial—we will also see that there is nothing ad hoc about this synthesis. Our thinking about radical skepticism has failed to take into account the very different demands imposed by underdetermination$_{RK}$-based and closure$_{RK}$-based radical skepticism, and for this reason our responses to radical skepticism are at best naggingly unsatisfying. Our way of dealing with the radical skeptical problem is thus crying out for a synthesis of just this sort. Furthermore, as I hope to make clear in part 4, the Wittgensteinian and McDowellian responses to radical skepticism are genuinely complementary, and so this is not merely a case of bolting the one onto the other in order to keep the anti-skeptical boat afloat. In particular, we can better live with the idea that all rational evaluation is essentially local insofar as we can show that the rational support that our beliefs enjoy is not always insular; and we can better live with the idea that our beliefs sometimes enjoy rational support that isn't insular insofar as we can show that all rational evaluation is essentially local.

PART 3

Epistemological Disjunctivism

～

> The considerations I have offered suggest a way to respond to scepticism about, for instance, perceptual knowledge; the thing to do is not to answer the sceptic's challenges, but to diagnose their seeming urgency as deriving from a misguided interiorisation of reason.
> —John McDowell, "Knowledge and the Internal," 890

CHAPTER 5

Epistemological Disjunctivism and the Factivity of Reasons

0. Introductory Remarks

In part 2 we witnessed an intriguing response to closure-based skepticism, inspired by Wittgenstein's writings. We also saw, however, that this proposal struggled to deal with the logically distinct challenge posed by underdetermination-based skepticism. The goal of part 3 is to explore a radical thesis regarding perceptual knowledge, known as *epistemological disjunctivism*. This proposal is rooted in the work of John McDowell and offers a distinctive response to the problem of radical skepticism. As we will discover, however, this way of dealing with the skeptical problem, while very powerful when applied to underdetermination-based radical skepticism, cannot be comfortably extended to closure-based radical skepticism. We are thus presented with two ways of responding to the skeptical paradox, each of which in fact confronts only one aspect of this problem.

Ultimately, my aim is to demonstrate that these two anti-skeptical proposals, while superficially very different, are not only compatible but also mutually supportive. In particular, when they are appropriately formulated and combined within the right framework, they jointly offer us a satisfactory answer to the radical skeptical paradox that we are here confronting, in both its guises. That is a task for part 4, however. In part 3, our focus will be an exploration of the strengths and weaknesses of epistemological disjunctivism as an anti-skeptical strategy.

1. Epistemological Disjunctivism in Outline

We will begin by setting out the distinctive element of McDowellian anti-skepticism, which is its defense of a particular view—*epistemological disjunctivism*—about what constitutes perceptual knowledge in paradigm cases.[1] Note that in what follows we will be less concerned with McDowellian exegesis than with the task of spelling out this proposal as best we can in order to amplify its anti-skeptical potential. (The upshot of this is that the position we will end up defending, while clearly McDowellian, may well not be a version of the position that the man himself would endorse.)[2]

Epistemological disjunctivism is the view that in paradigm cases of perceptual knowledge the knowledge in question enjoys a rational support that is both *factive* and *reflectively accessible*. In particular, it is the view that when one has perceptual knowledge in such cases, the reflectively accessible rational support one has for one's knowledge that p is that one *sees that p*. Note, however, that seeing that p is factive, just like knowing that p. That is, if one knows that p then it follows that p must be true; likewise if one sees that p, then p must be true.

The factivity claim that seeing that p entails p is not in itself controversial. One can *seem to see* that p without p being true, as happens when, for example, one is the victim of a hallucination. But genuine seeing that p requires the truth of p. Similarly, the claim that the rational support for one's believing that p must be reflectively accessible is also not usually thought to be controversial, and it is easy to see why. For if this rational support were not so accessible—if, in particular, it was opaque to one that one's belief enjoyed this rational support—then it would be hard to see why it would count as rationally supporting one's belief that p.[3]

What creates the controversy when it comes to epistemological disjunctivism is thus not these two theses in isolation, but rather their combination. In particular, what is controversial is the idea that one could have perceptual knowledge in virtue of rational support which is *both* factive *and* reflectively accessible at the same time.

We can get a sense of how idiosyncratic this view is by spelling out some of its implications. Consider the following pair of cases. On the one hand, we have a "good" case where the agent possesses paradigmatic perceptual knowledge. On the other hand, we have a corresponding "bad" case—such as a BIV case of the kind that we witnessed in part 1—where the agent's experiences are introspectively indistinguishable and in which she lacks perceptual knowledge of the target proposition (but nonetheless blamelessly supposes that she possesses such knowledge).[4] As we noted in chapter 2 (§7), a standard view about reflectively accessible rational support is that the agents in these pairs of good and bad cases possess essentially the same degree of reflectively accessible rational support for their beliefs.[5] This is the so-called new evil demon intuition, which we noted is held to be a cornerstone of what it means for rational support to be reflectively accessible. It is a prior commitment to this intuition that generates support for the insularity of reasons thesis. This is because with this intuition in play it follows that, even in the best case, the rational support enjoyed by one's everyday beliefs will inevitably be compatible with those beliefs being radically in error, as the rational support one has for one's beliefs even in paradigmatic perceptual conditions is never better than the rational support one has for one's beliefs in corresponding cases in which one is radically deceived.

Epistemological disjunctivism rejects this picture and holds instead that the rational support reflectively accessible to the agents in these pairs of cases is in fact fundamentally different. In the good case the agent possesses paradigmatic perceptual knowledge and so is in possession of rational support that is both reflectively accessible and factive. In the bad case, in contrast, she lacks such knowledge and hence lacks this type of rational support too (we will consider what, if any, rational support is available to the subject in the bad case below). The upshot is that the epistemological disjunctivist rejects the insularity of reasons thesis and, with it, the new evil demon intuition that underlies it.

As an illustration, consider the following pairing of "good" and "bad" cases. In the first case, the agent genuinely perceives that there is a tree before her in epistemically excellent conditions (there is no deception in play in the environment, her faculties are working normally, and so on). On the basis of this perception she forms the belief that there is a tree before her. In the second case, the agent is in a situation that is experientially introspectively indistinguishable from the first, and hence which blamelessly prompts her to form a belief in the same proposition with as much conviction as in the first case. Crucially, however, her belief is formed in highly suboptimal conditions. To make the contrast particularly clear, let us suppose that our agent in this second case is simply hallucinating that there is a tree before her and in fact is being visually presented with no specific object at all.

According to the new evil demon intuition, the rational support one's belief enjoys in the two cases is essentially the same. In particular, the rational support one's belief enjoys in the first ("good") case is no better than the rational support one's belief enjoys in the second ("bad") case. According to epistemological disjunctivism, in contrast, the rational support reflectively accessible to the agents in these two cases is very different. In particular, in the first case the agent's reflectively accessible rational support will be the factive ground that she sees that there is a tree before her, and she will have perceptual knowledge that there is a tree before her in virtue of possessing this rational basis for her belief.

But whatever the nature of the reflectively accessible rational support in the second case, it cannot be of this factive sort (aside from anything else, the target proposition is false in the second case). Moreover, notice that however we understand the rational support in the second case, it is not merely a "stunted" version of the rational support in the first case, as if the latter were just the former supplemented in some way with additional rational support. Rather, the two rational standings are radically different *in kind* (this is what makes this epistemological proposal *disjunctivist*).[6]

For many in epistemology, epistemological disjunctivism is simply untenable. In particular, on standard views in epistemology when dealing with pairs of experientially introspectively indistinguishable "good" and "bad" cases like this the verdicts we should draw are very clear. In particular, both standard epistemic externalist and internalist proposals would grant that the internalist epistemic support—typically, the reflectively accessible rational support—the agent has for her belief is common to both cases. After all, or so the thought runs, if the agent really cannot introspectively distinguish between the experiences in the two cases, then surely the reflectively accessible rational support for her belief in the two cases must be essentially the same (or, at the very least, the rational support in the good case cannot be any better than it is in the corresponding bad case).

Conversely, both standard epistemic externalist and internalist proposals would grant that insofar as there is a difference in the epistemic support that the agent's belief enjoys in these two scenarios, then it must be the case that the kind of epistemic support we have in mind is of an externalist rather than internalist variety. So, for example, it could well be that the agent in the good situation has better epistemic support for her belief than the agent in the corresponding bad situation in virtue of forming her beliefs in a more reliable fashion. Whether or not one's beliefs are reliably formed is, however, a purely external matter (usually, anyway), in that it is not reflectively accessible to the subject.

In terms of the epistemological disjunctivist idea that seeing that p could be one's epistemic support for perceptually knowing that p in a good case, the upshot is that on standard epistemological views a dilemma is posed. Either we take seriously that seeing that p constitutes factive epistemic support, in which case it cannot be the reflectively accessible rational support one has for one's belief (that privilege instead going to a related nonfactive epistemic standing, such as *seeming to see that p*). Or we take seriously that seeing that p constitutes the reflectively accessible rational support one has for one's perceptual knowledge in good cases, but in so doing opt for a revisionist understanding of what it is to see that p, such that it is no longer a factive notion. Either way, epistemological disjunctivism is simply not an option.

2. Three Core Problems for Epistemological Disjunctivism

What explains the widespread reluctance to take epistemological disjunctivism seriously as a plausible view? Elsewhere I have set out three core problems that this view appears to face and that, superficially at least, all appear fatal. I have then argued that all three problems are on closer inspection far from compelling, the result being that, despite the conventional wisdom on the matter, epistemological disjunctivism is a viable proposal after all.[7] I cannot hope to give a full account of these problems and how epistemological disjunctivism can evade them here, so what follows will be a mere overview of the issues in this regard.

First, there is the *basing problem*. On standard views about the relationship between seeing that p and knowing that p, seeing that p entails knowing that p on account of it merely being a way of knowing that p.[8] But if that's right, then how can seeing that p constitute one's epistemic *basis* for knowing that p, given that it involves citing something that is itself just a way of knowing that p? At most, it seems, one can appeal to seeing that p to *explain* how one knows that p, but not to indicate one's epistemic basis for knowing that p.

The basing problem takes it as granted that one's epistemic basis for knowledge cannot be itself a way of knowing, and that claim could be questioned. But I think there is an even better way of responding to this worry, which is to dispute the thesis that seeing that p entails knowing that p. For what is at the root of the basis problem is the thought that if seeing that p is essentially a way of knowing that p, then it cannot constitute one's epistemic basis for knowing that p. Accordingly, if we can argue that seeing that p is not essentially a way of knowing that p—that is, such that one can see that p while failing to know that p—then this ought to suffice to block the problem.

In order to see the attraction of this line of argument, we should note first that seeing that p is clearly robustly epistemic in a way that mere object seeing (i.e., merely seeing a barn, as opposed to *seeing that* there is a barn) is not. A child can count as seeing an object—a banana, say—without knowing what object she has seen. But a child cannot *see that* there is a banana before her without at least having some idea about what it is she is seeing. In particular, to count as seeing that there is a banana before one, one must possess the relevant conceptual repertoire. But if you not only see the object but also are able to conceptually classify the object too, then what stands in the way of you knowing the relevant proposition (e.g., that this is a banana)?

Seeing that p is thus much closer to knowing that p than merely seeing the corresponding object. That much is undeniable. But we should be wary about concluding on this basis that seeing that p entails knowing that p. In order to understand why, consider scenarios that, while being epistemically propitious from an objective perspective, are nonetheless epistemically poor from a subjective perspective. So imagine, for example, that one is genuinely visually presented with a banana in what is entirely normal conditions, and that one has the conceptual repertoire to correctly conceptually classify this object, but that one is told by someone one takes to be a reliable informant that what one is looking at is not a banana but rather a clever fake. One is thus faced with a defeater, albeit, unbeknownst to one, a *misleading* defeater.

In such a scenario, would one believe that the object before one is a banana? Surely not. Given that knowledge entails belief, it follows that one would not know this proposition either. But does one genuinely see a banana? That seems right. After all, one is indeed visually presented with a banana, and that is what is most important for object seeing. That is, one is seeing a banana, even though one doesn't think that one is seeing a banana. So the key question becomes whether one is *seeing that* there is a banana before one in this case.

I contend that it is at least plausible to suppose that one is. From an objective point of view, after all, there is nothing amiss with one's epistemic relationship to the facts; it is just that one has had the misfortune to be in receipt of a misleading defeater. Think of it this way: suppose that you subsequently found out that the defeater was misleading; wouldn't you now characterize your previous situation as one in which you *saw that* there was a banana ("ah, so I did see that there was a banana on the table after all!")? Misleading defeaters can be destructive to knowledge, but why should they be destructive to seeing that p? In particular, what would be wrong in such cases in contending that one genuinely sees that p in virtue of being in an objectively epistemically good scenario—the kind that would usually lead to paradigmatic perceptual knowledge, absent misleading defeaters—but that the presence of misleading defeaters means that nonetheless one lacks knowledge? But, of course, if the logical link between seeing that p and knowing that p is broken, then the basis problem inevitably loses its bite. In particular, the worry that seeing that p can't be an epistemic basis for knowing that p if it is merely itself a form of knowing that p is completely removed.[9]

The second problem facing epistemological disjunctivism is the *access problem*. This is the concern that such a view will directly generate a kind of "McKinsey-style" problem—that is, a problem of a parallel sort to that which is widely alleged to face the combination of first-person authority and content externalism.[10] In essence, the McKinsey problem concerns the fact that according to (some famous versions of) content externalism a prerequisite of one's beliefs having a particular content can be that a certain specific worldly fact (or facts) obtain. Given that content externalism is a philosophical thesis, it seems that it can be known a priori. But given first-person authority, that one has a belief with a certain content is also something that is plausibly in the market for reflective (and thus a priori) knowledge. Thus it seems that if both first-person authority and content externalism are true, then one ought to be able to come to know specific facts about one's environment simply through reflection. For many this would constitute a *reductio* of this conjunction of theses.

The parallel problem that faces epistemological disjunctivism concerns the fact that one can know a priori that seeing that p entails p. Thus, if one can come to know by reflection alone that one's rational support for one's belief that p—where p is a specific proposition about one's environment—is that one sees that p, then surely one can through further a priori reflection come to know that p itself. But, as with the McKinsey problem that faces the combination of content externalism and first-person authority, it seems incredible that one could come to know a specific fact about one's environment purely through reflection. This is the access problem.

In order to illustrate the access problem, consider a concrete case. Suppose one believes that John is at home, and that one's reflectively accessible rational support for this belief is that one sees that John is at home (i.e., this is a case of paradigmatic perceptual knowledge, as the epistemological disjunctivist describes it). Given that one also (we might assume) knows a priori that seeing that p entails p, it seems that one can further conclude, purely by undertaking a competent deduction (and hence by reflection alone), that John is at home. But now it seems that one is coming to know a specific empirical fact about one's environment purely by a reflective and thus nonempirical process, and that sounds absurd.

Fortunately, the access problem doesn't stand up to closer scrutiny. In particular, notice that seeing that p is itself an *empirical reason* for believing that p, since it is acquired by perception of the world. We should thus be immediately suspicious of the claim that reflecting on the nature of one's empirical reasons can provide one with an exclusively reflective (and thus nonempirical) route to empirical knowledge.

Of course, one might counter this point by arguing that what counts is just what the basis for the inferred belief amounts to. So, for example, suppose one sees that p, but one does not form a belief in the empirical proposition that p on this basis (a possibility that we granted above, on the way to arguing that seeing that p does not entail knowing that p). Now imagine that via a competent deduction from one's reflectively accessible factive reason, one forms a belief that p. Wouldn't this be an exclusively reflective route to knowledge that p (and thus a possible route to nonempirical knowledge of an empirical proposition)?

The problem with this line of argument, however, is with the idea that one can have reflectively accessible factive reasons and yet not believe the target proposition. There is no reason why the epistemological disjunctivist should subscribe to this view. Recall that the epistemological disjunctivist claim is only that in paradigmatic cases of perceptual knowledge one's rational support can consist of the factive reason that one sees that p. But in such cases it is already stipulated that the agent knows, and thus believes, that p on the basis of this rational support. In particular, while epistemological disjunctivists grant that in nonparadigm cases of perception seeing that p might not lead to one believing that p, they aren't committed to holding that in such cases the subject will have reflectively accessible access to the factive rational support in play.

So either one's knowledge that p is grounded in the empirical reason that one sees that p, in which case the subject obviously cannot have a purely reflective route to knowledge that p, or else it isn't so grounded, in which case the epistemological disjunctivist is not committed to this empirical reason being reflectively accessible to the subject. Either way, the access problem is neutralized.[11]

The third problem facing epistemological disjunctivism—which I think is a much deeper worry than the other two—concerns the fact that if one does have reflective access to factive reasons in cases involving paradigmatic perceptual knowledge, then it is hard to see how one can reconcile this claim with the undeniable truth that there are parallel indistinguishable scenarios in which one lacks a factive reason but where, nonetheless, one continues to blamelessly suppose that one possesses it.[12] As noted above, even the epistemological disjunctivist will grant that the good case in which one sees that there is a tree before one, and so knows this proposition on this reflectively accessible rational basis, can be indistinguishable from a parallel bad case where one is the victim of an illusion and merely thinks that one sees a tree (where, say, there is in fact no tree in one's visual field). But if one has reflective access to one's seeing that *p* in the good case, and one knows that this is only so in the good case, then surely one also knows that one is not in the bad case. But that's odd. If one can know just through reflecting on the nature of the rational support one's beliefs enjoy that one is in the good case rather than the bad case, then surely one *can* distinguish between good and corresponding bad cases after all. Of course, one can do this only in the good case, since in the bad case one doesn't have reflective access to the factive reason, but one might naturally contend that even this ought not to be possible. Call this the *distinguishability problem*.

In order to resolve the distinguishability problem, we need to recognize that there is a way of knowing that one is one scenario rather than a competing scenario that is not thereby a way of distinguishing between the two scenarios. In sloganizing form, we need to recognize that there is a way of knowing the difference that is not thereby a way of telling the difference. Indeed, as we will see, this is a distinction that all epistemologists should recognize, and not just epistemological disjunctivists.

Consider someone at the zoo who forms the belief that there is zebra before her on the basis of what she sees. We need not imagine that the epistemic support in question is in the form of factive reflectively accessible reasons; it could just be perceptual evidence of a familiar kind (e.g., it looks like a zebra, the sign above the enclosure says "zebra," and so on). If this is a normal member of the public (and not, say, a zoologist), then she wouldn't be able to perceptually distinguish this "zebra" scenario from an alternative scenario in which, due to a sophisticated deception, what she is being visually presented with is a cleverly disguised mule instead of a zebra.[13]

But even though our agent is unable to perceptually distinguish between these two scenarios—in particular, even though she would be unable to perceptually distinguish (at this distance, etc.) between a zebra and a cleverly disguised mule—does it follow that she cannot know that the former scenario obtains as opposed to the latter scenario? It is this entailment that I think we should query. For presumably our subject will likely have all manner of background evidence available to her that epistemically favors the "zebra" scenario over the alternative "cleverly disguised mule" scenario. This will include evidence regarding the plausibility of this deception, the likelihood of it being spotted, the penalties that would be imposed were it to be discovered, the lengths that one would need to go to in order to make this deception plausible (including the costs that one would incur), and so on. Collectively, these considerations surely provide a sufficient epistemic basis for preferring the "zebra" scenario to its locally skeptical alternative. But if that's right, then our subject can know that she is in the "zebra" scenario rather than the competing "cleverly disguised mule" scenario even though she cannot perceptually distinguish between these two scenarios—in particular, even though she cannot perceptually distinguish between zebras and cleverly disguised mules.

The point of the foregoing is that we need to distinguish between "discriminating" and "favoring" epistemic support. The additional considerations that our subject is able to bring to bear are specifically of the latter type, in that they favor one scenario over another without providing the subject with a means to perceptually tell the two scenarios apart. With this distinction in play, it ought to be clear how the epistemological disjunctivist should respond to the distinguishability problem. For the epistemological disjunctivist can now consistently grant that reflectively accessible factive rational support provides one with a means to know, in the good case, that one is in the good case rather than the bad case, in virtue of it presenting the subject with favoring epistemic support from which one can legitimately draw deductive inferences from. But the existence of this favoring epistemic support is entirely compatible with the fact that one lacks the means to discriminate between good and bad cases. Once one factors in a distinction between these two types of epistemic support, a distinction that all epistemologists should endorse, the distinguishability problem for epistemological disjunctivism thus disappears.[14]

There is undoubtedly more to say about these problems—indeed, as noted above, I've explored each of them at greater length elsewhere—but the foregoing should suffice to demonstrate that epistemological disjunctivism is at least a viable position. In what follows, we will therefore take its viability for granted and focus instead on its implications for the problem of radical skepticism.

3. Epistemological Disjunctivism qua Anti-skeptical Strategy

The anti-skeptical import of epistemological disjunctivism to the underdetermination$_{RK}$-based radical skeptical problem ought to be manifest. Consider again how we formulated that problem in chapter 2, in terms of a triad of collectively inconsistent claims:

THE UNDERDETERMINATION$_{RK}$-BASED SKEPTICAL PARADOX

(SU1) One cannot have rational support that favors one's belief in an everyday proposition over an incompatible radical skeptical hypothesis.

(SU2) The underdetermination$_{RK}$ principle.

(SU3) One has widespread rationally grounded everyday knowledge.[15]

The underdetermination$_{RK}$ principle at issue in (SU2) was formulated as follows:

THE UNDERDETERMINATION$_{RK}$ PRINCIPLE

If S knows that p and q describe incompatible scenarios, and yet S lacks a rational basis that favors p over q, then S lacks rationally grounded knowledge that p.

We noted at the end of chapter 2 that we would ideally like a response to the underdetermination$_{RK}$-based radical skeptical problem that rejected the first premise. For once this premise is granted, it is hard to see how we could possess the kind of rational support for our everyday beliefs that we typically suppose them to enjoy. What we seek, therefore, is a principled rejection of the claim that the rational support enjoyed by our beliefs in "good" cases is no better than the rational support we have for our beliefs in corresponding "bad" cases involving radical skeptical scenarios. Epistemological disjunctivism, via its rejection of the new evil demon intuition, and the insularity of reasons thesis which underlies it, offers us the resources to do just that.

To illustrate this point, take the example we used when we formulated this paradox in chapter 2, such that we consider the epistemic standing of one's "everyday" belief that one is currently seated at one's desk in light of the BIV radical skeptical hypothesis. According to epistemological disjunctivism, the rational support one has for one's belief that one is currently seated at one's desk will be (in paradigm cases of perceptual knowledge anyway) that one sees that one is seated at one's desk. Note that the factive rational support that one has in the good case for believing that one is seated at one's desk *entails* that one is not a BIV.

In contrast, if one were a BIV, then one's belief that one is currently seated at one's desk clearly cannot enjoy factive rational support, but must be much weaker (e.g., that it seems to one as if one is seated at one's desk, which is of course nonfactive rational support). It follows that by epistemological disjunctivist lights the rational support available to one in the good case is not on par with the rational support available to one in the corresponding bad case, but is in fact much stronger, and hence the new evil demon intuition is rejected.

We noted above that this rejection of a common level of rational support in good and corresponding bad cases is a core element of epistemological disjunctivism. But with this claim in play—in particular, the thesis that in good cases the rational support one has for one's beliefs can be factive, as opposed to merely nonfactive (as in bad cases)—we can block the underdetermination$_{RK}$-based skepticism argument at its outset. For according to epistemological disjunctivism, (SU1) is simply false.

In part 1 we argued that ideally we want an *undercutting* response to the radical skeptical problem that does not involve an independent commitment to a fundamental form of epistemological revisionism (as opposed to an *overriding* anti-skeptical proposal, which is so committed). Does epistemological disjunctivism satisfy this constraint? Arguably, it does. We've seen already that the view is a viable position, in that it doesn't succumb to the problems one might initially level at it. But that is of course consistent with it being an overriding anti-skeptical strategy, one that argues for a substantive form of epistemological revisionism as a means of evading the skeptical paradox. Indeed, one might think that epistemological disjunctivism must be committed to epistemological revisionism in virtue of it posing such a challenge to traditional ways of thinking about perceptual knowledge. This would, however, be a mistake.

The reason for this is that it is crucial to the defense of epistemological disjunctivism that this view is in fact more in keeping with our folk epistemological concepts than rival positions. In particular, epistemological disjunctivists claim that their proposal is the natural view that one would be led to were it not for the problems that are held to afflict such a position (i.e., the kind of problems that we outlined and critiqued above). That is, epistemological disjunctivists maintain that it is quite natural in ordinary language to appeal to factive rational support (i.e., that one sees that *p*) in support of one's perceptual knowledge in good epistemic conditions. Indeed, they argue that to appeal to anything short of factive rational support, as nonepistemological disjunctivists would demand, would be unnatural.

There is a lot of plausibility to this claim. For example, suppose I tell my manager over the phone that a colleague of mine is at work today (thereby representing myself as perceptually knowing this to be the case), and she expresses skepticism about this (perhaps because she falsely believes that my colleague always skips work when she isn't there). In response I might naturally say that I know that she's at work today because I can see that she's at work—she's standing right in front of me. Indeed, wouldn't it be odd for me to respond in this case, given the situation as described, by offering nonfactive rational support, such as by saying that *it seems to me as if* she is at work today (as if I'm not sure whether she is really there)?

With this point in mind, epistemological disjunctivists claim that it is only in response to the putative problems involved with taking this natural view seriously that epistemologists are led to adopt revisionary epistemological proposals, such as by claiming (in line with the insularity of reasons thesis) that the rational support one's perceptual beliefs enjoy in good cases can never be better than the kind of nonfactive rational support they enjoy in counterpart bad cases. In contrast, once we have determined that these putative problems are illusory—as we have argued in outline above (and as I have argued at greater length elsewhere)—then we are entitled to reject these forms of epistemological revisionism and return once more to the more natural view encapsulated by epistemological disjunctivism.

With epistemological disjunctivism so conceived, it represents an undercutting anti-skeptical strategy. In particular, epistemological disjunctivism claims that the plausibility of the key premise of the underdetermination$_{RK}$-based skeptical argument—that is, (SU1)—rests on theoretical assumptions that have been shown to be dubious. The idea that the rational support our everyday beliefs enjoy cannot favor those beliefs over radical skeptical alternatives is rooted not in our folk epistemological concepts, but rather in contentious theoretical moves that are made in light of the deficiencies that are mistakenly thought to be inherent to the very idea (embraced by epistemological disjunctivism) that in the right conditions one's perceptual beliefs can enjoy rational support that is both reflectively accessible and factive. As a result, once we demonstrate that these deficiencies are illusory, and thus that epistemological disjunctivism is a viable theoretical option, then the way is open to endorse our folk epistemological intuitions and in so doing reject (SU1). And of course once (SU1) is rejected, so too is underdetermination$_{RK}$-based radical skepticism.

The point is that the insularity of reasons thesis which underlies (SU1), far from being an uncontentious item of epistemological common sense, is in fact the product of dubious philosophical theorizing. In particular, we are led to adopt this thesis, and thereby revise our natural way of thinking about the rational support available to us in epistemically good conditions, only in response to theoretical moves that have been shown to be suspect. The path is therefore opened to offer an undercutting anti-skeptical response along epistemological disjunctivist lines.[16]

4. Radical Skepticism and Favoring/Discriminating Epistemic Support

So epistemological disjunctivism represents an undercutting anti-skeptical strategy that involves rejecting the theoretical basis for a key element in underdetermination$_{RK}$-based radical skepticism. In particular, epistemological disjunctivists hold that in paradigmatic cases of perceptual knowledge one's rational basis for an everyday belief, such as that one is seated at one's desk, can be the reflectively accessible factive reason that one sees that one is seated at one's desk. Since this is a factive reason, the rational support one has for one's everyday belief *does* favor the proposition believed over radical skeptical alternatives, contra premise (SU1) in the underdetermination$_{RK}$-based skeptical argument.

There are a few issues one might raise with this way of dealing with underdetermination$_{RK}$-based radical skepticism. For example, one might wonder why *factive* rational support is needed—that is, rational support that (in the cases that interest us anyway) actually *entails* the denials of skeptical hypotheses. After all, all that is required from a purely logical point of view to counter (SU1) is the claim that we have *better* rational support for our everyday beliefs over skeptical alternatives; such support needn't be factive.

Indeed, we might recall in this regard our discussion of favoring versus discriminating epistemic support from earlier. There we noted that as regards a local error possibility, such as the scenario that what one is looking at is not a zebra but a cleverly disguised mule, one is ordinarily in the position of having favoring epistemic support available to one that favors one's belief over the target error possibility. So although it might be true that one can't tell the difference between the scenario in which one is faced with a zebra as opposed to the scenario where one is faced with a cleverly disguised mule (because one cannot differentiate between zebras and cleverly disguised mules), this is nonetheless consistent with one being able to know that one is looking at a zebra rather than a cleverly disguised mule. As we put the point above, we need to distinguish between discriminating and favoring epistemic support, and recognize that sometimes we can know that one scenario obtains rather than another in virtue of the latter epistemic support rather than the former.

This distinction between discriminating and favoring epistemic support was held to be an entirely general one for epistemology, and hence not something endorsed only by epistemological disjunctivists (although it is a particularly useful distinction as far as epistemological disjunctivism is concerned since, as we saw, it enables the view to avoid the distinguishability problem). Indeed, the distinction was introduced not by appealing to factive rational support but merely by appealing to the kind of nonfactive background rational support that one typically has for one's beliefs (i.e., the general rational basis one has for treating the "zebra" scenario as more plausible than the competing "cleverly disguised mule" scenario). But this prompts the question of why we can't deal with underdetermination$_{RK}$-based skepticism in the same way as we dealt with the error possibility in play in the zebra scenario, and thereby argue that one can have better—albeit not factive—reasons to believe everyday propositions over radical skeptical alternatives.

The problem with this strategy lies in the very different scope of the error possibilities in play. The error possibility that one is in fact looking at a cleverly disguised mule rather than a zebra is a *local* skeptical scenario, in that it calls into question only a small subsection of one's beliefs. This is in contrast to a *radical* skeptical scenario, such as the BIV scenario, which calls a wide cross-section of one's beliefs into doubt. The reason why this distinction is relevant for our purposes is that the local skeptical scenario doesn't call into question one's background beliefs, and this is why it is legitimate to appeal to those beliefs when responding to this difficulty. That the creature before one is a cleverly disguised mule rather than a zebra doesn't in any way undermine the epistemic standing of one's beliefs about, say, the viability of such a deception.

Radical skeptical scenarios are very different, however, in that in virtue of the breadth of beliefs that they call into question, they bring into doubt one's background beliefs as well. So, for example, the skeptical scenario that one is not currently seated at one's desk but rather a BIV calls into question not just one's immediate beliefs about one's environment, but also one's background beliefs too. It would clearly be irrelevant, for instance, to respond to the BIV skeptical scenario by appealing to one's background beliefs about the plausibility of such scenarios (e.g., the viability, given one's beliefs about the current state of technological developments, that one could create a functioning BIV). After all, if one were a BIV then these background beliefs would also be the deceptive products of the vat, and so no more to be relied upon than one's immediate perceptual experiences.

The distinction between favoring and discriminating epistemic support by itself thus enables us only to deal with at most local skeptical scenarios.[17] In order to use this distinction to deal with radical skeptical scenarios, it is vital that we embed this distinction within epistemological disjunctivism. What we then get is the idea, distinctive to epistemological disjunctivism, that one can have factive rational support for one's everyday beliefs that favors—indeed *decisively* favors, given that the support is factive—those beliefs over radical skeptical alternatives. This is even while it remains true that one is unable to distinguish the target everyday scenarios from radical skeptical alternatives. Epistemological disjunctivism thus offers us not just favoring epistemic support, but also more specifically *factive* favoring epistemic support.

The reason why this is important is that factive favoring grounds will be incompatible with the skeptical hypotheses in question, and thus this particular evidence is not simply declared moot in the context of a skeptical hypothesis being raised. Raising the consideration that, for example, one has good reason for thinking that current technology could not support BIVs is clearly inappropriate in the context of the BIV skeptical hypothesis precisely because one would also believe that one had reasons of this sort if one were a BIV. That one is in possession of factive reasons—such as that one sees that one is seated at one's desk—that entail that one is not a BIV is different, however. For if one were a BIV then one would obviously not be in possession of factive reasons of this variety. Factive favoring reasons of the kind appealed to by epistemological disjunctivism are thus not contentious in the context of radical skepticism in the same way that nonfactive favoring reasons are.

Now one might baulk at this line of reasoning. For even while one might grant that these factive favoring reasons are not contentious in the same way as the corresponding nonfactive favoring reasons, one might well contend that they are still moot nonetheless. We can illustrate this point by considering how an appeal to factive favoring reasons can be problematic even when it comes to local skeptical possibilities.

Consider again the example described above of someone at the zoo who is confronted with a zebra-like creature housed within the zebra enclosure, and who therefore believes that she is looking at a zebra. Now imagine that someone raises the possibility that this creature our agent is looking at is in fact a cleverly disguised mule. Would it be appropriate for our agent to respond by dismissing this error possibility on the grounds that she can *see that* it is zebra? On the face of it at least, such a response seems highly problematic. After all, if the objector is right and the creature in question *is* a cleverly disguised mule, then of course it will no longer be true that our agent does *see that* it is zebra. Appealing to this factive favoring ground therefore appears moot. And if appealing to factive favoring grounds is problematic when it comes to local skeptical possibilities, then how can it be appropriate when it comes to radical skeptical possibilities?

There is, however, a crucial detail in the example just given that we need to make explicit. This is that it makes a big difference to how one ought to respond to the presentation of an error possibility—and, in particular, to the propriety of citing factive favoring reasons in this regard—whether the error possibility in question is *rationally motivated*. In normal conversational contexts, the only error possibilities that are raised are rationally motivated ones. That is, to go back to the zebra case, in raising the possibility that the creature at issue might be a cleverly disguised mule one is at least implicitly, if not explicitly, representing oneself as having some rational basis for thinking that this is an error possibility that should be taken seriously (e.g., that one has heard from a good source that a deception of this kind has recently happened in this zoo).

Responding to a rationally motivated error possibility by citing factive favoring support for one's belief is clearly moot, since such support does not at all speak to the error possibility in play. Indeed, the reasons that motivate consideration of the error possibility are also by their nature reasons to no longer regard oneself as seeing that there is a zebra before one, as opposed to merely seeming to see a zebra. Hence, so long as one lacks an independent rational basis to dismiss the rationally motivated error possibility in question, then one ought to no longer regard oneself as being in possession of the target factive rational support for one's perceptual belief.

Crucially, however, note that this is all in keeping with epistemological disjunctivism as we have described the view. For epistemological disjunctivists maintain that factive rational support of the relevant kind is reflectively available to agents only in *paradigm* cases of perceptual knowledge. Scenarios in which there are rationally motivated error possibilities in play clearly *aren't* epistemically paradigm, however, and so even where the evidence that motivates these error possibilities is misleading, such that the agent is at least potentially in a position to acquire perceptual knowledge (and so genuinely sees that p), it wouldn't follow by epistemological disjunctivist lights that this knowledge is supported by factive rational support.[18]

The interesting case from the epistemological disjunctivist perspective, therefore, is not one where the error possibility is rationally motivated, but rather one where it is clearly *not* rationally motivated. To begin with, consider the difference this makes to the propriety of responding to the "cleverly disguised mule" error possibility with factive rational support. Imagine that, contrary to the conventions of normal conversational interchange, someone raises the possibility that the creature before one is a cleverly disguised mule while nonetheless making it entirely explicit that she has no rational basis whatsoever for taking this error possibility seriously. It is, if you like, advanced merely as a *bare* error possibility, rather than as a rationally motivated error possibility. Would it now be problematic to appeal to the fact that one sees that the creature is a zebra? I don't see why it would be. Your interlocutor has, after all, offered you no reason for thinking that you are not in the excellent epistemic conditions that you take yourself to be in. With this in mind, why should one epistemically concede anything in response to this challenge?[19]

Of course, in saying that one can see that it's a zebra, one is not thereby suggesting that one can tell zebras and cleverly disguised mules apart. Indeed, in the interests of full disclosure one is likely to make this point explicit in any conversational interchange of this kind, in order to forestall possible confusion.[20] As we have seen, however, one can have knowledge in virtue of possessing favoring epistemic support even while lacking discriminatory epistemic support. Hence one's inability to tell zebras and cleverly disguised mules apart should not itself be any barrier to being able to know that the creature one is faced with is a zebra on the basis of factive favoring rational support, particularly since the only error possibility conversationally in play is completely lacking in rational motivation.

We are now in a position to apply all this back to the epistemological disjunctivist response to the problem of radical skepticism. In particular, we need to remember that radical skeptical hypotheses are *by their nature* bare—that is, rationally unmotivated—error possibilities.

Recall from part 1 that we saw that radical skepticism in its strongest form presents us with a putative paradox—namely, a contradiction which arises out of own epistemological concepts. As such, radical skepticism is not in the business of making empirical claims, but is rather concerned with demonstrating, on a purely a priori basis, how our own deeply held epistemological commitments are in logical tension. This is especially apparent when it comes to the skeptic's appeal to radical skeptical hypotheses. The radical skeptic is not claiming that there are reasons available for thinking that radical skeptical hypotheses obtain, but is rather merely demonstrating that our apparent inability to know that they don't obtain generates skeptical consequences.

Indeed, were the skeptic to argue for their radical skepticism by offering empirical grounds in support of radical skeptical hypotheses, then dealing with the skeptical problem would be so much easier. Radical skepticism, so construed, would no longer be a putative paradox that arises solely out of our own epistemological commitments, but would instead rest, in part, on additional empirical claims. But given that the skeptic's epistemic basis for these empirical claims would be itself undermined by the skeptical hypotheses in question, then this way of arguing for radical skepticism would be self-defeating. Radical skepticism of this stripe could be ignored with impunity.

It is thus not an incidental feature of radical skepticism that the error possibilities that it trades in are essentially rationally unmotivated. But with that point in mind, it is open to the epistemological disjunctivist to appeal to factive favoring grounds in the context of radical skeptical hypotheses in much the same way that one can legitimately appeal to factive favoring grounds in the context of rationally unmotivated local error possibilities. In particular, it is legitimate to respond to a radical skeptical hypothesis such as the BIV hypothesis by appealing to the fact that, say, one sees that one is seated at one's desk, just as one can respond to a local skeptical hypothesis such as the cleverly disguised mule hypothesis by appealing to the fact that one can see that the creature before one is a zebra.[21]

So once we make clear the way in which radical skeptical hypotheses are raised, it becomes apparent that it is legitimate to cite the factive favoring rational support that one has for one's perceptual beliefs in response to these hypotheses. Moreover, notice that this move is only available if one combines the distinction between favoring and discriminating epistemic support with a commitment to epistemological disjunctivism. In particular, this distinction by itself does not offer us a way of responding to underdetermination$_{RK}$-based radical skepticism.

A final point is in order on this score. One might object to the foregoing by arguing that to appeal to factive reasons is dialectically idle given that one's envatted counterpart will also regard herself as being in the good case, and hence will presumably cite her "factive" reason too. But notice that to insist that this makes a difference to whether factive reasons are dialectically appropriate in the good case is effectively to prejudge the case against epistemological disjunctivism. After all, every party to this debate—whether epistemological disjunctivism, classical epistemic internalism, or classical epistemic internalism—will grant that in the skeptical bad case one is, to put it bluntly, epistemically doomed. And of course we've already granted that the skeptical bad case is indistinguishable from the good case (though we have also noted that this is compatible with the epistemological disjunctivist claim that one has a way of knowing, in the good case, that one is in the good case and not the bad case). But unless we are assuming the falsity of epistemological disjunctivism from the outset—or, relatedly, taking the new evil demon intuition (which epistemological disjunctivism rejects) as sacrosanct—then it is hard to see why we should judge the rational standing of a subject's beliefs in the good case as being limited to the rational standing available for her counterpart's beliefs in the skeptical bad case. The point is that while factive rational support is unavailable to the subject in the skeptical bad case—though she will no doubt attempt to cite it nonetheless—that doesn't itself undermine the thought that one can legitimately cite the factive rational support that one genuinely has (according to epistemological disjunctivism anyway) in the good case.[22]

5. Concluding Remarks

In this chapter we have seen that, contrary to the prevailing wisdom on this score, epistemological disjunctivism represents a viable theoretical option when it comes to our understanding of perceptual knowledge. We have also seen that this proposal has direct application to the underdetermination$_{RK}$-based radical skeptical paradox. In particular, epistemological disjunctivism rejects the new evil demon intuition and the insularity of reasons thesis that underlies it, and hence is in a position to deny one of the claims that makes up this paradox.

Moreover, a key element of epistemological disjunctivism is the idea that this is a conception of perceptual knowledge which is rooted in our folk epistemic concepts, and which we are only driven to abandon in light of theoretical claims which the epistemological disjunctivist maintains are dubious on closer inspection. Epistemological disjunctivism can thus lay claim to being an undercutting anti-skeptical proposal.

Finally, we have noted how epistemological disjunctivism is able to trade on the general epistemological distinction that we have drawn between favoring and discriminating epistemic support. In particular, with this distinction in play the epistemological disjunctivist can explain why it can be legitimate for one to cite factive rational support in favor of one's perceptual beliefs even in light of the presentation of a radical skeptical hypothesis.

In order to fully develop this proposal, in the next chapter we will compare it to some other anti-skeptical proposals in the literature, with our focus remaining for the time being on underdetermination$_{RK}$-based radical skepticism. We will then turn to the question of how epistemological disjunctivism fares when it comes the closure$_{RK}$-based formulation of the radical skeptical problem.

CHAPTER 6

Epistemological Disjunctivism and Closure-Based Radical Skepticism

0. Introductory Remarks

In the last chapter we explored the merits of epistemological disjunctivism, both as an account of perceptual knowledge, and also as a putative undercutting anti-skeptical strategy. We saw that this proposal fared well when it came to underdetermination$_{RK}$-based radical skepticism. In this chapter we will further explore the epistemological disjunctivist anti-skeptical strategy by comparing it to some other anti-skeptical proposals in the literature. While our initial focus in this chapter will remain on underdetermination$_{RK}$-based radical skepticism, we will also examine how epistemological disjunctivism performs when it comes the closure$_{RK}$-based formulation of the radical skeptical problem. As we will see, epistemological disjunctivism struggles with this variety of radical skepticism.

1. Anti-skeptical Contrasts (I): Rational Support Contextualism

In chapter 2 we encountered the attributer contextualist response to radical skepticism, and found that proposal inadequate, in particular with regard to underdetermination$_{RK}$-based radical skepticism. Recall that this proposal argued that while assertions of knowledge ascription sentences express truths relative to normal contexts of epistemic appraisal (where the epistemic standards operative for "knows" are undemanding), assertions of those very same sentences in skeptical contexts of epistemic appraisal (i.e., contexts in which radical skepticism is at issue, and hence where the epistemic standards operative for "knows" are very demanding) express falsehoods. There is thus a sense in which radical skepticism is correct, in that the skeptical assertion that we generally lack knowledge will express a truth in the context of epistemic appraisal in which it is uttered. Even so, there is also a sense in which radical skepticism is wrong, for our everyday assertions of knowledge ascription sentences will tend to express truths.

The core difficultly that this proposal faces is that the problem of radical skepticism doesn't seem to in any way trade on a raising of the epistemic standards. That is, if the radical skeptic is right, then we fail to satisfy *any* epistemic standard for knowledge, even relatively low standards. We saw that we can bring this problem into sharp relief by considering how attributer contextualism would respond to underdetermination$_{RK}$-based radical skeptical paradox.

Recall that we can express the underdetermination$_{RK}$-based radical skeptical paradox in terms of the following collectively inconsistent triad:

THE UNDERDETERMINATION$_{RK}$-BASED SKEPTICAL PARADOX

(SU1) One cannot have rational support that favors one's belief in an everyday proposition over an incompatible radical skeptical hypothesis.

(SU2) The underdetermination$_{RK}$ principle.

(SU3) One has widespread rationally grounded everyday knowledge.

The underdetermination$_{RK}$ principle at issue in (SU2) was formulated as follows:

THE UNDERDETERMINATION$_{RK}$ PRINCIPLE

If S knows that p and q describe incompatible scenarios, and yet S lacks a rational basis that favors p over q, then S lacks rationally grounded knowledge that p.

Sticking to everyday contexts of epistemic appraisal in which assertions of knowledge ascription sentences express truths, we can see how attributer contextualists will retain (SU3), at least where that claim is suitably understood. But now we can ask the question: in virtue of what do such assertions express truths? That is, what epistemic desiderata are satisfied by the target beliefs to make these assertions true? In particular, do these beliefs enjoy rational support that favors them over skeptical alternatives, contra (SU1)? If attributer contextualists deny this, then unless they are willing to reject the underdetermination$_{RK}$ principle (and thus (SU2)) they are subject to underdetermination$_{RK}$-based radical skepticism, with all that this entails. But on what basis would attributer contextualists deny this principle? If, on the other hand, they argue that our everyday beliefs *do* enjoy such favoring rational support over skeptical alternatives—and, again, there is nothing in the attributer contextualist thesis itself that motivates this claim—then we will need to see the argument for this contention.

The point is that attributer contextualists need to explain which of (SU1) or (SU2) they reject, and why. Moreover, notice that insofar as attributer contextualists can motivate the rejection of either of these claims, then attributer contextualism will become an idle cog as an anti-skeptical strategy. After all, if we can make sense of why one of these claims is false, then that will suffice all by itself to block the underdetermination$_{RK}$-based radical skeptical paradox. Any additional appeal to attributer contextualism would be superfluous (except to the extent that it serves some diagnostic role in explaining how the skeptical problem comes about).

Note that it is of course the case that in asking this question—in engaging in this kind epistemological enterprise altogether—we are, according to the attributer contextualist, in a skeptical context of epistemic appraisal in which high epistemic standards apply, and hence any assertions of knowledge ascription sentences that we make will tend to express falsehoods. But we shouldn't let this fact distract us, since it is not materially relevant to the issues at hand. We can recognize this point about how attributer contextualism applies to assertions of knowledge ascription sentences in skeptical contexts of epistemic appraisal while nonetheless asking what epistemic desiderata are satisfied by an agent's beliefs in everyday contexts of epistemic appraisal where assertions of knowledge ascription sentences tend to express truths. And the crux of the matter is that insofar as the underdetermination$_{RK}$ principle is in play and these beliefs fail to enjoy rational support that favors the proposition believed over skeptical alternatives—in line with (SU1)—then the epistemic standing of these beliefs has been called into question.[1]

That, in any case, is roughly the line we took on the attributer contextualist anti-skeptical proposal in chapter 2. Now that we have epistemological disjunctivism on the table, however, we can consider a variant on the attributer contextualist anti-skeptical line that might fare better on this score. The key difficulty facing attributer contextualism as an anti-skeptical strategy is that while it generates the result that assertions of knowledge ascription sentences in everyday contexts of epistemic appraisal will tend to express truths, it does not back this up with a plausible epistemological story about how these assertions could express truths. That is, and especially bearing in mind the challenge to the epistemic standing of our beliefs that is posed by underdetermination$_{RK}$-based radical skepticism, in virtue of what do the beliefs in question count as knowledge?

But suppose we reconceived of attributer contextualism as being primarily concerned with the nature of the rational support available for our beliefs? In particular, imagine a form of attributer contextualism that maintained that the strength of rational support available to a subject could vary in response to changes in the context of epistemic appraisal. Relative to everyday contexts of epistemic appraisal, a subject could be truthfully ascribed very strong rational support for her beliefs, but relative to skeptical contexts of epistemic appraisal, in contrast, the very same subject could at best be truthfully ascribed only a very weak level of rational support for her beliefs. In this way one could maintain that the epistemic standards relevant to assessing the truth of assertions of knowledge ascription sentences don't vary from one context of epistemic appraisal to another, but that nonetheless whether or not these assertions express truths *is* a variable matter. Call such a view *rational support contextualism*.

In order for this proposal to fare better than a standard version of attributer contextualism, we need to suppose that in everyday contexts of epistemic appraisal the rational support that can be truthfully ascribed to an agent's belief can be factive in broadly the manner set out by epistemological disjunctivism. In this way rational support contextualism can lay claim to some of the anti-skeptical benefits that we saw accrued to epistemological disjunctivism in the last chapter, at least as regards underdetermination$_{RK}$-based radical skepticism. What happens on this view when radical skepticism is introduced to the context of epistemic appraisal is that the rational support that can be truthfully ascribed to a subject's beliefs shrinks to being merely nonfactive support (e.g., that it *seems to one as if p*, rather than that one sees that *p*). This is why although the epistemic standards for assessing knowledge ascriptions do not change, it is nonetheless the case that assertions of knowledge ascriptions sentences will tend to express truths in everyday contexts of epistemic appraisal and express falsehoods in skeptical contexts of epistemic appraisal.

This is broadly the view defended by Ram Neta (2002; 2003), although he describes his view in terms of evidence rather than reasons, a difference that we will set to one side here. Here is Neta's description of this proposal:

> Suppose that we are talking on the phone and I claim to know that my basement floor is all wet. You ask me what evidence I have that it's wet, and I reply that I can see that it's wet. Here, my evidence reaches all the way out to the fact: I can't see that my floor is all wet unless it is, in fact, all wet. There is, in this case, no epistemic gap between my evidence and my belief.

> Nonetheless, when we face certain skeptical challenges, we move into a context of epistemic appraisal in which we can truthfully say that our evidence fails to support our beliefs about the external world. Once we are in such a context, we can't find evidence for those beliefs, for none of our mental states count as evidence for such beliefs in that context. Thus, by issuing or confronting skeptical challenges, we create an epistemic gap between our beliefs about that world and our evidence for them. (Neta 2003, 27)

Here we get the essentials of the view. Exchanging talk of evidence with talk of reasons, Neta is claiming that relative to everyday contexts of epistemic appraisal the rational support one has for one's beliefs can be factive, in essentially the manner that epistemological disjunctivism proposes, but that relative to skeptical contexts of epistemic appraisal this rational support diminishes to the point of being nonfactive. This is why, relative to skeptical contexts of epistemic appraisal, the radical skeptic's claim that we lack knowledge expresses a truth (because such nonfactive rational support fails to favor our everyday beliefs over radical skeptical alternatives).

By allowing subjects to be truthfully ascribed factive rational support in everyday contexts of epistemic appraisal, rational support contextualism can plausibly evade the concern we raised above regarding the standard attributer contextualist anti-skeptical strategy. In particular, on this view we can explain why the underdetermination$_{RK}$-based skeptical challenge doesn't go through, since in everyday contexts of epistemic appraisal subjects *can* be truthfully ascribed rational support that is strong enough to conflict with (SU1). Thus the underdetermination$_{RK}$ principle can hold, and yet radical skepticism can nonetheless be resisted. Moreover, this view brings with it the usual advantage of attributer contextualist accounts, in that it can explain why radical skepticism can seem so compelling. After all, on this proposal radical skepticism is in a sense entirely correct, in that relative to contexts of epistemic appraisal in which radical skeptical error possibilities are at issue assertions of knowledge ascription sentences will tend to express falsehoods.

When it comes to radical skepticism, rational support contextualism thus has a key advantage over standard versions of attributer contextualism, in that it incorporates a plausible response to the specifically underdetermination$_{RK}$-based version of the radical skeptical paradox. Nonetheless, there are a number of problems with rational support contextualism, many of them shared with standard versions of attributer contextualism.[2]

First, like attributer contextualism, there is the worry that it is too simple a solution to the problem in hand. Recall that the attributer contextualist treatment of radical skepticism invited the response that if this problem simply trades on a raising of the epistemic standards applicable to the evaluations of knowledge ascription sentences, then surely this is something that we would have spotted long before now. Could we really have been so ignorant about how such a central term as "knows" functions? The same kind of worry surfaces with regard to rational support contextualism. If the extent of the rational support one's beliefs enjoy is straightforwardly responsive to contextual factors in this way, such that the problem of radical skepticism turns on this kind of context sensitivity, then isn't this something that we would have realized long ago?

A second problem that rational support contextualism shares with attributer contextualism concerns how it endorses an epistemic hierarchy of contexts. Recall that attributer contextualism concedes that radical skepticism, qua position, is correct relative to the high epistemic standards that are operative in skeptical contexts of epistemic appraisal. The same is also true of rational support contextualism, though here this claim is mediated by an appeal to the context sensitivity of our attributions of rational support. This concession severely undermines the anti-skeptical credentials of the view.

Recall our discussion of Wittgenstein's account of the structure of reasons from chapter 3, where we contrasted this proposal with the ordinary language response to radical skepticism, as found in the work of thinkers such as J. L. Austin (1961). We noted there Barry Stroud's (1984) point that radical skepticism, qua paradox, is entirely consistent with the claim that there are significant differences between our everyday practices of epistemic appraisal and the kinds of epistemic appraisal undertaken by the radical skeptic. After all, it is open to the radical skeptic to contend that the latter is a purified version of the former, such that if only we applied our epistemic principles in a thoroughgoing fashion—that is, if only we weren't impeded by practical limitations of time, creativity, and so on—then we would be led to adopt radical skeptic standards of epistemic evaluation. We noted that this was a point that Wittgenstein saw but the ordinary language response to radical skepticism misses. For while both emphasize the differences between our quotidian and radical skeptical practices of epistemic appraisal, only the Wittgensteinian account of the structure of reasons demonstrates that the latter simply cannot be a purified version of the former (indeed, that the latter is deeply incoherent, in that it aspires to an impossible ideal).

This point clearly has application to rational support contextualism (and, for that matter, attributer contextualism). For once we concede that radical skeptical epistemic assessments are relative to higher epistemic standards than normal epistemic assessments, then it is hard to resist the conclusion that radical skepticism is indeed offering us a genuine paradox. In particular, it seems to follow that relative to a purified version of our everyday standards of epistemic appraisal, a version that we have no way of insulating ourselves from, radical skepticism, qua position, is correct.

The contrast with the epistemological disjunctivist response to radical skepticism is telling in this regard. For what the epistemological disjunctivist is contending is that our everyday practices of paradigmatically treating the rational support agents have for their beliefs as factive is in fact entirely in order as it is. The story the radical skeptic tells us about why we should reject this quotidian picture turns out to trade on theoretical claims that the epistemological disjunctivist argues are highly dubious. There is thus no need to concede anything to the radical skeptic on this score, much less grant, as rational support/attributer contextualism does, that the radical skeptic effectively occupies the epistemic high ground.[3]

This point is clearest when it comes to the underdetermination$_{RK}$-based radical skeptical paradox. According to epistemological disjunctivism, it simply isn't true that one of our fundamental epistemological commitments is that the rational support we have for our everyday beliefs fails to favor those beliefs over radical skeptical alternatives. One of the key claims that make up the relevant radical skeptical inconsistent triad—namely, (SU1)—can thus be rejected. And notice that the rejection of this claim is not relativized to a particular context of epistemic appraisal. Rather, the contention is the underdetermination$_{RK}$-based radical skeptical paradox is illusory, in that it essentially turns on a dubious theoretical thesis that has been falsely presented as one of our fundamental epistemological commitments.

Notice that in making this point we needn't deny that when one is in the grip of the problem of radical skepticism it can seem to one as if the rational support that is available to one has shrunk to the nonfactive (e.g., to the merely phenomenal). And of course, insofar as one believes that the rational support that is available to one is of this kind, then obviously one can no longer know everyday propositions in virtue of possessing the target factive rational support. The point, however, is that in such a case one is not now in the kind of paradigm epistemic conditions in which, according to epistemological disjunctivism, factive rational support is available.[4] Moreover, notice that this is a completely *self-imposed* epistemic exile, in that there is in fact a strong philosophical basis for resisting this concession to the radical skeptic. That's just the point of the anti-skeptical diagnosis that epistemological disjunctivism puts forward, that in conceding this much to the radical skeptic one is in effect allowing oneself to be hoodwinked. Thus although it is undeniably possible to get oneself into such an epistemically concessive state of mind, there is a sound philosophical basis to resist the charms of the radical skeptic in this regard, and hence we should do so.[5]

In responding to rational support contextualism and attributer contextualism in this way we are implicitly supposing that the view should be thought of as an *undercutting* anti-skeptical strategy, such that its appeal to everyday contexts of epistemic appraisal is meant to undermine the very idea that radical skepticism presents us with a genuine paradox (in that what the radical skeptic presents as one of our fundamental epistemic commitments is instead merely the product of faulty philosophical theory). And yet we could just as easily think of contextualist responses to radical skepticism of this kind as being *overriding* anti-skeptical strategies that offer us independent reasons to reject one of the core intuitive claims as issue in the radical skeptical paradox. (Indeed, we explored the option of conceiving of attributer contextualism along these lines in chapter 2.) Even then, I don't think we will find the revisionist story put forward by these contextualist proposals as being compelling enough to effectively function as part of an anti-skeptical strategy. Moreover, as we noted in chapter 1, overriding anti-skeptical strategies are inevitably much less palatable than their undercutting counterparts. Hence if there is a plausible undercutting anti-skeptical strategy available—such as the kind of proposal offered by epistemological disjunctivism as regards the underdetermination$_{RK}$-based radical skeptical paradox—then there's very little incentive to explore overriding anti-skeptical strategies.

A further problem facing rational support contextualism as an anti-skeptical proposal concerns the dialectical effectiveness of the appeal to contexts of epistemic appraisal. For notice that the anti-skeptical work is in fact done by the claim that relative to everyday contexts of epistemic appraisal agents can be properly said to be in possession of factive rational support for their beliefs. But if we can make sense of this idea at all, then why do we need to appeal to contexts of epistemic appraisal, at least as far as underdetermination$_{RK}$-based radical skepticism goes? After all, this idea all by itself will block this form of radical skepticism, as we noted above in our discussion of epistemological disjunctivism. So what is added by the appeal to contexts of epistemic appraisal?

The rational support contextualist will no doubt contend that the contextualist element of the view is required in order for the proposal to have diagnostic appeal. The thought would be that without this aspect of the thesis there is not a plausible story in play regarding why the radical skeptic's assertions about our epistemic position can initially strike us as true. But we have already noted some deficiencies in the diagnostic element of the view, so this consideration is hardly decisive. Moreover, the relevant contrast is not merely with a view that allows factive rational support, à la epistemological disjunctivism, but that does not in addition offer any further anti-skeptical diagnostic story. Rather, the contrast is with such an alternative view *when allied to* its own anti-skeptical diagnostic story, which is exactly how we have developed the epistemological disjunctivist anti-skeptical proposal (at least as regards the underdetermination$_{RK}$-based radical skeptical paradox).

I contend that the epistemological disjunctivist diagnosis of where (underdetermination$_{RK}$-based) radical skepticism goes awry is much to be preferred, for at least two reasons. First, unlike rational support contextualism it offers us a straightforward and compelling undercutting response to the problem of (underdetermination$_{RK}$-based) radical skepticism. And, second, while on both views the anti-skeptical weight in this regard is carried by a claim about how our everyday beliefs can enjoy factive rational support, epistemological disjunctivism is not also burdened with a problematic and concessive appeal to contexts of epistemic appraisal (and in particular the idea of a skeptical context of epistemic appraisal).

When it comes to underdetermination$_{RK}$-based radical skepticism, epistemological disjunctivism is thus much more plausible, all things considered, than rational support contextualism. That said, as we will see below, once we consider not just underdetermination$_{RK}$-based radical skepticism but also closure$_{RK}$-based radical skepticism, then the dialectical situation shifts somewhat toward views like rational support contextualism (and attributer contextualism too, for that matter). This is because epistemological disjunctivism struggles to handle this form of radical skepticism, but rational support contextualism fares better in this respect. As we will further see in chapter 7, however, the solution to this is not to abandon epistemological disjunctivism in favor of rational support contextualism, but rather to recognize the role that epistemological disjunctivism needs to play within a wider anti-skeptical strategy.[6]

2. Anti-skeptical Contrasts (II): Contrastivism

A second kind of proposal that shares some features with rational support contextualism, and that can also be usefully compared with epistemological disjunctivism, is the *contrastivist* response to radical skepticism, as most prominently defended by Jonathan Schaffer (2004; 2005; 2007; 2008).[7] Like rational support contextualism, contrastivism is also often described as a form of attributer contextualism, although this description is in this case controversial.[8]

According to contrastivism, knowledge is to be understood not in the usual way as a binary relation between a subject and a proposition, but rather as a ternary relation between a subject, a proposition, and a contrast proposition. On this view, there is no such thing as knowledge that p *simpliciter*. Instead, knowledge is always to be understood as knowledge that p *rather than* q. Here is Schaffer:

> It is widely assumed that knowledge is a binary relation of the form Ksp. The project of understanding knowledge then becomes the project of completing the schema "s knows that p iff. . . ." The traditional epistemologist supposes that there is *one* Ksp relation. [. . . The contrastivist says that there is *none*—the assumption that knowledge is a binary relation is an error due to the seductive pull of the surface grammar of a special form of utterance.
>
> . . . Contrastivism is the view that knowledge is a ternary relation of the form Kspq, where q is a contrast proposition. (Schaffer 2004, 76–77)

We can get a better handle on what Schaffer has in mind in this regard by seeing the view in action with regard to the problem of radical skepticism. Here is what Schaffer writes in this regard, where for the "dogmatist" we can plug in most standard forms of (neo-Moorean) anti-skepticism:

> Does G. E. Moore know that he has hands? *Yes*, says the dogmatist: Moore's hands are right before his eyes. *No*, says the skeptic: for all Moore knows he could be a brain-in-a-vat. *Yes* and *no*, says the contrastivist: *yes*, Moore knows that he has hands rather than stumps; but *no*, Moore does not know that he has hands rather than vat-images of hands.
>
> The dogmatist and the skeptic suppose that knowledge is a *binary, categorical* relation: s knows that p. The contrastivist says that knowledge is a *ternary, contrastive* relation: s knows that p rather than q. (Schaffer 2005, 235)

In particular, contrastivism claims that knowing that p rather than q is a matter of being able to *discriminate* between p and q.[9] In this way, the contrastivist can account for the pull of radical skepticism without thereby conceding that we lack everyday knowledge. That is, our everyday knowledge that we have hands is perfectly fine, in that this is, presumably, knowledge that we have hands in contrast to mundane alternatives that are easy to discriminate between. In contrast, the radical skeptic is right that we don't have knowledge that we have hands as opposed to radical skeptical alternatives, such as the BIV hypothesis, since in this case we lack the relevant discriminative capacities.

Note that the claim that we can conceive of our knowledge along contrastive lines in this way is not itself controversial. In particular, we need not dispute that it is true of some agents that they (contrastively) know that they have hands rather than some contrasts (e.g., stumps) but do not (contrastively) know that they have hands rather than some other contrasts (e.g., vat-hands). What makes contrastivism a controversial thesis that is in tension with standard ways of thinking about knowledge is the further claim that knowledge is *only* to be understood contrastively. Why should we opt for such a claim?[10]

To begin with, let's set the problem to radical skepticism to one side and consider the merits of the view more generally. One advantage to contrastivism in this regard is that it seems to offer a very natural way of explaining perceptual knowledge. Think again of the "zebra" case that we encountered in chapter 5 (§2), where we have an agent faced with what looks like a zebra in a clearly marked zebra enclosure. Does our agent know that this creature is a zebra? Normally we would want to answer positively to this question, but matters become more complicated once we introduce the error possibility that the creature is a cleverly disguised mule. After all, by hypothesis, this agent cannot perceptually discriminate between zebras and cleverly disguised mules. Everyone can thus agree on at least this much: this agent can perceptually discriminate this zebra from lots of other nonzebra items (such as elephants), but she cannot perceptually discriminate zebras from cleverly disguised mules. There is thus an uncontentious sense in which our agent perceptually knows that what she is looking at is a zebra *rather than*, say, an elephant, but that she doesn't perceptually know that what she is looking at is a zebra rather than a cleverly disguised mule.

So far so good for the contrastivist, though as yet there isn't anything particularly controversial on the table. To make this claim controversial, we would need to add that there is nothing that our agent knows *simpliciter* in this case. What would prompt us to adopt the stronger claim?

Well, one clear motivation would be if we thought that there was a fundamental tension between our intuition that this agent would ordinarily know that what she is looking at is a zebra in these conditions, and the claim that she is unable to know that what she's looking at is a zebra once the cleverly disguised mule error possibility is introduced. As we noted in chapter 5, once the closure principle (in some form) is in play, then it is very easy to set up a tension between these two claims, in that once we grant that our agent knows that what she is looking at is a zebra, then it's just a short step to the further claim that she also knows that what she is looking at is not a cleverly disguised mule. But given that our agent cannot perceptually discriminate between zebras and cleverly disguised mules, this latter claim is questionable, and hence it calls into question whether we should attribute to her knowledge that what she is looking at is a zebra.

Adding the further contrastivist claim that there is no such thing as knowledge *simpliciter*—for example, knowledge *simpliciter* that the creature before one is a zebra—offers us a way of getting off this particular philosophical seesaw, albeit a highly revisionist solution. As we noted in chapter 5 (§§2 & 4) in our discussion of favoring versus discriminating epistemic support, however, there is a more straightforward way of dealing with the problem posed by the zebra case.

The crux of the matter is that we can treat the agent's knowledge in this case as requiring different kinds of epistemic support depending on the error possibilities at issue. In normal conditions, our agent can know *simpliciter* that what she sees is a zebra in virtue of being able to perceptually discriminate between zebras and other items that could plausibly be in the neighborhood (e.g., elephants, etc.). Unless cleverly disguised mules are the kinds of thing that could plausibly be in the neighborhood, then our agent doesn't need to be able to perceptually discriminate between zebras and cleverly disguised mules in order to know that what she see is a zebra.

Once the cleverly disguised mule error possibility is introduced, however, and our agent recognizes its incompatibility with what she currently believes, then it is incumbent upon her to rationally exclude this scenario. But that doesn't require the ability to perceptually discriminate zebras from cleverly disguised mules. Instead, it requires only that our agent can draw on relevant background evidence to the extent that she has a better rational basis (i.e., favoring grounds) for believing that what she sees is a zebra rather than a cleverly disguised mule. (Alternatively, as we also saw in chapter 5, for the epistemological disjunctivist it might simply involve the citing of a relevant factive reason, at least insofar as the error possibility has not been rationally motivated.) In this way, our agent will—ordinarily anyway—be able to know both that what she is looking at is a zebra and that it is not a cleverly disguised mule. (And insofar as she is unable to know the latter proposition, then she will lose her knowledge of the former proposition.) Moreover, notice that we can capture this claim without having to adopt any form of epistemological revisionism, since there is no appeal here to contexts of epistemic appraisal (whether along attributer contextualist or rational support contextualist lines) or a retreat to a contrastivist construal of the knowledge relation. Instead all we are appealing to is the familiar idea that being aware of incompatible error possibilities can make rational demands on one—albeit, as we've just seen, rational demands that are easy to meet. Finally, recall that this point does not trade on epistemological disjunctivism or any other specific epistemological proposal, but is rather an entirely general thesis about the nature of the epistemic support available to agents in cases like this.

Once we recognize that there is in fact nothing particularly problematic or mysterious about the agent's epistemic situation in the zebra case, what motivation is left for the revisionism advanced by contrastivism? Of course, we have bracketed the problem of radical skepticism here, and so that could be brought back into the frame as a motivating consideration. But notice that if the case for contrastivism as an epistemologically revisionist proposal rests squarely on the kind of anti-skepticism it offers, then that severely diminishes its dialectical effectiveness as an overriding anti-skeptical strategy. After all, the litmus test for anti-skeptical strategies of this kind is that they can offer compelling independent motivations for the epistemological revisionism that is being proposed in response to the problem of radical skepticism. If the motivation for this revisionism boils down to the need to deal with the problem of radical skepticism, then this isn't going to be very persuasive.

Even setting this dialectical issue to one side, there is also the further point that we now have a proposal on the table—epistemological disjunctivism—according to which we can make sense of how agents can know everyday propositions over radical skeptical alternatives. This proposal is cast in terms of the possession of (factive) favoring rational support rather than discriminative capacities, but nonetheless this proposal offers us a way of accounting for our knowledge in this regard without resort to the kind of epistemological revisionism advanced by contrastivism. Moreover, recall that this is meant to be an undercutting response to the problem of radical skepticism (in its underdetermination$_{RK}$-based form at any rate), in that on this view the radical skeptical paradox is not bona fide, but instead trades on dubious theoretical claims that are masquerading as common sense. Epistemological disjunctivism thus has significant dialectical advantages over contrastivism as an anti-skeptical proposal.

Of course, we haven't yet spelled out how epistemological disjunctivism deals with the closure$_{RK}$-based radical skeptical problem, so there is potential for the scales to turn back more in contrastivism's favor in this regard. We will return to compare and contrast epistemological disjunctivism and contrastivism with regard to closure$_{RK}$-based radical skepticism below.[11]

3. Anti-skeptical Contrasts (III): Dogmatism

We now come to a third kind of anti-skeptical proposal that has been influential in the literature. This is known as *dogmatism*, and its foremost exponent is Jim Pryor (2000).[12] Here is Pryor's statement of this view:

> The dogmatist about perceptual justification says that when it perceptually seems to you as if p is the case, you have a kind of justification for believing p that does not presuppose or rest on your justification for anything else, which could be cited in an argument . . . for p. To have this justification for believing p, you need only have an experience that represents p as being the case. No further awareness or reflection or background beliefs are required. (Pryor 2000, 519)

Thus far, the view may seem relatively unobjectionable, in that it does seem fairly plausible to suppose that its seeming to one as if p can give one reason to perceptually believe that p, and thus support a justified perceptual belief that p.

Where the view becomes controversial is with regard to how this basic thought is developed, particularly with regard to radical skepticism. The dogmatist maintains that the immediate justification for perceptually believing that p that arises out of it seeming to one as if p can suffice for perceptual knowledge. In particular, it provides defeasible support for perceptual knowledge that p, such that so long as there are not suitable defeaters present, then one perceptually knows that p. Furthermore, it is maintained that from this perceptual knowledge a subject can undertake closure-style inferences and thereby come to know the denials of radical skeptical hypotheses, such as the BIV hypothesis. Indeed, although dogmatists don't express the point in these terms, they would presumably allow that the corresponding inferences involving the closure$_{RK}$ principle are fine too. Hence, subjects can in this way come to have rationally grounded knowledge of the denials of radical skeptical hypotheses by undertaking competent deductions from their knowledge of everyday propositions, where this latter knowledge is rationally grounded in the relevant perceptual seemings claim.

We thus get a particularly robust form of neo-Mooreanism. Unlike the externalist neo-Mooreanism that we have previously encountered (e.g., in chapter 1), this proposal maintains not just that we can have knowledge of the denials of radical skeptical hypotheses, but also that we can have *rationally grounded* knowledge of the denials of radical skeptical hypotheses. Moreover, in contrast to the entitlement reading of hinge propositions that we examined in chapter 3, the claim is precisely that the rational support available for our beliefs in the denials of radical skeptical hypotheses can be dependent upon the defeasible rational support that we have for our everyday beliefs along with the relevant competent deduction. Unlike the entitlement reading, then, there is thus no need to deny the closure$_{RK}$ principle.

Consider first the suggestion that the immediate (defeasible) justification one gains for one's perceptual belief that p from its seeming to one as if p can generate rationally grounded knowledge that one is not the victim of a radical skeptical hypothesis. At first blush, this can appear like little more than epistemic magic. We can bring this worry into sharper relief by asking how, specifically, the dogmatist would respond to the underdetermination$_{RK}$-based radical skeptical paradox. In particular, here is the crucial question: would the dogmatist concede that we lack rational support for our everyday perceptual beliefs that favors those beliefs over radical skeptical alternatives, in line with (SU1)?

It seems that the dogmatist must answer this question in the negative. Consider the pairing of an everyday perceptual belief and a radical skeptical hypothesis that we used in chapter 1: that one is presently seated at one's desk as opposed to being the victim of the BIV radical skeptical hypothesis. According to the dogmatist, both one's belief that one is presently seated at one's desk and one's belief that one is *not* the victim of the BIV radical skeptical hypothesis could amount to rationally grounded knowledge. But if that's right, then it surely follows that one has a better rational basis for believing that one is presently seated at one's desk than for believing that one *is* a BIV. The dogmatist is thus committed to rejecting (SU1).

Here is the crux. Whereas the epistemological disjunctivist has a sophisticated story to tell both how (SU1) could be false, and also why we might have thought that it was true, the dogmatist position, true to its name, has nothing so substantial to offer. Let us state the matter baldly: why should its merely seeming to one as if p give one better rational support for believing that p than for believing that one is the victim of a known to be incompatible radical skeptical hypothesis? Indeed, without the epistemological disjunctivist's account of why the new evil demon intuition, and the insularity of reasons thesis that underlies it, is false, it is hard to see how the dogmatist can make any plausible case for why agents can possess this favoring rational support.

Note that the complaint I am raising here is *not* that the introduction of radical skeptical hypotheses defeats the defeasible rational support for believing that p, which the dogmatist claims accrues in virtue of it seeming to one as if p. In fact, I think we should grant to the dogmatist—in line with what we argued in chapter 5 (§4) regarding rationally unmotivated error possibilities—that the mere raising of an error possibility does not suffice to introduce a defeater. So the point is not that the dogmatist's would-be rational support for rationally grounded knowledge that p is defeated by the introduction of the radical skeptical hypothesis.[13] The claim is rather that the dogmatist is committed to treating the subject's rational basis for believing that p as favoring this belief over radical skeptical alternatives, and yet the subject's rational basis for believing that p according to the dogmatist simply doesn't seem remotely robust enough to fulfill this requirement.

Epistemological disjunctivism, in contrast, doesn't face this problem. This is because this view has a story to tell about how the rational support for our everyday beliefs can be factive in nature, such that it does favor those everyday beliefs over radical skeptical alternatives. This, coupled with the diagnostic story the epistemological disjunctivist offers regarding why we should reject (SU1), puts epistemological disjunctivism into a much stronger dialectical position with regard to radical skepticism than dogmatism.

We will return below to the comparison of epistemological disjunctivism and dogmatism qua anti-skeptical strategies, this time with regard to the closure$_{RK}$-based radical skeptical paradox. As we will see, although epistemological disjunctivism has its problems in this regard, dogmatism is at least no better off on this front, and arguably offers an anti-skeptical strategy that is even less palatable.[14]

4. A Weakness in Epistemological Disjunctivism

I do not doubt that many will find the epistemological disjunctivist anti-skeptical proposal that we set out in chapter 5 unsatisfying. In particular, the idea that it is legitimate to regard factive favoring reasons as adequate responses to the presentation of radical skeptical hypotheses will surely strike many as dubious. As we will see, I have some sympathy for this way of reacting to the epistemological disjunctivist treatment of radical skepticism, since I agree that the account is problematic in a fundamental respect. But we need to carefully identify what is the source of the disquiet in this case, since some of the reasons why we might find this response to radical skepticism dubious are themselves suspect on closer inspection.

For example, we might find the appeal to factive favoring reasons in the context of radical skepticism problematic because we imagine that citing factive favoring grounds in this way is tantamount to (falsely) representing oneself as being able to discriminate between the scenario in which one finds oneself and the target skeptical scenario. We have already noted, however—see chapter 5, §4—that even when presented with rationally unmotivated error possibilities, one should still be wary about citing factive favoring rational support in an unqualified fashion, since it is apt to generate misleading conversational implicatures. In this case, for example, it would usually be more appropriate to qualify one's assertion to make clear that in putting forward this factive favoring rational support one is not thereby representing oneself as being able to discriminate between current conditions and radical skeptical alternatives.

But it is not clear to me that we should in any case be thinking of the debate with the radical skeptic in terms of assertion and counterassertion in the first place. It is natural to characterize what is taking place in the "zebra" case in terms of some sort of conversational exchange between our agent and the (local) skeptic, but that is because we are implicitly supposing that the error possibility raised is rationally motivated. Once we imagine that it is completely lacking in rational motivation, then the conversational exchange becomes at best somewhat artificial.

This is even more so when it comes to the problem of radical skepticism. For as we have emphasized at a number of junctures, radical skepticism is not best thought of as a position—indeed, so construed it isn't a particularly challenging philosophical problem at all—but rather as a putative paradox, where this is a problem that arises out of our own fundamental epistemic commitments. Accordingly, there is something very dubious about characterizing the debate with the skeptic in terms of our explicitly offering counterassertions in response to the skeptic's assertions. The dispute with the "skeptic" is in fact a quarrel that is completely internal to our own conceptual realm, and hence it is an argument with ourselves. While we can represent this debate in terms of a clash with an imagined adversary, we should bear in mind that strictly speaking there isn't anyone that we are arguing with. The issue of the conversational propriety, or otherwise, of our anti-skeptical assertions is thus to a large extent completely by the by.

But if the awkwardness of the epistemological disjunctivist response to radical skepticism does not lie in this area, then where does it lie? I think we can see the source of the problem once we consider how epistemological disjunctivism squares up to the closure$_{RK}$-based formulation of radical skepticism. Recall that we formulated this version of the skeptical paradox in chapter 1 in terms of the following collectively inconsistent triad of claims:

THE CLOSURE$_{RK}$-BASED RADICAL SKEPTICAL PARADOX

(SC1) One is unable to have rationally grounded knowledge of the denials of radical skeptical hypotheses.

(SC2) The closure$_{RK}$ principle.

(SC3) One has widespread rationally grounded everyday knowledge.[15]

The closureRK principle at issue in (SC2) was in turn formulated as follows:

THE CLOSURE$_{RK}$ PRINCIPLE

If S has rationally grounded knowledge that p, and S competently deduces from p that q, thereby forming a belief that q on this basis while retaining her rationally grounded knowledge that p, then S has rationally grounded knowledge that q.

We have seen how epistemological disjunctivism responds to underdetermination$_{RK}$-based radical skepticism, but how does it deal with the closure$_{RK}$-based formulation of the problem?

Epistemological disjunctivism will obviously endorse (SC3), so the question is which of (SC1) and (SC2) do they reject? Let's start with

(SC1). Could epistemological disjunctivism reject this claim? Since epistemological disjunctivism holds that one can have perceptual knowledge that enjoys factive rational support—that is, rational support that entails the falsity of a radical skeptical hypothesis, such as the BIV hypothesis—it follows (contra the first premise of the underdetermination$_{RK}$-based skeptical paradox, (SU1)) that one can have better rational support for, say, one's belief that one is currently seated at one's desk than for the hypothesis that one is a BIV. As we noted in chapter 2, however, while this claim at least *suggests* the rejection of (SC1), in that it implies that an agent can know the denials of radical skeptical hypotheses, it does not entail it. This is because one can in principle have better (and even factive) reasons for believing a proposition over an alternative scenario, and know what one believes, without thereby knowing that the alternative scenario does not obtain. The epistemological disjunctivists' rejection of (SU1) therefore does not commit them, by itself anyway, to rejecting (SC1). There is thus at least the logical space available to them on this score to maintain that agents are unable to know the denials of skeptical hypotheses as (SC1) alleges, even though they do possess rational support for their everyday beliefs that favors those beliefs over skeptical alternatives.

Although accepting (SC1) is at least a possibility for epistemological disjunctivism, it is clearly not a comfortable option to pursue. For this would on the face of it mean rejecting (SC2), and thus the closure$_{RK}$ principle. We have seen, however, that the case for this principle appears watertight. How could a competent deduction from one's rationally grounded knowledge, which is by its nature an exemplary rational process, *undermine* the rational standing of one's beliefs thereby deduced, such that the inferred beliefs do not amount to rationally grounded knowledge? The case for (SC2) thus looks irresistible. This brings us back to what the epistemological disjunctivist wants to say about (SC1). For while it might not follow from the epistemological disjunctivists' rejection of (SU1) that (SC1) must be denied, unless they wish to reject (SC2), and thus the closure$_{RK}$ principle, then it seems that they are committed to opposing (SC1) after all.

So, given the choice between rejecting the closure$_{RK}$ principle, (SC2), and denying (SC1), the course of least resistance as far as the epistemological disjunctivist is concerned is to opt for the latter. Indeed, faced with these two options, the epistemological disjunctivist would be wise to *embrace* this option and argue that the ability to reject (SC1) is a considerable advantage of the view, in virtue of its anti-skeptical ramifications.[16] This is, however, much easier said than done.

The reason for this is that the epistemological disjunctivist's rejection of (SC1) seems far too strong. As we noted in chapter 1, we have a deep-seated intuition that (SC1) is true. In particular, we intuitively have no rational basis at all for regarding radical skeptical hypotheses as false. But consider now the rational basis on which the epistemological disjunctivist rejects (SC1). This includes a factive rational basis for one's everyday beliefs that entails the falsity of radical skeptical hypotheses, combined with the exemplary rational process of competent deduction at issue in the closure$_{RK}$ principle. The upshot is surely rationally grounded knowledge that one is not the victim of a skeptical hypothesis—that one is not a BIV, say—which is supported by factive rational grounds. Far from lacking any rational basis for believing that we are not victims of radical skeptical hypotheses, according to epistemological disjunctivism, so conceived, we in fact have a *decisive* rational basis for these anti-skeptical beliefs. The worry, of course, is that this anti-skeptical conclusion seems far too robust.

There is nothing to stop the epistemological disjunctivist simply embracing this point as a mere *consequence* of their view, rather than a count against it. But it does at least suggest that we should step back and see if there are not other options available to us here. In particular, are there not ways of retaining the core idea behind epistemological disjunctivism—namely, that there can be perceptual knowledge supported by factive rational support, rational support that favors the proposition believed over even skeptical alternatives—which does not require the epistemological disjunctivist to in addition claim that we can know the denials of radical skeptical hypotheses? As we will see in the next chapter, the logical space we are seeking here is indeed available. In order to occupy it, however, we will need to combine epistemological disjunctivism with the Wittgensteinian response to radical skepticism that we explored in part 2.

5. Epistemological Disjunctivism and Its Competitors

At this juncture it will be worthwhile to compare epistemological disjunctivism as an anti-skeptical proposal with the three anti-skeptical strategies we looked at earlier: rational support contextualism, contrastivism, and dogmatism. We noted there that epistemological disjunctivism generally fares much better than competing anti-skeptical approaches when it comes to the underdetermination$_{RK}$-based radical skeptical paradox. Matters are not so straightforward, however, once we extend our anti-skeptical remit to cover the closure$_{RK}$-based radical skeptical paradox too. The reason for this is that most other kinds of anti-skepticism aim to avoid precisely the kind of epistemic immodesty that epistemological disjunctivism seems committed to.

This is certainly true of rational support contextualism and contrastivism, both of which avoid at least an all-out commitment to our having rationally grounded knowledge of the denials of radical skeptical hypotheses (much less knowledge of these propositions that is rationally grounded in factive reasons). According to rational support contextualism, for example, in undertaking a competent deduction from one's rationally grounded everyday knowledge to belief in the denial of a radical skeptical hypothesis, the subject must inevitably shift to a skeptical context of epistemic evaluation. Relative to this context of epistemic evaluation, however, it is no longer the case that one has rationally grounded knowledge of the everyday proposition (because one's rational support shrinks to the merely nonfactive). In this way rational support contextualism, like its sister view attributer contextualism, can maintain that there is no context of epistemic evaluation relative to which an agent counts as having rationally grounded knowledge of the denials of radical skeptical hypotheses. Moreover, this claim is consistent not only with the closure$_{RK}$ principle but also with agents generally possessing rationally grounded knowledge of everyday propositions relative to nonskeptical contexts of epistemic appraisal. Insofar as we grant that it is a weakness in epistemological disjunctivism that it is committed to the epistemic immodesty of contending that we can have rationally grounded knowledge of the denials of radical skeptical hypotheses, then in this respect at least rational support contextualism has a dialectical advantage over epistemological disjunctivism as an anti-skeptical strategy.

Contrastivism also avoids the claim that agents can have rationally grounded knowledge of the denials of radical skeptical hypotheses. Indeed, since such knowledge is by its nature binary in form, contrastivism generates this result simply in virtue of its rejection of knowledge as a binary, as opposed to a ternary, relation. More specifically, contrastivism contends that while agents can know everyday propositions in contrast to nonskeptical contrast propositions, they cannot know these propositions in contrast to skeptical contrast propositions (i.e., propositions that concern radical skeptical hypotheses).

The challenge facing contrastivism is to explain how it can account for the intuitions driving the closure$_{RK}$ principle. Since this principle concerns a noncontrastivist conception of knowledge, the contrastivist must reject it. Even so, it will be desirable for the view to put in its place a suitably "contrastivized" version of this principle and show that this can satisfy the intuitions that motivated the closure$_{RK}$ principle. This is exactly what contrastivists have attempted to do. While I do not find what the contrastivists have proposed in this regard compelling, it would take me too far afield to argue for this claim here.[17]

Instead, let me simply make a concession to the contrastivist similar to the one I made to the rational support contextualist, which is that at least as regards closure$_{RK}$-based radical skepticism contrastivism has dialectical advantages over epistemological disjunctivism. More precisely: to the extent that contrastivism can retain the motivations for the closure$_{RK}$ principle while avoiding the epistemic immodesty of epistemological disjunctivism, then it has significant dialectical advantages over epistemological disjunctivism when it comes to dealing with the closure$_{RK}$-based radical skeptical problem.[18]

That leaves dogmatism. Fortunately for epistemological disjunctivism, this is one anti-skeptical proposal that doesn't fare better when it comes to closure$_{RK}$-based radical skepticism. For one thing, dogmatists are committed to essentially the same kind of epistemic immodesty that epistemological disjunctivists are committed, in that they allow that agents can have rationally grounded knowledge of the denials of radical skeptical hypotheses. This commitment on the dogmatism's part is arguably both more and less problematic than the parallel commitment made by the epistemological disjunctivist, and for related reasons.

It is arguably *less* problematic since at least the dogmatist isn't claiming, with the epistemological disjunctivist, that one has a factive rational basis for excluding radical skeptical hypotheses. But it is also arguably *more* problematic since without such a factive rational basis it is even harder to stomach the idea that one can have rationally grounded knowledge of such propositions. In particular, how can the kind of nonfactive defeasible rational basis that the dogmatist has in mind suffice for rationally grounded knowledge of the denials of radical skeptical hypotheses? I think we can thus reasonably conclude that dogmatism is at least no better off than epistemological disjunctivism when it comes to closure$_{RK}$-based radical skepticism, and it may well be significantly worse off.

We will return to consider these three competitor anti-skeptical proposals again briefly in chapter 7. While we have just noted that at least two of these competitor proposals have advantages over epistemological disjunctivism, we will see in the next chapter that these advantages disappear once we recast epistemological disjunctivism as part of a wider anti-skeptical strategy that incorporates the Wittgensteinian insights that we gleaned in part 2.

6. Concluding Remarks

In this chapter we have seen that the Achilles' heel of epistemological disjunctivism as an anti-skeptical strategy lies in the response that it offers to the closure$_{RK}$-based radical skeptical paradox. In particular, whereas the epistemological disjunctivist's claim that one can possess a rational grounding for one's everyday beliefs that favors those beliefs over radical skeptical alternatives is well motivated, such that epistemological disjunctivism can evade the problem posed by underdetermination$_{RK}$-based radical skepticism, a stronger epistemological thesis is required to deal with closure$_{RK}$-based radical skepticism, and this thesis isn't well motivated. In particular, what is required is the idea that one can have rationally grounded knowledge of the denials of radical skeptical hypotheses, and such a claim appears epistemically immodest in the extreme.

Is there a way for the epistemological disjunctivist to demur from advancing this stronger thesis while still being in a position to offer a response to closure$_{RK}$-based radical skepticism? As we will see, there is a positive answer available for this question. In order for this positive answer to be available, however, we need to understand how epistemological disjunctivism can be combined with the Wittgensteinian account of the structure of reasons that we encountered in part 2.

PART 4

Farewell to Epistemic Angst

> Scepticism is thus a resting-place for human reason, where it can reflect upon its dogmatic wanderings and make survey of the region in which it finds itself, so that for the future it may be able to choose its path with more certainty. But it is no dwelling-place for permanent settlement.
> —Kant, *Critique of Pure Reason*, A761/B789

> To be sure there is justification; but justification comes to an end.
> —Wittgenstein, *On Certainty*, §192

CHAPTER 7

Farewell to Epistemic Angst

0. Introductory Remarks

The goal in this final part of the book is to bring together the main threads of discussion from the previous three parts to offer a unified solution—a *biscopic* proposal, as I describe it (for reasons that will become apparent)—to the two formulations of the radical skeptical problem that we have been engaging with. To this end, we will need to revisit some of the key points raised in the previous three parts in order to set the scene for our resolution of radical skepticism. Once the solution has been expounded, we will then explore it further by considering some natural objections that might be raised for the view and comparing it with rival proposals.

1. Recap: The Problem of Radical Skepticism

We will begin by reminding ourselves of the main features of the radical skeptical problem that we have set out. First, let's look again at the two formulations of the radical skeptical paradox that we offered. Here is the triad of collectively inconsistent claims that is at issue in the closure$_{RK}$-based version of the radical skeptical paradox:

THE CLOSURE$_{RK}$-BASED RADICAL SKEPTICAL PARADOX

(SC1) One is unable to have rationally grounded knowledge of the denials of radical skeptical hypotheses.

(SC2) The closure$_{RK}$ principle.

(SC3) One has widespread rationally grounded everyday knowledge.

The closure$_{RK}$ principle at issue in (SC2) is in turn formulated as follows:

THE CLOSURE$_{RK}$ PRINCIPLE

If S has rationally grounded knowledge that p, and S competently deduces from p that q, thereby forming a belief that q on this basis while retaining her rationally grounded knowledge that p, then S has rationally grounded knowledge that q.

The closure$_{RK}$-based version of the radical skeptical problem is a putative paradox precisely because all three of the claims that make up this problem are highly intuitive (especially given that this puzzle is cast in terms of rationally grounded knowledge). And yet, of course, they can't possibly all be true.

Now consider the collectively inconsistent triad of claims that we saw constitutes the underdetermination$_{RK}$-based version of the radical skeptical paradox:

THE UNDERDETERMINATION$_{RK}$-BASED SKEPTICAL PARADOX

(SU1) One cannot have rational support that favors one's belief in an everyday proposition over an incompatible radical skeptical hypothesis.

(SU2) The underdetermination$_{RK}$ principle.

(SU3) One has widespread rationally grounded everyday knowledge.

The underdetermination$_{RK}$ principle at issue in (SU2) is formulated as follows:

THE UNDERDETERMINATION$_{RK}$ PRINCIPLE

If S knows that p and q describe incompatible scenarios, and yet S lacks a rational basis that favors p over q, then S lacks rationally grounded knowledge that p.

Again, we have a putative paradox on our hands here, in that all three claims that make up the underdetermination$_{RK}$-based version of the radical skeptical problem are highly intuitive (especially given that this puzzle is cast in terms of rationally grounded knowledge), and yet they can't all be true.

We saw in part 1 that although these two skeptical puzzles are closely related to one another, they are in fact logically distinct. In particular, we argued that the closure$_{RK}$ principle is in an important sense logically stronger than the underdetermination$_{RK}$ principle, in that it in effect demands that one be able to have rationally grounded knowledge of the denials of radical skeptical hypotheses as opposed to merely being in possession of rational support that favors one's everyday beliefs over radical skeptical alternatives. More generally, we noted that the logical differences between these two radical skeptical puzzles meant that we shouldn't take it for granted that an adequate response to the one form of radical skeptical paradox was thereby a response to the other.

We noted too that the underdetermination$_{RK}$ principle is a very weak epistemic principle, in that it is equivalent to what we termed the rational ground* principle:

THE RATIONAL GROUND* PRINCIPLE

If S has a rationally grounded belief that p, and S knows that p entails q, then S lacks a rational basis for belief that not-q.

This principle demands that one cannot have an all-things-considered rational basis to believe both a proposition and a known to be incompatible alternative, and hence that having such a rational basis for believing a proposition entails lacking a rational basis for believing the alternative. So, for example, one cannot have an all-things-considered rational basis for believing both that one has hands and that one is a handless BIV, such that if one has such a rational basis for believing that one has hands, then one lacks a rational basis for believing that one is a handless BIV. Note just how weak this claim is. It is not the claim that one *has* a rational basis for believing that one is *not* a handless BIV, but rather the claim that one *lacks* a rational basis for believing that one *is* a handless BIV. And yet such an undemanding principle turns out to be logically equivalent to the underdetermination$_{RK}$ principle, which demonstrates just how weak the latter principle is.

We also noted that these two logically distinct radical skeptical paradoxes trade on two very different core ideas about the nature of rational support. The closure$_{RK}$-based radical skeptical paradox appeals to what we called the *universality of rational evaluation thesis*. This is the idea that there is no in principle limitation on rational evaluation, such that global rational evaluations are perfectly legitimate. A commitment to this thesis is reflected in the closure$_{RK}$-based skeptical challenge in that it makes use of closure$_{RK}$-based inferences that take us from the kind of local rational evaluations at issue when we rationally evaluate our everyday beliefs to the wholesale rational evaluations that are in play when we consider the radical skeptical hypotheses that are known to be inconsistent with these everyday beliefs.

In contrast, the underdetermination$_{RK}$-based radical skeptical paradox turns on a very different idea about the nature of reasons, which we labeled the *insularity of reasons thesis*. This is the claim that the rational support that we have for our everyday beliefs about the world around us is by its nature such that it is compatible with one's beliefs being radically false. As we saw, this thesis is manifested in terms of the widespread endorsement of the new evil demon intuition. It is a commitment to the insularity of reasons thesis that underwrites (SU1) in the underdetermination$_{RK}$-based radical skeptical paradox. More specifically, underdetermination$_{RK}$-based radical skepticism turns upon this thesis since without it the underdetermination$_{RK}$ principle doesn't have any radical skeptical import.

We also distinguished between responses to radical skepticism that are *undercutting* and those that are *overriding*. In short, what makes a response radical skepticism undercutting is that it maintains that it is not a bona fide paradox at all, but rather smuggles contentious theoretical claims into the setup of the skeptical argument, disguised as common sense. Overriding anti-skeptical strategies, in contrast, grant that the skeptical problem is a genuine paradox—in the sense that it is arising out of our most fundamental epistemological commitments, but argue nonetheless that we have adequate independent grounds to offer the kind of epistemic revisionism that would block the skeptical argument. We argued that undercutting anti-skeptical strategies are to be preferred to overriding anti-skeptical strategies, all things considered.

We offered some further desiderata when it came to anti-skeptical strategies. Given the plausibility of the underdetermination$_{RK}$ and closure$_{RK}$ principles, we would ideally want a response to radical skepticism that found a way of retaining these principles. In particular, we argued that an optimal response would enable us to exploit the logical difference between the two skeptical arguments noted above. That is, we would find a way to argue, contra the insularity of reasons thesis, that we do have rational support for our quotidian knowledge that favors the proposition believed over radical skeptical alternatives. We would thus be able to block underdetermination$_{RK}$-based radical skepticism without having to reject the underdetermination$_{RK}$ principle. At the same time, it would be preferable to nonetheless demur from claiming that we have rationally grounded knowledge of the denials of radical skeptical hypotheses. The challenge would therefore be to find a way of taking this line while at the same time retaining the closure$_{RK}$ principle and yet even so evading the closure$_{RK}$-based radical skeptical paradox.

On the face of it this looks to be an impossible set of desiderata, particularly this last move regarding closure$_{RK}$-based radical skepticism. On this score, the thought would be to somehow disentangle the closure$_{RK}$

principle from the universality of rational evaluation thesis, such that we could retain the former while denying the latter. That is, we allow the general principle that where belief is acquired by making competent deductions from one's rationally grounded knowledge, then that belief amounts to rationally grounded knowledge, while nonetheless insisting, on a principled basis, that there are limits to the extent of one's rational evaluations, such that one cannot acquire rationally grounded knowledge of the denials of radical skeptical hypotheses in this fashion.

Finally, we noted that we would ideally want an integrated treatment of these two radical skeptical problems. For even though these problems turn on epistemic principles that are logically distinct, they are nonetheless clearly closely related difficulties. In particular, an anti-skeptical strategy that dealt with only one of these problems would not be intellectually satisfying. Furthermore, if one offered responses to each of these problems that turned out to be in tension with one another, then that would clearly be problematic.

We thus have two radical skeptical paradoxes, both of which look on the face of it hard to respond to (and which will almost certainly require their own anti-skeptical strategy). Moreover, we also have a set of anti-skeptical desiderata that looks like an aspiration for the impossible. Nonetheless, we will now see that there is a way of offering a response to these two radical skeptical paradoxes that adequately disarms both skeptical puzzles, and does so in an integrated and mutually supportive fashion.

2. The Biscopic Proposal: Epistemic Angst Avoided

Recall the Wittgensteinian position that we outlined in part 2. This was primarily a response to the closure$_{RK}$-based formulation of the skeptical paradox. On the specific rendering of the position that we settled upon it responded to this paradox in a distinctive way by arguing that one could reject (SC2) while nonetheless retaining the closure$_{RK}$ principle that is alleged to underwrite it. With (SC2) rejected, one is then in a position to endorse the highly intuitive (SC1). Indeed, it was an explicit part of this Wittgensteinian position to embrace (SC1), since on this view it was part of the very nature of the rational support that our beliefs enjoy that one could not have rationally supported knowledge of the denials of skeptical hypotheses. This was because the denials of skeptical hypotheses codify our über hinge commitment that we are not radically and fundamentally mistaken in our beliefs, and we saw that it was core to this proposal that our commitments to propositions which codify the über hinge commitment—that is, our hinge commitments—were by their nature exempt from rational evaluation.

Interestingly, it was precisely because of the essentially arational nature of our hinge commitments that our inability to know the denials of skeptical hypotheses was not, via the closure$_{RK}$ principle, in tension with our widespread rationally grounded knowledge of everyday propositions. The closure$_{RK}$ principle, after all, concerns rationally grounded knowledge, and thus rationally grounded belief, that is acquired via the rational process of competent deduction from prior rationally grounded knowledge. And yet our hinge commitments cannot be the result of any rational process, but rather express prior visceral commitments on our part, commitments that must be in place in order to create the rational arena in which rational evaluations function. This is why it is a mistake to even conceive of our hinge commitments as being (knowledge-apt) beliefs, since a propositional attitude that is in principle insensitive to rational considerations cannot be a (knowledge-apt) belief.

The upshot is that one can retain the closure$_{RK}$ principle while also endorsing (SC1) and (SC3). The problem lies rather with (SC2), and in particular with the claim that (SC2) is underwritten by the closure$_{RK}$ principle. The closure$_{RK}$ principle has application only to competent deductions that generate rationally grounded knowledge, and thus rationally grounded belief, from prior rationally grounded knowledge. But this means that this principle simply has no application to our hinge commitments, such as our commitments to the denials of radical skeptical hypotheses. It follows that one cannot derive, via the closure$_{RK}$ principle, the claim at issue in (SC2) that if one is unable to have rationally grounded knowledge of the denials of skeptical hypotheses, then one must lack rationally grounded knowledge of everyday propositions.

At the heart of this Wittgensteinian anti-skeptical proposal is the idea that all rational evaluation is an essentially local phenomenon. More specifically, the claim is that the very possibility of rationally evaluating one's beliefs presupposes arational hinge commitments that are beyond rational evaluation. Indeed, Wittgenstein argues that it is in the nature of rational support that it be local in this fashion, such that the very idea of a universal rational evaluation (whether positive or negative, Moorean or radically skeptical) is simply incoherent, and the product of faulty theorizing. This is why our commitments to the denials of radical skeptical hypotheses are not in the market for being rationally grounded knowledge (indeed, given that these commitments are not knowledge-apt beliefs, they are not in the market for knowledge *simpliciter*).

More generally, on this view the universality of rational evaluation thesis—which we have seen is presupposed in closure$_{RK}$-based radical skepticism—is rejected, and rejected because it is exposed as being the product of defective philosophy masquerading under the guise of common sense. The shift from ordinary local rational evaluations to the kind of wholesale rational evaluations that take place when one, for example, considers radical skeptical hypotheses is not a harmless extension of scope, but rather a shift from an intelligible practice rooted in our ordinary epistemic practices to one that is simply incoherent. Since all rational evaluation presupposes arational hinge commitments that are by their nature exempt from rational evaluation, this puts an in principle constraint on the extent of rational evaluations. In particular, it excludes the kind of wholesale rational evaluations that call into question our hinge commitments, and that are the stock in trade of the radical skeptic.

Hence, the universality of rational evaluation thesis has to go. The Wittgensteinian account of the structure of rational evaluation shows us why an unrestricted version of this thesis is untenable, since it exposes its dubious philosophical commitments. But rejecting this thesis (so construed) does not require us to reject, or otherwise refine, the closure$_{RK}$ principle since, as we have just noted, when our hinge commitments are properly understood they cannot play the role required by the radical skeptic in closure$_{RK}$-based inferences.[1]

On the face of it, the Wittgensteinian conception of the structure of rational evaluation is antithetical to the epistemological disjunctivist account according to which rational support can be factive. Whereas the former view emphasizes the essential limitations of rational evaluation, the latter view holds in contrast that in an important sense reasons are not as limited as we hitherto (guided by a faulty philosophical picture) supposed. On closer inspection, however, it becomes clear that there is no essential conflict between these two accounts. Rational evaluation could be essentially local in the Wittgensteinian sense, and yet reasons could also be factive in the way that epistemological disjunctivism describes. What would be ruled out by combining these views would be the possibility that our hinge commitments could be rationally evaluated, such that we can have rationally grounded knowledge of the denials of radical skeptical hypotheses. On the combined view, reasons could still be factive, but only when set within local rational evaluations.

The mere logical compatibility of these two views is not primarily what interests us, however. Rather, what we seek is a way of combining these proposals such that they are mutually supportive. We have already seen in outline how thinking of factive reasons as also being embedded within essentially local rational evaluations can help epistemological disjunctivism. In particular, we noted in the last chapter that epistemological disjunctivists would ideally like to exploit the logical gap between the following two claims:

(i) The rational support one's everyday perceptual beliefs enjoy factively favors those beliefs over radical skeptical alternatives.

(ii) One's commitments to the denials of skeptical hypotheses are to be understood in terms of rationally grounded—indeed, *factively* rationally grounded—knowledge.

Epistemological disjunctivists actively endorse (i), but would rather avoid thereby also endorsing (ii), which is a far less plausible claim, one that seems to incorporate an undue degree of epistemic immodesty.

Treating rational support, even factive rational support, as embedded within essentially local rational evaluations offers a way of retaining (i) while rejecting (ii). The route to (ii), after all, goes via a closure$_{RK}$-style inference, and on the Wittgensteinian account of rational evaluation this principle simply has no application to hinge commitments such as our commitments to the denials of skeptical hypotheses. By allying themselves to the Wittgensteinian account of rational evaluations, then, epistemological disjunctivists are thereby free to respond to the closure$_{RK}$-based skeptical argument by rejecting not (SC1) but rather (SC2). Moreover, they can do so while retaining their support for the closure$_{RK}$ principle. What is rejected is thus not our powerful intuitions in support of (SC1) or the closure$_{RK}$ principle, but rather the theoretical presuppositions about the nature of rational evaluations (i.e., their universality) that inform the way in which the closure$_{RK}$ principle is held to generate (SC2).

The Wittgensteinian account of rational evaluations can thus be combined with epistemological disjunctivism in order to make the latter a more compelling response to the problem of radical skepticism, one that can accommodate both closure$_{RK}$- and underdetermination$_{RK}$-based formulations of radical skepticism. Importantly, the support relations between these two anti-skeptical proposals also flow in the opposite direction, in that by adding epistemological disjunctivism to the

Wittgensteinian account of rational evaluations the latter is better placed to deal with some of the difficulties that it faces.

In particular, recall from part 2 that one fundamental worry about the Wittgensteinian account of the structure of rational evaluation is that while it fares well when applied to closure$_{RK}$-based radical skepticism (because it offers a principled basis on which to reject the universality of rational evaluation thesis), it struggles with underdetermination$_{RK}$-based radical skepticism. As we saw, merely noting the essential locality of rational evaluations does not give one any purchase at all on the concern that the rational support that our everyday beliefs enjoy fails to favor those beliefs over skeptical alternatives. Relatedly, noting that our commitments to the denials of skeptical hypotheses are not in the market for knowledge (much less rationally grounded knowledge) is by the by in this regard, since the underdetermination$_{RK}$ claim employed by the radical skeptic does not presuppose that one should be able to have knowledge of these propositions (the latter being a logically stronger claim).

But when the thesis that rational evaluations are essentially local is combined with the factivity of reasons thesis as expressed by epistemological disjunctivism, a response to the underdetermination$_{RK}$-based skeptical argument immediately becomes available. In particular, it is now no longer true that the rational support one's everyday beliefs enjoy must be such as to fail to favor those beliefs over radical skeptical alternatives, as this formulation of the skeptical problem contends. By allying the Wittgensteinian account of rational evaluations to epistemological disjunctivism, one can in a principled way reject the insularity of rational evaluation thesis and thereby resist underdetermination$_{RK}$-based radical skepticism.

The addition of epistemological disjunctivism to the Wittgensteinian account of the structure of rational evaluations is also advantageous on another front. To be told that all rational evaluation is essentially local can at least *sound* like a fairly fundamental concession to radical skepticism. As we saw in part 2, we need to understand this claim in terms of a wider thesis about how radical skepticism, and standard forms of anti-skepticism too, are buying into a theoretical picture about the nature of rational evaluations which is simply untenable. Thus what looks like a severe limitation on the nature of the rational support enjoyed by our beliefs is in fact no such thing, as rational evaluations simply could not function as the radical skeptic/traditional anti-skeptic supposes. Even so, the claim that rational evaluations are essentially local is much easier to live with if it is combined with the claim that reasons can be factive. For if it is both the case that all rational evaluations are local and that all rational support is insular (in line with the insularity of reasons thesis), then that is clearly to offer a much weaker thesis about the nature of the rational support enjoyed by our beliefs than would be the case if factive rational support were held to be available.

Notice too that the undercutting elements of these two anti-skeptical strategies are also mutually supportive. On the one hand, the Wittgensteinian claim that the closure$_{RK}$-based skeptical argument trades on an illicit commitment to (an unrestricted version of) the universality of rational evaluation thesis undercuts the motivation for the closure$_{RK}$-based skeptical paradox. On the other hand, the epistemological disjunctivist claim that the underdetermination$_{RK}$-based skeptical argument trades on an unsupported commitment to the insularity of reasons thesis undercuts the motivation for the underdetermination$_{RK}$-based skeptical paradox. Collectively, then, both formulations of the skeptical paradox are shown to rest on contentious theoretical assumptions that we should discard.

I call this combined account a *biscopic* proposal. The reason for this is that it conveys the essential features of how I understand the skeptical problem and its resolution. For if my take on the skeptical paradox is correct, then we have in effect been viewing it hitherto through, as it were, one eye only. Without realizing, we have been inspecting the skeptical problem first through the lens of closure$_{RK}$-based skepticism (unwittingly guided by the universality of rational evaluation thesis), and then again through the different lens of underdetermination$_{RK}$-based skepticism (unwittingly guided, this time, by the insularity of reasons thesis), without realizing that these are importantly different formulations of the skeptical problem. In short, we have been engaging with the relevant philosophical terrain while lacking an accurate representation of that terrain. This has meant, for example, that we have evaluated the effectiveness of different anti-skeptical approaches without both eyes on the problem, which is why we have tended to overestimate—and in some cases, such as the Wittgensteinian and epistemological disjunctivist approaches, underestimate, or at least misunderstand—their import to this philosophical difficulty.

The biscopic approach to the problem set out here, in contrast, recognizes that there are two distinct formulations of the skeptical problem on display. Accordingly, it explicitly acknowledges that this problem needs a dual solution, one where the two anti-skeptical proposals are not merely combined, but also fully integrated, as two lines of sight might be. The result is a fully fledged response to the problem of radical skepticism, at least as that problem is typically understood in contemporary epistemology. Epistemic *angst* has thus been avoided.

3. Some Anti-skeptical Contrasts

We are now in a position to revisit some of the specific anti-skeptical accounts that we have encountered while setting out our own stall to see exactly how they are deficient relative to the biscopic proposal offered here. In particular, it will be useful to reconsider those views that we saw in chapter 6 offered some anti-skeptical mileage with regard to at least one of the formulations of radical skepticism.

Let's begin with rational support contextualism. Recall that this proposal contended that the extent of the rational support enjoyed by one's beliefs depended on the context of epistemic appraisal. In particular, relative to everyday contexts of epistemic appraisal, this rational support can be factive, but relative to skeptical contexts of epistemic appraisal it will be nonfactive. The upshot of this point is that whether or not an ascription of knowledge expresses a truth will depend on whether the context of epistemic appraisal is skeptical or everyday. In particular, if it is the former, then the ascription will likely express a falsehood. We thus get a particular rendering of the attributer contextualism that we encountered in chapter 2.

We saw that this proposal struggles to deal with underdetermination$_{RK}$-based radical skepticism, at least when compared with epistemological disjunctivism. If we can make sense of the idea that agents can have factive rational support for their beliefs, then what is gained by incorporating this thesis into a contextualist proposal that makes core concessions to the radical skeptic? In particular, if we buy the undercutting anti-skeptical line that epistemological disjunctivism offers us as regards the underdetermination$_{RK}$-based radical skeptical paradox, then what possible motivation could there be to concede that relative to skeptical contexts of epistemic appraisal ascriptions of knowledge tend to express falsehoods?

We also noted, however, that the dialectical situation becomes much more complicated once we bring in closure$_{RK}$-based radical skepticism, and it is easy to see why. After all, if the epistemological disjunctivist extends her anti-skeptical line to this form of radical skepticism by contending that we can have rationally grounded knowledge of the denials of radical skeptical hypotheses, then it can look like an unduly strong response to the problem of radical skepticism. As we noted, epistemological disjunctivism, so construed, seems committed to embracing a kind of *epistemic immodesty*, in that intuitively we are unable to have rationally grounded knowledge of these propositions.

In contrast, according to rational support contextualism, the context of epistemic appraisal in which radical skeptical hypotheses are raised is one in which factive rational support is no longer possessed, and thus one in which ascriptions of knowledge will tend to express falsehoods. As a result, this proposal can avoid making the kind of unduly bold antiskeptical claim that the epistemological disjunctivist seems committed to. Rational support contextualism is thus on this front at least *epistemically modest*.

Rational support contextualism therefore has advantages over epistemological disjunctivism when it comes specifically to closure$_{RK}$-based radical skepticism. The dialectical situation changes somewhat, however, once we combine epistemological disjunctivism with the Wittgensteinian account of the structure of rational evaluation as part of our biscopic proposal. For on the biscopic view we are now in a position to also demur from the epistemically immodest claim that we can have rationally grounded knowledge of the denials of radical skeptical hypotheses. It remains the case that the rational support paradigmatically enjoyed by one's perceptual beliefs is factive, and of course such factive rational support will provide the agent with a rational basis that decisively favors those everyday perceptual beliefs over skeptical alternatives. But, crucially, there is now no route from this claim to the stronger, and epistemically immodest, thesis that one has a factive rational basis for believing the denials of radical skeptical hypotheses. This claim is blocked by the Wittgensteinian account of the structure of rational evaluation. There is thus no reason for preferring rational support contextualism over our biscopic anti-skeptical proposal, since the latter fares better than the former as regards both formulations of radical skepticism.

Moreover, notice that the Wittgensteinian account of why we are unable to have rationally grounded knowledge of the denials of radical skeptical hypotheses engages with the radical skeptical problem at a much greater level of depth than rational support contextualism. The Wittgensteinian claim is motivated via appeal to a rich undercutting anti-skeptical diagnosis that highlights the essential role of hinge commitments in our systems of rational evaluation. Rational support contextualism, in contrast, merely offers us a relatively thin anti-skeptical diagnosis that appeals to the very particular epistemic standards that are at issue in specifically skeptical contexts of epistemic appraisal. Nowhere is this more apparent than in the way rational support contextualism grants the legitimacy of the skeptical context of epistemic appraisal, whereas the Wittgensteinian approach explains why the very idea of such a kind of universal epistemic appraisal is incoherent.

Inferential contextualism, which we encountered in chapter 4, arguably fares better than rational support contextualism on this score, in that at least it recognizes the relevance of Wittgenstein's discussion of hinge commitments to the radical skeptical problem. As we saw in chapter 4, however, this proposal goes awry in offering a faulty conception of these commitments, in particular to the extent that it allows that the radical skeptic inhabits a legitimate context of epistemic appraisal that incorporates its own specific hinge commitments. We argued in chapter 4 that the very idea of such a legitimate skeptical context of epistemic assessment is problematic even by the lights of inferential contextualism (because even the skeptical hinge commitments need to be at least true if the context is to be legitimate, and yet if inferential contextualism is right then they simply cannot be true). In any case, it is certainly problematic by our lights, since on the account of hinge commitments that we have offered the radical skeptic is attempting a kind of rational evaluation that is simply impossible. As we just noted with regard to rational support contextualism, we can thus straightforwardly dismiss such a context of epistemic appraisal as incoherent.

We also noted in chapter 4 that at the root of the problems facing inferential contextualism was a failure to properly distinguish between closure$_{RK}$-based and underdetermination$_{RK}$-based radical skepticism. While the inferential contextualist's rejection of universal rational evaluations offers a way of dealing with the former problem, in order to deal with the latter problem one needs to confront the insularity of reasons thesis. We saw that there was a partial, and implicit, recognition of this point in terms of how proponents of inferential contextualism try to extract a claim about *epistemic priority* from the Wittgensteinian thesis that all rational evaluation is local. In particular, they argue that there is no fixed epistemic priority in play when it comes to empirical knowledge, such that it is not necessary that knowledge of the external world should be ultimately based on knowledge of one's own mental states.

In response, we argued that one in fact cannot extract epistemic priority from the Wittgensteinian thesis, in that there was nothing to prevent the possibility that it is *both* true that all rational evaluation is local *and* that all worldly knowledge is ultimately based on knowledge of one's own mental states. Furthermore, while one might initially suppose that allowing that the rejection of such a fixed epistemic priority might give one a handle on underdetermination$_{RK}$-based radical skepticism—in that one could argue that the source of this problem is that one is forced to ground one's empirical knowledge in knowledge of one's mental states—this proved to be illusory. What matters for underdetermination$_{RK}$-based radical skepticism is that one can deny the insularity of reasons thesis, and such a denial does not follow from a rejection of a fixed epistemic priority regarding empirical knowledge. In particular, it could be true that one's rational support in the good case is no better than in the corresponding skeptical bad case, and yet it is possible nonetheless to sometimes ground knowledge of the external world in knowledge other than of one's own mental states.

It is thus crucial that the Wittgensteinian account of the structure of rational evaluation is both allied to the right conception of our hinge commitments, and also wedded to epistemological disjunctivism such that it offers us the dialectical resources to reject the insularity of reasons thesis. The crucial point is that one cannot derive the rejection of this thesis from the Wittgensteinian account of hinge commitments alone. The structure of rational evaluation can be essentially local and yet nonetheless also accord with the insularity of reasons of thesis. When it comes to radical skepticism, we thus need Wittgenstein *and* epistemological disjunctivism—namely, the biscopic proposal.[2]

Now consider the dialectical situation with regard to contrastivism. Recall that contrastivists hold that knowledge is to be understood not as a binary relation between a subject and a proposition, but rather as a ternary relation among a subject, a proposition, and a contrast proposition. In short, there is no such thing as knowledge that *p simpliciter*; there is, rather, knowledge that *p rather than q*.

We saw in chapter 6 that epistemological disjunctivism fares much better than contrastivism when it comes to underdetermination$_{RK}$-based radical skepticism. In particular, we argued that much of the impetus toward adopting such a revisionary proposal is removed once we recognize the important distinction between favoring and discriminating epistemic support, a distinction that we claimed all epistemologists should endorse (i.e., and not just epistemological disjunctivists). For example, this distinction enables us to explain why a subject can know that the creature before her is a zebra and not a cleverly disguised mule even though she cannot perceptually discriminate between zebras and cleverly disguised mules. There is thus no need to retreat, in line with contrastivism, to the claim that there is no such thing as the subject knowing *simpliciter* that the creature before her is a zebra, much less do we need to claim (as the contrastivist contends) that the subject's knowledge is relative only to certain very specific contrast propositions (e.g., that she knows only that the creature before her is a zebra rather than an elephant, and so on).

Once we extend our focus to the closure$_{RK}$-based radical skeptical problem, however, one might think that contrastivism is on stronger ground. After all, the contrastivist has an explanation of why one can never have rationally grounded knowledge of the denials of radical skeptical hypotheses, since no one has binary knowledge of this sort. Moreover, no one has the relevant ternary knowledge either, given that it's impossible to perceptually discriminate between good cases and corresponding skeptical bad cases. So, for example, according to contrastivism one can know that one has hands as opposed to having stumps (since one can discriminate between the two scenarios), but one cannot know that one has hands as opposed to being a handless BIV (since one cannot discriminate between the two scenarios). Contrastivism can thus accommodate the kind of epistemic modesty that we noted was desirable in this regard, in contrast to the manifest epistemic immodesty that epistemological disjunctivism seems committed to when applied by itself to the closure$_{RK}$-based radical skeptical problem.

One issue that we might raise for contrastivism on this score is whether it can sufficiently accommodate the intuitions that underlie closure-style principles, such as the closure$_{RK}$ principle. In line with our discussion of contrastivism in chapter 6, however, let us grant for the sake of argument that contrastivists have a successful story to tell in this regard.[3] Even if we grant this much to contrastivism, it loses any dialectical advantage it might gain over epistemological disjunctivism as an anti-skeptical proposal once the latter view is wedded to the Wittgensteinian account of the structure of rational evaluation as part of our biscopic proposal. For one can now avoid the epistemic immodesty that epistemological disjunctivism alone was committed to, and do so without having to deny the closure$_{RK}$ principle or adopt the revisionism of contrastivism. In particular, one can claim that one's everyday perceptual beliefs enjoy rational support that decisively favors those beliefs over radical skeptical alternatives without thereby having to suppose that one's hinge commitments to the denials of radical skeptical hypotheses are in the market for (rationally grounded) knowledge.

Finally, we come to the dogmatist position. Recall that dogmatism is the view that its perceptual seeming to one as if *p* can provide one with a defeasible justification for believing that p, and thus rationally grounded perceptual knowledge that p. Moreover, recall that the dogmatist contends that one can legitimately infer from this rationally grounded perceptual knowledge that p, via a closure$_{RK}$-style inference, that one has rationally grounded knowledge of the denials of radical skeptical hypotheses that are inconsistent with p.

As we noted in chapter 6, one of the striking features of dogmatism is how epistemically immodest it is. Epistemological disjunctivism when not wedded to the Wittgensteinian account of the structure of rational evaluation draws a similar epistemically immodest conclusion, of course, but at least it does so on a much stronger rational basis—namely, factive reflectively accessible reasons rather than mere perceptual seemings. Accordingly, dogmatism does not seem any better off than a straightforward epistemological disjunctivist anti-skeptical strategy on this score. Once epistemological disjunctivism is wedded to the Wittgensteinian account of the structure of rational evaluation, however, then the view is at a severe dialectical disadvantage, since our combined biscopic anti-skeptical proposal completely avoids the epistemic immodesty advocated by dogmatism.

The biscopic combination of epistemological disjunctivism and the Wittgensteinian account of the structure of rational evaluation thus offers us not just a compelling response to the skeptical problem in its own right, but also a response that fares much better than its anti-skeptical rivals, even those proposals that gain a purchase on at least one of the formulations of the skeptical problem.

4. Concluding Postscript: Epistemic Vertigo

We began this book with epistemic *angst*; we have concluded with its cure.

Nonetheless, I want to close with a question regarding the nature of our epistemic condition, given this resolution to the radical skeptical problem. With the radical skeptical problem dealt with, does this mean that we can return to a state of epistemic innocence, on par with how we conceived of our epistemic position prior to engaging with the skeptical problem? One might think that the answer to this question is straightforwardly yes, but, as we will see, I'm not convinced that matters are quite so straightforward.

One point that we should note from the beginning is that it clearly does follow from the fact that the paradox is resolved that there is nothing epistemically amiss (on this score at any rate) with the beliefs and commitments held by those who have never engaged with this problem, and who thus never left a state of epistemic innocence. But, of course, this point is inapplicable to us, since we have engaged with this problem, and therein lies the rub.

Still, one might protest that engagement with the problem of radical skepticism shouldn't make a difference on this score. After all, one point that we have noted in our dealings with the skeptical puzzle is that at a most basic level we are psychologically incapable of taking skeptical doubt seriously. We are, if you like, "hardwired" to be anti-skeptics. This fact, coupled with our possession of an undercutting response to the skeptical problem, may well seem to suffice to expunge all trace of the skeptical problematic from our intellectual lives.[4]

I don't think that matters are quite so simple, however. The reason for this lies in the Wittgensteinian element of our anti-skeptical approach. For notice that in the state of epistemic innocence we are completely unaware of the essential locality of rational evaluation. This is not to say, of course, that we instead take it for granted that rational evaluation can be universal; rather, the point is that we just do not have any theoretical beliefs about our overall epistemic standing. Once we have engaged with the skeptical problem and appreciated how it should be resolved, however, then we also have to take on board the essential locality of rational evaluation. Recognizing this limitation, even while at the same time understanding that it is an unavoidable feature of our epistemic position, is bound to have an impact on how we conceive of our epistemic condition. In short, it is one thing to quite properly employ an essentially local system of rational evaluation without ever recognizing that it is essentially local, and another thing entirely to come to realize that one's system of rational evaluation is local in this fashion (even if one is at the same time convinced that systems of rational evaluation are by their nature local).

Elsewhere, I have referred to this intellectual anxiety induced by radical skepticism, even when in possession of an undercutting solution to the problem, as *epistemic vertigo*.[5] Roughly, the idea is that a by-product of the very process of engaging with radical skepticism, even when successfully engaging with this problem, is that it involves a kind of reflection—a kind of *epistemic ascent*, if you will—that can induce intellectual anxiety. Just like normal vertigo—or *acrophobia*, to be more accurate—it can be tremendously difficult, if not impossible (practically speaking), to shake off the fear in question, even once one recognizes that one has nothing to be afraid of (the best that one can hope for is usually a way of managing this fear, not of removing it altogether).[6] I think something very similar often occurs after our engagement with radical skepticism, even when the problem is resolved. Our engagement with the problem, and the associated epistemic ascent, leads us to seek an overall perspective on our epistemic position, and this generates intellectual anxiety. But even once we are assured that there is nothing to fear and that our epistemic position is as secure as one might reasonably expect (and certainly not subject to the specific threats outlined by the radical skeptic anyway), the anxiety might well remain.

Note too that epistemic vertigo is analogous to vertigo *simpliciter* in another respect, in that they are both rooted in perfectly rational fears. Being high up when unsecured is obviously a source of immediate risk, and hence something to be feared. No wonder, then, that it is common to be afraid of heights even when knowing full well that there is no risk involved. Similarly, having a commitment that lacks a proper rational grounding is a legitimate source of epistemic anxiety, and we witness this phenomenon all the time when it comes to particular commitments that we hold ("Can I really trust what X is telling me about Y, given that I know so little about X?"; "Can it really be true that p, given that the media are currently reporting otherwise?"; and so on). Following the analogy through, epistemic vertigo plays on a perfectly legitimate anxiety about epistemic risk, but is in effect the pathological form of this anxiety, which is to say that it is no longer reflecting rational concerns.[7]

This may well seem to be courting mystery. If the problem is resolved, then why isn't that the end of the matter? Well, in the most important sense it *is* an end of the matter, at least to the extent that there is now no philosophical problem to be resolved. And as I noted above, the epistemic position of those who haven't engaged with this problem is not just perfectly in order as it is (in this regard anyway), but they also will not be subject to epistemic vertigo. The point I am trying to make by appeal to the phenomenon of epistemic vertigo is more psychological than philosophical, in that it describes the particular phenomenology involved when one has resolved the skeptical puzzle.

Moreover, notice that I am *not* suggesting, as others have done in the debate about radical skepticism, that there is something inherently dubious, in the sense of skepticism-inducing, about taking a detached perspective on one's epistemic position, at least in some specific respect (e.g., as regards a certain subject matter).[8] More precisely, my view is that there is nothing essentially problematic about adopting a detached perspective on one's epistemic position so long as it does not lead one to attempt to undertake universal rational evaluations, and I take it to be at least possible to do the former without succumbing to the latter temptation (even though, as Wittgenstein reminds us, it is very easy to slip from the former to the latter).

Hence on my view the radical skeptical problem we have been discussing really is resolved, *period*. So why should there be any phenomenological vestige of intellectual anxiety remaining? I think the answer to this question lies in the fact that radical skepticism, while being in many ways very unnatural (e.g., in attempting to doubt even our hinge commitments, and in being illicitly based upon contentious theoretical assumptions), nonetheless arises out of very natural intellectual inclinations and aspirations (just as vertigo arises out very rational considerations, as we noted above). The drive to step out of one's ordinary ways of believing and reasoning—and, more generally, one's ordinary ways of thinking and acting—and thereby effect a detached perspective on those particular ways of believing and reasoning, is an entirely natural intellectual inclination, after all, one that underpins much of philosophy (indeed, it underlies most, if not all, intellectual enterprises). Moreover, once we have adopted this perspective, the aspiration to go on to discover the universal rational foundations of our beliefs—and thereby adopt a *completely* detached perspective—is very natural too. Indeed, the latter aspiration can look on the surface of things to be little more than a variant of taking a detached perspective on some aspect of one's epistemic position. It takes the philosophical skill of someone like Wittgenstein to help us to see how the project of undertaking a fully general rational evaluation of one's beliefs is in fact very different from the (epistemologically benign) project of taking a detached perspective on some aspect of one's epistemic position, in that it covertly buys into a dubious theoretical picture.

Given that such natural intellectual inclinations underlie the ascent to skepticism-friendly reasoning, it should be no wonder that our recognition that the kind of rational support at issue in a universal rational evaluation is unavailable can have such a giddying effect, even once we explicitly disengage the detached epistemic perspective from the attempt to undertake universal rational evaluations. Natural aspirations are hard to shake, and one cannot in any straightforward way unlearn what one has discovered about one's epistemic position. If reason cannot alter our hinge commitments, then it is unsurprising that it is also unable to completely eradicate our naturally arising anxieties, whether they be phobias like acrophobia or intellectual anxieties like epistemic vertigo. So even though there is a cure available for epistemic *angst*, there is also a sense in which *angst* of a certain kind—that is, epistemic vertigo—may remain even once the cure has been swallowed.[9]

Still, we should not allow this talk of epistemic vertigo to sidetrack us from the central point in hand, which is that the kind of radical skepticism that we have been engaging with has been neutralized. Insofar as epistemic vertigo is a genuine phenomenon—that is, not simply a description of my own idiosyncratic psychological state when engaging with the skeptical problem—then it would explain why resolving the radical skeptical problem does not return one back to the state of epistemic innocence. It would not show that there is anything amiss with the biscopic resolution of radical skepticism on offer. To repeat: we began with epistemic *angst*, and we have concluded with its cure.

Notes

Introduction

1. In my view, Pyrrhonian skepticism requires a completely separate treatment from Cartesian skepticism. This is for a number of reasons, but the main issue is that it is not a paradox but rather a distinctive kind of ethical position (which means, among other things, that the scope of the doubt is significantly constrained). In contrast, I follow Conant (e.g., 2004; 2012) in thinking that Cartesian and Kantian forms of skepticism are related in important ways. Although I don't have the space to address this issue here, I think Humean skepticism is hard to place with regard to other forms of skepticism precisely because it has elements of all three kinds of radical skepticism just listed. Henceforth, where I refer to "skepticism" or "radical skepticism" without qualification, then it is the particular Cartesian variety of this problem, as it is cast in the contemporary epistemological debate, that I have in mind.

2. That's not to say that I think anti-luck epistemology is in doubt, only that its application to the problem of radical skepticism is limited. For some of my recent defenses of anti-luck epistemology, which is now embedded within a view of knowledge I call *anti-luck virtue epistemology*, see Pritchard (2007a; 2007c; 2009a; 2012a; 2012c; 2013c; forthcoming–a) and Pritchard, Millar, & Haddock (2010, chaps. 1–4).

3. Henceforth, "OC." See, for example, Pritchard (2005g; 2011f; 2012e; 2014a; forthcoming–d).

4. See especially Pritchard (2012b). See also Pritchard (2007b; 2008b; 2009f).

5. Many thanks to all those people who have suggested alternative names (I'd thank everyone individually, but the list is far too large). Alas, in the end none of the names proposed had the crucial dual virtue of both being aesthetically pleasing and conveying the particular point that I wanted to make.

6. Which, note, is not to say that the skeptical problem is able to generate real radical skeptical doubt. This point will become much clearer later on in the book once we encounter Wittgenstein's account of our hinge commitments.

7. I think this relates to Cavell's (1988, chap. 6) famous remark, in the context of radical skepticism, about the "uncanniness of the ordinary."

8. Note that this point is entirely compatible with Wittgenstein's (1953, §124) oft-cited claim that philosophy "leaves everything as it is." If this solution to radical skepticism is right, then there really is nothing amiss (on this front anyway) as regards our ordinary epistemic practices.

Chapter 1. Radical Skepticism and Closure

1. It is, of course, an interesting question how much affinity there is between Cartesian skepticism, as it is understood in the contemporary epistemological literature, and the kind of radical skepticism explored by Descartes himself, though I will not be getting into this issue here. For a useful discussion of this issue, see

Luper (2011). See also Gaukroger (2011). As I noted in the introduction, there are, of course, other significant forms of radical skepticism. In the first instance I have in mind Pyrrhonian skepticism, which does not proceed by offering philosophical arguments as such, much less philosophical theses, but rather puts forward a piecemeal, and yet unrestricted, method of doubt. But there is also a broadly Kantian form of radical skepticism which I think is very important too. Very roughly, this is skepticism about the very idea that one could entertain contentful thoughts about an external world. (There is also Humean skepticism, though as I remarked in the introduction, this is harder to classify relative to the other main forms of radical skepticism. See Beebee (2011) for a useful recent overview of Humean skepticism). Although these forms of radical skepticism do feature in the contemporary debate, they do not nearly have the same profile as the broadly Cartesian form of radical skepticism that we will be concerned with in this book. I take the challenge posed by these forms of radical skepticism to be distinctive, and so deserving of a separate treatment. That said, if the anti-skeptical proposal that I set out in this work is sound, then it will at the very least make the task of dealing with the Pyrrhonian and Kantian skeptical challenges much easier (though I'm afraid the reader will have to take this on trust, as I won't be arguing for this claim here). For some representative contemporary work on Pyrrhonian skepticism, see Bett (2011) and the essays collected in Machuca (2011). For some of my own engagements with this variety of skepticism, see Pritchard (2000*b*; 2011*d*; 2013*b*). For some helpful recent works that engage with both Pyrrhonian and Cartesian forms of radical skepticism, see Fogelin (1994), Williams (2001*b*), Gascoigne (2002), and Hazlett (2013). See Forster (2010; cf. Forster 2011) for an important recent work on Kantian skepticism, but note that his discussion of what he calls "veil of perception skepticism" doesn't quite correspond to the kind of radical skepticism I have just described as Kantian. Indeed, this is a point on which this work has been critiqued—see, for example, Chignell & McLear (2010). For an influential treatment of Kantian skepticism more in keeping with my description of it, see McDowell (1994*b*). See also Conant (2004; 2012). For a general overview of the contemporary debate regarding radical skepticism, see Pritchard (2002*c*). For a recent annotated bibliography of the contemporary literature on radical skepticism, see Pritchard (2010*b*).

2. I first started referring to the problem posed by this form of radical skepticism in terms of *epistemic angst* in Pritchard (2005*b*, passim; 2005*e*; 2008*c*). Since completing this manuscript, Ernie Sosa has alerted me to the fact that in early work he used the phrase "meta-epistemic *angst*" to refer to a general epistemological outlook that he claims derives from Roderick Chisholm's writings. See Sosa (1991, 209n).

3. Note that I use the term "perceptual" here in the broad sense that it includes all sensory perception (i.e., and not just visual perception), including proprioception.

4. If you wish, add to the BIV scenario that the agent concerned has only recently become envatted. So construed, the kind of content externalist considerations put forward against BIV-based radical skepticism by Putnam (1981, chap. 1) and others are thereby neutralized. For further discussion of the relationship between content externalism and radical skeptical hypotheses, see Brueckner (2012).

5. This claim is actually logically stronger than we need, in that the following would suffice for our purposes:

($S_1 1^*$) One does not know that one is not a BIV.

The version of the radical skeptical paradox that employs the stronger formulation is, however, more perspicacious, and hence we will stick with this formulation in what follows. The skeptic, after all, is not claiming that it is a mere incidental epistemic lack on our parts that we fail to know the denials of radical skeptical hypotheses, as if we could have this knowledge if only we were smarter, were more attentive, made more inquiries, etc. The skeptical claim is rather that this is an *in principle* epistemic lack on our part. See also notes 6, 9, and 10.

6. I noted above—see note 5—that ($S_1 1$) could be replaced with a weaker claim, ($S_1 1^*$), without loss. With the weaker claim in play, however, it is also true that ($S_1 2$) could be replaced with a weaker claim without loss as well:

($S_1 2^*$) If one does not know that one is not a BIV, then one does not know E.

($S_1 2^*$), after all, would suffice to generate the required logical tension between ($S_1 1^*$) and ($S_1 3$). See also note 9.

7. This is essentially the formulation of the closure principle put forward by Williamson (2000a, 117) and Hawthorne (2005, 29). See also David & Warfield (2008).

8. As it happens, DeRose's point was in fact targeted at the previous formulation of the closure principle (i.e., where knowledge is closed under knowledge entailment), but this doesn't matter for our purposes.

9. As noted in notes 5 and 6, there is also a logically weaker version of this skeptical paradox available, which proceeds as follows:

THE RADICAL SKEPTICAL PARADOX (I^*)

($S_1 1^*$) One does not know that one is not a BIV.

($S_1 2^*$) If one does not know that one is not a BIV, then one does not know that E.

($S_1 3$) One knows that E.

10. As noted above in note 5, all we actually need to generate the paradox is that one *does not* know the denials of skeptical hypotheses (as opposed to cannot).

11. See Stroud (1984) for a seminal contemporary discussion of the problem of radical skepticism qua paradox. As he famously put the point—see Stroud (1984, 82)— radical skepticism falls out of "platitudes" that "we would all accept," but which are collectively inconsistent. Wright (1985; 1991) makes a similar point, and also expands on the dialectical implications of treating radical skepticism as a paradox rather than as a philosophical position. Consider, for example, this passage:

> [T]he best philosophical paradoxes . . . signal genuine collisions between features of our thinking that go deep. Their solution has therefore to consist

in fundamental change, in taking up conceptual options which may have been overlooked. . . . [T]he traditional sceptical arguments, in their strongest forms, are such paradoxes. (Wright 1985, 429–30)

We will be discussing the idea of radical skepticism as a paradox again in chapter 3 (§2), when we look at Wittgenstein's distinctive response to this problem. See also Pritchard (2014*c*).

12. For more on undercutting and overriding anti-skeptical strategies, see Pritchard (2012*b*, pt. 3, §6). A very similar way of thinking about these issues is offered by Cassam (2007*a*). He argues that we should recast skeptical problems in terms of "how possible?" questions, and then distinguishes different levels of response to this problem. This is basically equivalent to recasting the radical skeptical argument into a paradox, as I explain in Pritchard (2009*e*). Moreover, Cassam then goes on to distinguish (among other things) between obstacle-overcoming and obstacle-removing anti-skeptical strategies, which is roughly equivalent to our distinction between overriding and undercutting anti-skeptical strategies. For another related, and influential, discussion of the dialectical situation with regard to the radical skeptical problem, see Williams (1991, chap. 1).

13. Another way of expressing this point—due to Schiffer (1996, 330)—is that if radical skepticism poses a genuine paradox then there is no "happy face" solution to this problem, only a "sad face" solution, because it would mean that there is indeed a "deep-seated incoherence" within our pretheoretical epistemological commitments.

14. Famously, Dretske (1970) and Nozick (1981) denied a version of the closure principle—essentially, they denied, respectively, the two cruder formulations of the closure principle offered above—though their reasons for denying this principle as they formulated it do not carry over to the more nuanced formulation of the principle that is at issue here—i.e., one that essentially involves a competent deduction on the part of the subject. For some useful critical overviews of the numerous grounds that have been offered in the literature for denying various closure-style principles, see Collins (2006), Kvanvig (2006), Brueckner (2010*a*), and Luper (2010). For a recent discussion of the merits of the closure principle, see the exchange between Dretske (2005*a*; 2005*b*) and Hawthorne (2005). Note that I am setting aside here the particular difficulties that beset so-called multi-premise closure principles. See Hawthorne (2004, passim) and Collins (2006, §1) for discussion on this issue. We will be considering an anti-skeptical proposal (the *entitlement reading* of Wittgenstein's *On Certainty*) that has some broad affinities with the "nonclosure" strategy in chapter 3, §5.

15. Although nothing depends on this here, this way of understanding epistemic internalism is explicitly along *accessibilist*, as opposed to *mentalist*, lines, where mentalism is the other dominant way of characterizing epistemic internalism in the contemporary literature. For two key defenses of accessibilism, see Chisholm (1977) and BonJour (1985, chap. 2). For the core defense of mentalism, see Conee & Feldman (2004). For some useful discussions of the debate between accessibilists and mentalists, see Steup (1999), Pryor (2001, §3), BonJour (2002), Pappas (2005), and Poston (2008). Note that henceforth I will take it as given, unless otherwise specified, that rational support meets this accessibilist requirement.

16. For a key defense of process reliabilism, see Goldman (1986), though note that Goldman wouldn't endorse the crude rendering of the process reliabilist thesis that we have just offered in the main text. For a very useful recent survey of work on reliabilism, see Goldman (2008).

17. Note that in part 3 we will be questioning whether even by epistemic internalist lights it follows that one lacks a rational basis for believing (and thus knowing) that one is not a BIV.

18. I think the first usage of this label to describe this kind of anti-skeptical proposal is found in Pritchard (2002c).

19. For helpful discussion of Moore's contributions to epistemology, see Baldwin (1990, chap. 9; 1993). For some useful discussions of neo-Mooreanism, see, for example, Sosa (1999), Black (2002; 2008), and Pritchard (2002d; 2005b; 2007b). For a survey of the literature on Mooreanism and neo-Mooreanism, see Carter (2012).

20. In the contemporary literature the closure principle is often contrasted with the so-called transmission principle—see, e.g., Davies (2004) and Wright (2004c)—and one might think that the latter is effectively identical with the closure$_{RK}$ principle here formulated. There is a subtle difference, however. For whereas the closure$_{RK}$ principle merely demands that competent deductions from rationally grounded knowledge generate rationally grounded knowledge, the transmission principle demands in addition that *the very same* rational basis for knowledge of the entailing proposition should be a rational basis for the entailed claim. This is a more specific thesis. For our purposes, however, all that matters is that the subject's knowledge of the deduced proposition is no less rationally grounded, and we can bracket the issue of whether a particular rational basis has been "transmitted" across the competent deduction. It could be, for example, that the competent deduction itself transforms the rational basis for the agent's knowledge of the entailing and entailed proposition. For more on this issue, see Pritchard (2014a). See also Klein (1981; 1995), whose discussion of closure-style principles is relevant here. Note that we will be examining the style of anti-skepticism that is based around a rejection of the transmission principle in its own right in chapter 3, §5.

21. We will be further discussing the possibility of denying the closure$_{RK}$ principle on epistemic externalist grounds in chapter 3, §4. For further discussion of the relationship between epistemic externalism and closure in the context of radical skepticism, see Pritchard (2002b).

22. For further discussion of abduction more generally, including critiques of this form of reasoning, see Lipton (1991) and Douven (2011).

23. See Vogel (1990, 659) for an example of an abductivist response to the problem of radical skepticism that appeals to simplicity.

24. Indeed, if we are to weigh the simplicity of an explanation in ontological terms—i.e., in terms of how many entities it commits us to—then the skeptical hypothesis will presumably count as much simpler than the everyday scenario.

25. For example, it is often claimed that the way we typically evaluate testimony involves abductive inferences. See Adler (1994) and Lipton (1998).

26. See Lipton (1998) for a seminal account of the centrality of abduction to scientific reasoning.

27. BonJour (e.g., 1999) is the clearest articulation of such a rationalist approach to abductivism, though in offering this approach he appeals to a number of independently contentious claims. See Beebe (2009) for an excellent critical discussion of BonJour's abductivism.

28. See Vogel (1990) for an influential defense of an abductive response to the problem of radical skepticism. See also BonJour's (e.g., 1999) defense of this line of response, which is surveyed and discussed by Beebe (2009) and McCain (2012). For critical discussion of abductivism, see Fumerton (1992), Neta (2004b), and the exchange between Fumerton (2005) and Vogel (2005).

Chapter 2. Radical Skepticism and Underdetermination

1. Note that—as with, mutatis mutandis, our formulation of closure-based radical skepticism in chapter 1—($S_3$1) is in fact formulated much more strongly than we actually need, for it would suffice for the skeptic's purposes that we merely *do not* have this favoring epistemic support, rather than that we cannot have it. The stronger claim better captures what the skeptic is maintaining, however, in that the thesis in play is not merely that there is some incidental epistemic lack on our part, one that could potentially be rectified, such as by making further inquiries. The claim is rather that there is an *in principle* epistemic lack at issue. See also notes 3, 5, and 6.

2. Recall that we discussed abductive treatments of radical skepticism in chapter 1, and explicitly understood these proposals as attempting to demonstrate that one has a stronger rational basis for one's everyday beliefs over radical skeptical alternatives. In doing so we were effectively treating them as being applied primarily against a radical skeptical claim like ($S_3$1). We noted that such proposals are highly problematic, however, and at best constitute overriding anti-skeptical strategies. Accordingly, we will set this style of anti-skepticism to one side here.

3. As with our formulation of ($S_3$1)—see note 1 above—this is actually stronger than we need in order to generate the skeptical paradox. In particular, it would suffice for the antecedent that one *does not* (as opposed to cannot) have a rational basis that favors one's belief that E over the BIV hypothesis.

4. For some of the main discussions of underdetermination-style principles and their role in radical skeptical arguments, see Yalçin (1992), Brueckner (1994), Cohen (1998), Byrne (2004), Vogel (2004), and Pritchard (2005b, pt. 1; 2005f). See also Pritchard (2012d).

5. As noted in notes 1 and 3 above, there is actually a weaker formulation of this paradox available, which goes as follows:

THE RADICAL SKEPTICAL PARADOX (III*)

($S_3$1*) One does not have rational support that favors one's belief that E over the BIV hypothesis.

($S_3$2*) If one does not have rational support that favors one's belief that E over the BIV hypothesis, then one does not know that E.

($S_3$3) One knows that E.

6. As noted above—see note 1—it would actually suffice for this paradox that one merely *does not* have this favoring rational support (i.e., as opposed to cannot).

7. For some of the key defenses of attributer contextualism, see DeRose (1995), Lewis (1996), and Cohen (2000). For some useful overviews of this position, see DeRose (1999), Brady & Pritchard (2005), Black (2006), and Rysiew (2011a; 2011b). Note that this kind of attributer contextualism is very different from the superficially similar view defended by Williams (1991). See Pritchard (2002c; 2002e) for a comparative discussion of these two types of contextualism. See also Black (2006). We will be looking at Williams's proposal in its own right in chapter 4.

8. That's not quite right, of course, in that in order to "talk past" someone one (usually, anyway) has to at least be talking *with* the person, and the contrast we just drew was between a skeptical conversational context and a normal, nonskeptical conversational content—i.e., two distinct conversational contexts. Still, the general idea that the radical skeptical problem on this view trades on a misunderstanding—i.e., on something purely semantic—should be clear.

9. Note that in what follows I will talk not of conversational contexts specifically (although this is the usual terminology employed by attributer contextualists), but rather more generally of contexts of epistemic appraisal (which leaves it open whether such contexts need to be specifically conversational). Nothing hangs on this shift of terminology for our purposes (indeed, arguably it makes the attributer contextualist position more palatable). See also note 12.

10. See Heller (1999) for a nonstandard version of attributer contextualism that in addition denies the closure principle. For a critique of this proposal, see Pritchard (2000a).

11. For a very honest response to this problem from a prominent attributer contextualist, see Cohen (2000), who argues that we must regard our beliefs in the denials of radical skeptical hypotheses as having an a priori status. As even Cohen concedes, however, this is not a comfortable dialectical move for the attributer contextualist to make. See also Cohen (1999). For more on the contrast between attributer contextualism and neo-Mooreanism as regards (roughly) the present formulation of the skeptical problem, see Pritchard (2005c; 2005d).

12. Note the potential importance of our terminological shift from expressing attributer contextualism in terms of conversational contexts to formulating the view in terms of contexts of epistemic appraisal (see note 9). After all, in considering radical skeptical hypotheses one might not actually be in a particular *conversational* context at all, at least where that is understood as something involving actual conversation between two or more people. Still, I think we can charitably interpret attributer contextualism such that whatever applies to conversational contexts will carry over—somehow, the details need not concern us here—into relevantly analogous nonconversational contexts of epistemic appraisal.

13. This is the reason why attributer contextualism doesn't face the problem of "abominable conjunctions"—see DeRose (1995)—which we saw in chapter 1 (§1) afflicted views that deny the closure principle. Recall that abominable conjunctions concern the assertion of sentences that simultaneously affirm an instance of one's everyday knowledge while also denying that one has knowledge

of the denial of a skeptical hypothesis that is clearly inconsistent with that everyday knowledge. According to attributer contextualism, the key to resolving this problem is to realize that the introduction of the skeptical hypothesis in the second conjunct effectively ensures that the relevant context of epistemic appraisal is a skeptical one, where high epistemic standards are in play. So while attributer contextualists hold that there are everyday contexts of epistemic appraisal relative to which the assertion of the first conjunct expresses a truth, there is no single context of epistemic appraisal relative to which the assertion of the conjunction as a whole expresses a truth.

14. Actually, I think the idea that the "conversational air" can simply clear in this way is far from straightforward. This is the so-called problem of epistemic descent, as explained in Pritchard (2001a). I will be setting this concern to one side in what follows, however.

15. I believe the first to make this point was Schiffer (1996). Note that this is now part of a cluster of related (semantic/linguistic) objections that are made to attributer contextualism. See, for example, Stanley (2005, chap. 2) on whether "knows" is a gradable adjective like "flat" or "tall" as (some canonical versions of) attributer contextualism suggest. There is also the related issue of whether attributer contextualism correctly describes our everyday practices of asserting knowledge ascription sentences. For further criticism in this direction, see Pritchard (2001a; 2005a). For a helpful overview of the contemporary literature regarding both issues, see Rysiew (2011b, esp. §4).

16. We will return to this issue in chapter 4 when we explore inferential contextualism, and in chapter 6 when we will examine rational support contextualism.

17. One finds variants of this particular charge against the attributer contextualist response to radical skepticism in a number of places. See, for example, Feldman (1999; 2001) and Kornblith (2000).

18. For a related critique of the attributer contextualist treatment of radical skepticism, see Sosa (2011, chap. 5). Note that, for now, I have set aside the distinctive kind of attributer contextualism that is proposed by Neta (2002; 2003) and the related *contrastivist* position put forward by Schaffer (2004; 2005). Neta's view is distinctive in being a specifically *evidential* version of the view, one that allows agents to have factive evidential support for their empirical beliefs relative to everyday contexts of epistemic appraisal. Schaffer's proposal is that knowledge is to be understood as an essentially contrastive notion, with the relevant contrast determined by the context of epistemic assessment. I will be exploring these proposals in chapter 6 in the context of epistemological disjunctivism (where Neta's view will be described as *rational support contextualism*).

19. That's not quite right, of course, in that all we have actually shown is that what is in effect an *instance* of the one principle in the context of the skeptical problem entails a corresponding *instance* of the other (which, given that we are interested in these principles only in terms of their application to the skeptical problem, is really all we need for our purposes). But it ought to be clear nonetheless from the argument just given that the general point that the closure$_{RK}$ principle entails the underdetermination$_{RK}$ principle holds. Here is the argument, where p is some arbitrary proposition and q depicts a scenario known by the subject to be incompatible with p (note that I've kept the original numberings for the claim, even despite the shift in content):

(P1) *S* has rationally grounded knowledge that *p*. [Premise]

(P2) *S* has rationally grounded knowledge that not-*q*. [From (P1), Closure$_{RK}$]

(P3) *S*'s rational support favors her belief that *p* over *q*. [From (P1), (P2)]

20. Of course, in principle at least, it is possible to reject the underdetermination$_{RK}$ principle even while leaving intact a weaker restricted version of this principle, which nonetheless generates the same radical skeptical puzzle. Put more precisely, then, what is required is not merely a rejection of the underdetermination$_{RK}$ principle, but rather a rejection of this principle that specifically blocks the skeptical puzzle generated by this principle. That is, one needs to expressly argue that rationally grounded knowledge of a quotidian proposition, such as that one is presently seated at one's desk, is compatible with a lack of favoring rational support for this belief over skeptical alternatives like the BIV scenario. (The same point applies, mutatis mutandis, to responses to the closure$_{RK}$-based skeptical paradox that proceed by rejecting the closure$_{RK}$ principle.)

21. There are a number of puzzles concerning the apparent rationality of believing incompatible propositions, including known to be incompatible propositions, such as the original (Kyburg) lottery puzzle and the preface paradox. So, to take the example of the preface paradox, it seems that I can have a rational basis for believing that there are some mistakes in my book, while also having a rational basis for believing each and every proposition in that book. But note that the incompatibility in question here is not in direct conflict with the rational ground or rational ground* principles. In order to generate a direct conflict one would need to add additional claims—such as that where one has an individual rational basis for belief in a series of propositions one thereby has a collective rational basis for believing the set of propositions as a whole (this is known as the "agglomeration principle" in the literature)—but these additional claims are themselves contentious. In any case, I will be setting this broader issue to one side in what follows. The locus classicus for discussions of the lottery paradox is Kyburg (1961). For further discussion of this paradox, see Sorensen (2002; 2011, §3). The locus classicus for discussion of the preface paradox is Makinson (1965). For two helpful overviews of this paradox in a specifically epistemological context, see Sorensen (2002; 2011, §4). See also Christensen (2004) and Kaplan (2013) for two very different accounts of the ramifications the rejection of the agglomeration principle has for our understanding of the requirements of rationality. I discuss the relevance of preface-style paradoxes to a certain form of disagreement-based skepticism in Pritchard (2013*b*).

22. Strictly speaking, the negation of (P3*) is the claim that *it is not the case* that *S has* rational support for the belief that she is a BIV, rather than what we have here (viz., that *S* does *not* have rational support for the belief that she is a BIV). Although generally speaking one should be wary about importing negations into claims in this way, it ought to be clear that nothing rides on our doing so in this particular case. If readers prefer, they can suppose that there is an intermediate step between (P4*) and (P5*), whereby we move from the strictly formulated negation of (P3*) to the formulation offered in (P5*).

23. As noted above—see note 19—the foregoing doesn't strictly speaking demonstrate that these two principles are logically equivalent, in that all that has actually been shown is that an instance, in the context of the skeptical problem, of the one principle is logically equivalent to a corresponding instance of the other principle. It is, however, really only the equivalence between the two principles in the skeptical context that matters to us. Moreover, and again as before, the general claim nonetheless holds (in this case the logical equivalence), and holds on the same grounds. So, for the purists, here is the entailment from the underdetermination$_{RK}$ principle to the rational ground* principle, where (as before) p is some arbitrary proposition and q depicts a scenario known by the subject to be incompatible with p (and again, as before, note that I've kept the original numberings for the claim, even despite the shift in content):

(P1*) S has rationally grounded knowledge that p. [Premise]

(P2*) S's rational support favors her belief that p over the alternative that q. [From (P1*), Underdetermination$_{RK}$]

(P3*) S has rational support for believing that q. [Assumption for *Reductio*]

(P4*) S's rational support does not favor her belief that p over the alternative that q. [From (P3*)]

(P5*) S does not have rational support for believing that q. [From (P2*), (P3*), (P4*), RAA]

And here is the entailment from the rational ground* principle to the underdetermination$_{RK}$ principle:

(P1**) S has rationally grounded knowledge that p. [Premise]

(P2**) S does not have rational support for believing that q. [From (P1**), Rational Ground*]

(P3**) S has rational support for her belief that p. [From (P1**)]

(P4**) S's rational support favors her belief that p over the alternative that q. [From (P2**), (P3**)]

24. Indeed, one can think of the insularity of reasons thesis as the epistemic aspect of the more general idea of the "veil of perception," an idea that also has a metaphysical component, concerning the very nature of our perceptual experiences. Like the metaphysical aspect of this problem, which maintains that our perceptual experiences fall short of direct contact with an external world, the insularity of reasons thesis highlights a sense in which the rational standing of our perceptual beliefs regarding the external world also falls short, in that even in the best case it is compatible with widespread falsity in one's beliefs about the nature of that world and one's relationship to it.

25. The loci classici in this regard are Lehrer & Cohen (1983) and Cohen (1984). For a helpful general discussion of the new evil demon intuition and its epistemological significance, see Littlejohn (2009). See also Bach (1985) and Engel (1992).

Chapter 3. Wittgenstein on the Structure of Rational Evaluation

1. The foregoing gloss on Moore's general line with the skeptic, while broadly accurate, nonetheless misses out a number of subtleties regarding Moore's position, particularly with regard to his "Proof of an External World" (Moore 1939). For a more detailed discussion of Moore's contributions to epistemology, see Baldwin (1990, chap. 9). For a recent survey of contemporary work on Moore's proof, see Carter (2012).

2. Indeed, as we will see, Wittgenstein would similarly claim that the game of *believing* presupposes certainty too.

3. There are obvious affinities here with the anti-skeptical use of the principle of charity made by Davidson (e.g., 1977; 1983). I will be commenting on these affinities in chapter 4, §5.

4. Although the "hinge" metaphor is the dominant symbolism in the book, it is accompanied by various other metaphors, such as the following: that these propositions constitute the "scaffolding" of our thoughts (OC, §211); that they form the "foundations of our language-games" (OC, §§401–3); and also that they represent the implicit "world-picture" from within which we inquire, the "inherited background against which [*we*] distinguish between true and false" (OC, §§94–95). Henceforth, I will follow most commentators of *On Certainty* in making use of the hinge metaphor. As will become apparent in due course, however, this metaphor may not be the most apt, in that it implies that we can change our hinge commitments at will (just as we might change the hinges on a door). At least on my reading of Wittgenstein, in contrast, there is nothing remotely optional about our hinge commitments.

5. There is, of course, far more to be said about Austin's treatment of skepticism, though this is not the place to undertake such an exploration. For some helpful recent discussions of Austin's epistemology, see the exchange between Travis (2005*a*) and Millar (2005), and also Travis (2008), Kaplan (2011*a*; 2011*b*), and Lawlor (2013). See also Longworth (2012, §3).

6. I further discuss this aspect of Wittgenstein's thinking, in the context of the very different treatments of radical skepticism offered by Austin (1961) and Stroud (1984), in Pritchard (2011*f*, §1; 2014*c*). I return to this contrast between Wittgenstein's approach to radical skepticism and that associated with ordinary language philosophy below—see chapter 6—as part of a critique of rational support contextualism and attributer contextualism.

7. This is sometimes known as "Russell's Hypothesis"—see Russell (1921, 159).

8. A further worry about the Wittgensteinian account of the structure of rational evaluation is that it might license epistemic relativism. For on this view can't there be distinct epistemic systems that incorporate different hinge commitments and thus generate opposing rational beliefs? But if that is possible, then how is a disagreement among two parties who adhere to these respective epistemic systems to be rationally resolved? We will be exploring this issue in its own right in the next chapter (§3) in the context of the inferential contextualist view that is advocated by Williams (1991) and that is inspired by Wittgenstein's remarks on hinge propositions in *On Certainty*. For an important recent discussion of the relationship between Wittgenstein's stance on hinge commitments and epistemic

relativism, see Williams (2007), to which Pritchard (2010c; cf. Pritchard 2009b) is effectively a response. See also Kusch (2010) and the significant new treatment of this issue offered by Coliva (2010, passim).

9. Just to be clear: in calling this view, and other subsequent views, a "reading" I am not suggesting that it is being explicitly put forward as an interpretation of Wittgenstein's *On Certainty*. Often, as in this case, such "readings" are merely *inspired* by the text.

10. For further discussion of the epistemic externalist development of Wittgenstein's account of the structure of rational evaluation, see Pritchard (2001b; 2005g; 2011f; forthcoming–d). For an influential contextualist variant of the externalist reading, see Williams (e.g., 1991). I discuss Williams's view further below—see especially chapter 4, §3 and §7.

11. Note that DeRose's own "abominable conjunctions" were specifically targeted at putative counterexamples to the closure principle for knowledge rather than the closure principle for rationally supported knowledge (i.e., the closure$_{RK}$ principle).

12. For a key defense of process reliabilism, see Goldman (1986). For a very useful recent survey of work on reliabilism, see Goldman (2008).

13. For a prominent defense of virtue epistemology explicitly cast along epistemic externalist lines, see Greco (1999; 2000; 2003; 2007). See also Sosa (1991; 1998; 2007; 2009; 2011) for a defense of an influential version of virtue epistemology that is broadly speaking in the epistemic externalist camp. See Axtell (1997) for a helpful critical overview of epistemic externalist and epistemic internalist versions of virtue epistemology. For more on (basis-relative) modal conditions on knowledge, see Nozick's (1981) defense of a sensitivity condition, and Sosa's (e.g., 1999) defense of a safety condition. I explore the prospects of such modal conditions on knowledge—including specifically safety-based theories of knowledge—in a number of places. See Pritchard (2002d; 2005b, passim; 2007a; 2008d; 2009c, passim; 2009d; 2012c; 2013c; forthcoming–a).

14. The foremost exponent of this kind of proposal is Wright. See, especially, Wright (2004c; cf. Davies 2004). See also Wright (1985; 1991; 2000; 2002; 2003a; 2003b; 2004a; 2004b; 2007; 2008a; 2008b). For some helpful discussions of Wright's proposal, see Davies (2004), Coliva (2012), Pryor (2012), Williams (2012), and Zalabardo (2012). Note that this notion of epistemic entitlement is very different from that defended by Burge (1993; 2003) and Peacocke (2003). See Altschul (2011) for a useful survey of these three different conceptions of epistemic entitlement.

15. The entitlement strategy is often formulated in terms of the rejection of the "transmission" principle for knowledge rather than in terms of the rejection of what we are terming the closure$_{RK}$ principle. As noted in chapter 1—see note 20—the two principles are subtly different, with the closure$_{RK}$ principle being if anything the (marginally) logically weaker principle of the two. Given their similarity, and the fact that of the two the closure$_{RK}$ principle is the logically weaker if either is, for our purposes nothing of consequence is lost by focusing on the closure$_{RK}$ principle.

16. In earlier work—see, for example, Pritchard (2005g)—I pressed such a claim myself. See also Jenkins (2007) and Pedersen (2009).

17. Even Williamson (2000a), who holds that knowledge cannot be analyzed in terms of belief plus some other conditions (such as truth and an epistemic condition like justification), nonetheless holds that knowledge entails belief. See Williamson (2000a, §1.5). For a useful taxonomy of different ways of thinking about belief, see Stevenson (2002).

18. In this regard, consider Radford's (1966) famous example of the diffident schoolboy who knows the answer to the question he is asked, but who, it is claimed, doesn't believe it because he doesn't think he knows it. Even if we grant that there is knowledge in the absence of belief here (which is of course contentious), it remains that the schoolboy is not at all agnostic about the truth of the target proposition—of all the options available, it is explicit to the example that he is inclined toward regarding a very specific answer as being the correct one. The point of the case is not that the schoolboy is agnostic about whether the answer he gives is correct (since that would undermine the claim that the schoolboy has knowledge), but rather that he doesn't have the kind of confidence in this regard that we would usually associate with having knowledge.

19. See in particular Wright (2004c, 194) for his discussion of "rational trust" in this regard. (The "rational" element in "rational trust" will be explored in more detail below.) See also Wright (2008b).

20. The avowedly transcendental response to radical skepticism offered by Sosa (2011, chap. 8) has some commonalities with Wright's entitlement proposal, particularly to the extent that one is meant to be able to derive a rational basis for rejecting skeptical hypotheses from the fact that endorsing them would lead to incoherence. As such, it suffers from many of the problems that we have seen beset Wright's account, as I explain in Pritchard (forthcoming–b). For a more sympathetic treatment of Sosa's proposal, see Neta (forthcoming).

21. In the contemporary literature, the entitlement reading is often contrasted with a proposal known as *dogmatism*. See, for example, Pryor (2000; 2004; 2012). See also Wright (2007) for a response to dogmatism on behalf of the main proponent of the entitlement reading, and Williams (2013) for a helpful critical appraisal of both Wright's view and the alternative dogmatist proposal. Since dogmatism is not offered as a view that is inspired by Wittgenstein's *On Certainty*, I have not explored it here. I will, however, be discussing dogmatism in part 3—see chapter 6, §3—where I will be critically contrasting it with an epistemological disjunctivist account of perceptual knowledge.

22. This type of proposal has been recently expounded in some detail in Moyal-Sharrock (2004). See also the highly influential earlier work by McGinn (1989; cf. McGinn 2008; 2011) which takes a similar line. See also Wright (1985), Stroll (1994; 2005) and Phillips (2005). For a very useful critical discussion of the nonpropositional reading, see Coliva (2010).

23. As a number of commentators have noted (e.g., Williams 2004d), we need to carefully distinguish between Wittgenstein's remarks in the first notebook that makes up *On Certainty* (i.e., up to §65), and the rest of the text. This is because the first notebook seems more concerned with Moore (1925) than with the later Moore (1939). This is significant for our purposes because the first Moore text is effectively dealing with idealism, and thus with the assertion of claims which purport to refute this philosophical thesis, while it is the latter text which

is focused on the kind of everyday certainties which we now think as distinctively "Moorean." Wittgenstein's line in the first notebook regarding Moore's rejection of idealism is very clearly that Moore's assertions in this respect are nonsense. In particular, the claim is not that Moore has taken ordinary empirical expressions which have a legitimate use in normal contexts and employed them out of context, but rather that he is putting normal terms to an entirely illegitimate theoretical use. Here is Wittgenstein:

> "A is a physical object" is a piece of instruction which we give only to someone who doesn't yet understand what "A" means, or what "physical object" means. Thus it is instruction about the use of words, and "physical object" is a logical concept. (Like colour, quantity, . . .) And that is why no such proposition as: "There are physical objects" can be formulated.
>
> Yet we encounter such unsuccessful shots at every turn. (OC, §36; cf. §§35 & 37)

In saying that physical objects exist, as if this were a normal empirical claim, Moore is thus simply making a meaningless assertion. Moreover, notice that in contrast with an assertion like "I have two hands," Wittgenstein's contention is that there is *no* conversational context where this assertion expresses an ordinary empirical proposition. Given these clear differences between the target of the first notebook of *On Certainty* and the later notebooks, I think we would do well to bracket the "nonpropositionalism" of the first notebook. In particular, one might agree with Wittgenstein that a statement like "There are physical objects" is meaningless and yet nonetheless be willing to argue that a statement like "I have two hands," even when asserted in a Moorean fashion to make an anti-skeptical point, is nonetheless meaningful.

24. Though see Coliva (2010) for an insightful critique of the nonpropositional reading of *On Certainty*. See also my remarks in note 23 above.

25. Of course, there is also the further issue of how best to understand the nonsense that results on this view when one attempts to express one's hinge commitment in the form of an assertion. Is it, for example, just plain nonsense, or is it somehow philosophically significant nonsense (if such a thing is possible)? For more on this issue, see the exchange between Conant (1998) and McGinn (2002).

26. For a development of a radically context-sensitive account of meaning which is in large part inspired by Wittgenstein's work, see Travis (1989; 2001; 2006). See also Travis (2008), where the influence of Austin's work is more in the foreground. For discussion of the anti-skeptical merits of this way of thinking about meaning, see Putnam (2001; 2012) and the exchange between Travis (2005a) and Millar (2005). See also Williams (2004a).

Chapter 4. Hinge Commitments

1. See note 8 for a qualification of the claim that our hinge commitments are in their nature unresponsive to rational considerations. Also, remember that we are treating the notion of belief in play, unless qualified, as knowledge-apt belief (i.e., the specific notion of belief which is a constituent part of knowledge).

2. Of course, exactly how one should understand the claim that beliefs are in their nature responsive to rational considerations is controversial—what it means, to use the parlance in the literature, for the *telos* of belief to be truth—but we do not need to get into that issue here. For our purposes we only need to note that a propositional attitude which is completely unresponsive to rational considerations, and which cannot be the result of a rational process, would not qualify as a belief—at least insofar as we are interested in the notion of belief that is component part of knowledge—and that claim is surely uncontroversial. For some of the key works on the debate about the relationship between truth and belief see Wedgwood (2002), Shah (2003), and Shah & Velleman (2005). See also Pritchard (2011c; 2014d) and the essays collected in Matheson & Vitz (2014).

3. This particular line of response was put to me by Crispin Wright.

4. Note that the fourfold taxonomy of readings of *On Certainty* offered in this chapter and the last is not meant to be exhaustive, but merely representative of some of the main lines of thought in this regard. For example, there is also the so-called *therapeutic reading* of *On Certainty* which is offered by Conant (1998), whereby the radical skeptic's assertions are strictly senseless. Although this has some affinities with the nonpropositional reading which we discussed in the last chapter, many have distinguished these two proposals (e.g., Coliva 2010). For an intriguing feminist interpretation of Wittgenstein's work as whole, including *On Certainty*—which is perhaps best described more broadly as an *anti-modernist* reading—see Tanesini (2004). For an excellent recent discussion of the various interpretations of *On Certainty* in the contemporary literature, see Coliva (2010). See also Brenner & Moyal-Sharrock (2005) and Pritchard (2011f; forthcoming-a). Note that the "inferential contextualist" reading of *On Certainty* offered by Williams (1991) will be discussed below in §3 and §7, and the "naturalistic" reading of *On Certainty* offered by Strawson (1985) will be discussed in §4.

5. I say "radically *and* fundamentally" here to stress both the *extent* and the *depth* of the error involved. Note that there are technical issues in play here regarding how best to "weigh" the overall truth of one's beliefs. In particular, one cannot simply do so by counting the number of true beliefs that one has (insofar as one can make any sense of the idea counting beliefs in the first place), although it is often implicitly supposed by contemporary epistemologists that this is possible. For discussion of this point, which bears on the so-called trivial truths problem in epistemology, see Treanor (2014). See also Pritchard (2014d). For further discussion about how one is to "weigh" truth in one's beliefs given that one cannot do it in purely numerical terms, see Treanor (2013). For two different perspectives, see Sider (2011) and Hazlett (2014).

6. This is a point that Wittgenstein emphasizes on a number of occasions. Consider, for example, this passage:

> If my friend were to imagine one day that he had been living for a long time past in such and such a place, etc. etc., I should not call this a mistake, but rather a mental disturbance, perhaps a transient one.
>
> Not every false belief of this sort is a mistake. (OC, §§71–72; cf. OC, §§54; 155–58)

7. In particular, we should be wary about construing our hinge commitments in such a way that they license epistemic relativism. I will be returning to this issue in the next section when we will be exploring the inferential contextualist view that is advocated by Williams (1991) and that draws its inspiration from Wittgenstein's remarks on hinge propositions in *On Certainty*.

8. This is the extent to which one's hinge commitments can be indirectly responsive to rational considerations. Rational considerations can lead one to change one's beliefs, after all, and as one's beliefs change so the personal hinge commitments that codify one's (unchanging) über hinge commitment might alter. The point remains, however, that even one's personal hinge commitments are not directly responsive to rational considerations in the way that one's beliefs are.

9. Interestingly, notice that by the lights of the nonbelief reading, we can in fact capture a version of the universality of rational evaluation thesis that is harmless. For while we are rejecting the idea of universal rational evaluations—where this covers *all* the propositions we are committed to (i.e., that we regard as true)—we have also noticed that a significant body of our commitments are not to be thought of as (knowledge-apt) beliefs. Thus, insofar as we think of the universality of rational evaluation thesis as only applying to beliefs, then it can be endorsed, even by Wittgensteinian lights. Such a formulation of the universality of rational evaluation thesis would be entirely harmless from a skeptical point of view, however, in that one could not use it to motivate, via the closure$_{RK}$ principle, the relevant bridging claim in the closure-based skeptical argument (because this bridging claim by its nature involves the rational evaluation of a hinge commitment). See also note 14 below.

10. Or, at least, whatever restrictions there are won't be epistemic ones. There might be psychological restrictions on inferences of this kind, for example, in that at some point one is unable even to form the relevant beliefs since their contents have become too complex.

11. Stroud (1984) defends a simple version of the closure$_{RK}$ principle*, which he attributes to Descartes. The advantage of this principle over closure-style principles that don't entail iterativity for rationally grounded knowledge is that it can be used to generate radical skepticism that is based both on those radical skeptical scenarios that trade on massive error (such as the ones we are focusing on here, like the BIV scenario) and those radical skeptical scenarios that don't trade on massive error (such as dreaming-based radical skepticism). For critical discussion of this type of closure principle in the context of Stroud's proposal, see Wright (1991; cf. Pritchard 2001*c*). For further discussion of Stroud's approach to radical skepticism in general, see Pritchard & Ranalli (forthcoming–*a*). For an influential recent treatment of dreaming-based radical skepticism, see Sosa (2007, chap. 1). For more on iterativity for knowledge, see Kelp & Pedersen (2011).

12. For further critical discussion of multi-premise closure-style principles, and their relation to their single-premise counterparts, see Hawthorne (2004, passim) and Collins (2006, §1). See also Pritchard (2013*b*) for a critical discussion of the status of multi-premise closure in the context of just the sort of "track-record"-style argument that is being envisaged here.

13. One might be tempted to classify our hinge commitments as *aliefs*. This is a kind of belief-like propositional attitude that has been most prominently

defended by Gendler (2008a; 2008b). Very roughly, aliefs are spontaneous judgments that are (at least typically) in tension with what one actually believes. For example, at high altitude and looking down, and overcome with acrophobia, one might instinctively judge that one is in danger, even while being perfectly aware that one is entirely safe. The instinctive judgment that one is in danger is in this case an alief, whereas the judgment that one is safe is a belief. Given that our hinge commitments are entirely visceral, there is certainly a prima facie case for regarding them as aliefs. Ultimately, however, I think that it is probably best to not treat them as aliefs. For one thing, as just noted, aliefs are typically understood as being in tension with our beliefs, but of course our hinge commitments by definition cannot be in tension with what we believe. Moreover, and I think more importantly, there is nothing in the notion of an alief that means that it is in its nature unresponsive to rational considerations (though in practice they often are, as the acrophobia case just give illustrates). In contrast, this is a defining feature of our hinge commitments. For some useful critical studies of alief, see Nagel (2012) and Mandelbaum (2013). For a helpful overview of different ways of thinking about beliefs, see Stevenson (2002). See also chapter 7, note 9.

14. An alternative way of putting this point—as suggested in note 9 above—is that the universality of rational evaluation thesis is ambiguous in a crucial respect. Construed as a claim about the rational evaluation of one's beliefs, specifically, it is not in conflict with Wittgenstein's account of the structure of rational evaluation, but neither can it be used to generate the radical skeptical paradox. In order for it to have this import to the skeptical problem, it needs to be construed as a more general thesis about our commitments (i.e., not just our beliefs, but also our hinge commitments). But so construed the thesis is in conflict with the Wittgensteinian account of the structure of rational evaluation.

15. I have developed the nonbelief reading of Wittgenstein's *On Certainty* in a number of works. See especially Pritchard (2012e; 2014a; forthcoming–d). For an application of this proposal to the epistemology of religious belief, see Pritchard (2011e; forthcoming–c). See also Coliva (2010) for the development of a similar reading of *On Certainty* that retains many of the main features of the nonpropositional reading while nonetheless allowing that our hinge commitments can be cast along propositional lines. Since developing the nonbelief reading, I have come across remarks in Campbell (2001, 96) which might suggest a similar approach to our hinge commitments. In particular, in setting forth a particular account of delusions, he discusses these commitments and notes that they are "not normal factual beliefs," which comes very close to making the point that I want to make that they are not to be thought of in terms of knowledge-apt belief.

16. See especially Williams (1991). See also Williams (1988a; 1993; 2001b), and his earlier monograph, Williams (1977). For a useful symposium on Williams (1991), see the exchange among Rorty (1997), Vogel (1997), and Williams (1997). See also the discussion of this exchange offered by Pritchard & Ranalli (2013). I discuss Williams's treatment of radical skepticism in a number of places—see, for example, Pritchard (2002e; 2005d; 2010c; 2011f).

17. I first described Williams's view as inferential contextualism in Pritchard (2002e). It is interesting question how attributer contextualism and inferential contextualism relate to one another. One overarching difference between the

two views is that whereas the former is primarily a semantic thesis, the latter is an epistemological thesis (at least insofar as this characterization includes the metaphysics of epistemology). So even if, for example, inferential contextualism turned out to entail a form of attributer contextualism, as is plausible, it would still be a mistake to conclude that the former is just a variant of the latter. I comment on a further difference between the two views in the main text below. For additional discussion of these two forms of contextualism, see Williams (2001a; 2004b; 2004c). See also Pritchard (2002c; 2002e).

18. For a different characterization of Williams's conception of epistemic priority, see Ribeiro (2002).

19. A good point of comparison in this regard—a comparison that Williams himself draws—is the contextualist account of justification offered by Annis (1978).

20. Or, at the very least, Williams regards closure-based radical skepticism as simply being a variant of underdetermination-based radical skepticism rather than logically distinct, where the latter connects most directly with the "veil of perception," and thus with issues concerning epistemic priority that are Williams's focus. See, for example, Williams (1991, chap. 8) where he discusses the former form of radical skepticism in some detail. See also Williams (2010, 196).

21. This won't come as a surprise to Williams, for he is quite explicit that his notion of a methodological necessity, while inspired by Wittgenstein's remarks on hinge commitments in *On Certainty*, is not meant to be an interpretation of this notion. See Williams (1991, chap. 1).

22. Similar points apply to other putative methodological necessities of historical inquiry (or, for that matter, any other specific inquiry). Consider, for example, Williams's claim that one such methodological necessity of this kind of inquiry concerns the general veracity of historical documentation. Notice that if there were a systematic deception in play with regard to all "official" testimony regarding the past, then that would almost certainly be in conflict with one's über hinge commitment. A commitment to the absence of such a systematic deception is thus a plausible manifestation of one's general über hinge commitment. It follows that one will tend to regard historical documentation as generally veracious. By casting the commitment in question as being specifically concerned with *historical* documentation, Williams makes it look as if this is a commitment that is peculiar to a particular context of inquiry. But closer inspection of the kind of commitment in play reveals that it is no such thing, but rather just the manifestation of the more general über hinge commitment.

23. We will return to the issue of a hierarchy of contexts as it applies to attributer contextualism in chapter 6, where we will be examining a related view called rational support contextualism.

24. That his conception of the structure of rational evaluation might lead to epistemic relativism of this kind is certainly a problem that Wittgenstein grapples with in *On Certainty*. Consider, for example, this famous passage:

Where two principles really do meet which cannot be reconciled with one another, then each man declares the other a fool and a heretic.

I said I would "combat," the other man,—but wouldn't I give him *reasons*? Certainly; but how far do they go? At the end of reasons comes *persuasion*. (Think of what happens when missionaries convert natives.) (OC, §§611–12)

I explore Wittgenstein's treatment of epistemic relativism in more detail in Pritchard (2010c). Note that there are interesting issues here regarding Wittgenstein's broader approach to the epistemology of religious belief—not just in *On Certainty*, but also as it figures in his other work, such as Wittgenstein (1966)—and how this interrelates both with his views about hinge commitments in *On Certainty* and with topics such as epistemic relativism. See Nielsen (1967) and Phillips (1976) for two influential accounts of Wittgenstein's putatively fideistic approach to the epistemology of religious belief. I offer my own particular *quasi-fideistic* reading of Wittgenstein in this regard in Pritchard (2011e). See also Pritchard (forthcoming–c; cf. Pritchard 2000c), where I examine the relevance of Wittgenstein's views in this regard in the context of the religious epistemology proposed by John Henry Newman (1979), an epistemology that was arguably a key influence on Wittgenstein's thinking in *On Certainty*. See also Kienzler (2006), which offers a fascinating discussion of the influence of Newman on Wittgenstein, and Plant (2011), which offers a naturalistic reading of Wittgenstein's epistemology of religious belief that he claims enables Wittgenstein to avoid charges of epistemic relativism.

25. Oddly, later on in the very same page cited here Williams seems to assert the very *opposite* of this claim and deny that there can be epistemic incommensurability. I discuss Williams's ambivalent approach to these issues, including the logical tension between these two passages, at length in Pritchard (2010c). See also note 26.

26. It should be noted that Williams's views on how inferential contextualism and epistemic relativism interrelate are complex. He has argued at length that the former is in fact the "antidote" to the latter (see Williams 2007), and yet as we have noted he also seems to endorse epistemic incommensurability, which is the very kind of thing that generates epistemic relativism. I explore Williams's account of how inferential contextualism relates to epistemic relativism in detail in Pritchard (2010c). See also note 25.

27. Note that we will be returning to further consider Williams's inferential contextualism below (§7), when we will be examining how it fares with regard to underdetermination$_{RK}$-based radical skepticism.

28. As Byrne (2004, 302) quips, the idea that radical skeptical doubts are idle in this sense, and hence can be ignored, "is a curious view for an erstwhile Waynflete Professor of Metaphysics, to say the least." For more on Strawson's response to radical skepticism, see the exchanges between Putnam (1998) and Strawson (1998a) and between Sosa (1998) and Strawson (1998b). One interesting exegetical question when it comes to Strawson's later naturalistic response to radical skepticism is how it relates to his earlier treatment of this problem in Strawson (1959). For further discussion of this question, see Callanan (2011). See also Stern (2003) and Cassam (2008).

29. We should note an affinity between the anti-skeptical stance offered by Strawson and the entitlement reading of *On Certainty* that we explored earlier. In particular, we noted that the most prominent exponent of the entitlement reading

explicitly advances this view as a response to a genuine problem posed by the radical skeptic. Here is the relevant passage from Wright again, arguing that the entitlement strategy (as we have described it)

> concedes that the best sceptical arguments have something to teach us—that the limits of justification they bring out are genuine and essential—but then replies that, just for that reason, cognitive achievement must be reckoned to take place *within such limits*. The attempt to surpass them would result not in an increase in rigour or solidity but merely in cognitive paralysis. (Wright 2004c, 191)

Like Strawson's naturalistic reading of *On Certainty*, the entitlement strategy concedes that the skeptical paradox is a bona fide paradox, but argues on independent theoretical grounds that there is a revisionary way of approaching matters that resolves the puzzle. In this sense, Strawson's naturalistic interpretation of *On Certainty* is perhaps better grouped with the entitlement reading than the nonbelief reading.

30. For the twists and turns, see Pritchard (2013a). See also note 31.

31. Davidson's initial inclination was to couch this anti-skeptical proposal in terms of an appeal to an "omniscient interpreter" (see Davidson 1977; 1983), but in light of various critiques of this way of expressing the argument, he retreated to the broadly transcendental version of his anti-skepticism that we will be exploring here. See especially Davidson (1999), which is a response to Stroud (1999). For some of the main critiques of the omniscient interpreter argument, see, for example, Vermazen (1983), Foley & Fumerton (1985), Brueckner (1986; 1991), Rorty (1986), Williams (1988b), and Ludwig (1992). For more on Davidson's approach to radical skepticism more generally, see Pritchard (2013a) and Pritchard & Ranalli (2013).

32. Indeed, as noted above—see notes 9 and 14—there is a plausible rendering of the universality of rational evaluation thesis that is compatible with the Wittgensteinian account of the structure of rational evaluation, at least on the nonbelief reading, so there is a sense in which the proponent of this view can retain a commitment to this thesis.

33. Or, at the very least, he regards closure-based radical skepticism as simply being a variant of underdetermination-based radical skepticism, rather than a logically distinct radical skeptical paradox. See note 20.

Chapter 5. Epistemological Disjunctivism and the Factivity of Reasons

1. Note that epistemological disjunctivism should be kept apart from the more familiar form of disjunctivist view in the philosophy of perception, which is best classed as a *metaphysical* rather than epistemological thesis. It would take us too far afield to discuss metaphysical disjunctivism here, much less the logical relationship between this form of disjunctivism and its epistemological relative. I discuss these questions at some length in Pritchard (2012b, pt. 1), where I argue that epistemological disjunctivism doesn't entail metaphysical disjunctivism. See also Pritchard (2008b) and Pritchard & Ranalli (forthcoming–b). This nonentailment claim has also been defended (at least in its most general

form) by Snowdon (2005), Millar (2007; 2008b), Byrne & Logue (2008), and McDowell (2008, 382n). In particular, the claim in this regard is often that epistemological disjunctivism is compatible with a causal theory of perceptual experience, as defended, for example, by Grice (1961) and Strawson (1974). For further discussion of the logical connections between metaphysical and epistemological disjunctivism, see Haddock & Macpherson (2008b), Byrne & Logue (2009b), Fish (2009), and Soteriou (2009, esp. §2.4). See also Brogaard (2010) and Dorsch (2011). For some of the key defenses of metaphysical disjunctivism, see Hinton (1967a; 1967b; 1973), Snowdon (1980–81; 1990–91), and Martin (1997; 1998; 2002; 2004; 2006). See also the essays collected in Haddock & Macpherson (2008a) and Byrne & Logue (2009a). For an important recent exchange on metaphysical disjunctivism, see Hawthorne & Kovakovich (2006) and Sturgeon (2006).

2. Indeed, I know from personal correspondence that there are some features of epistemological disjunctivism, as I describe the view, that McDowell would not endorse. I discuss how epistemological disjunctivism is rooted in McDowell's work in Pritchard (2012b, passim). See also Pritchard (2003; 2007b; 2008b; 2009e) and Neta & Pritchard (2007).

3. For a key defense of such an "accessibilist" conception of rational support, see Chisholm (1977). See also BonJour (1985, chap. 2) and also chapter 1, note 15. For further discussion of the epistemic externalism/internalism distinction in light of epistemological disjunctivism, see Neta & Pritchard (2007) and Pritchard (2007b; 2008b; 2009e; 2011b; 2012b, passim).

4. For further discussion of "good" and "bad" cases, including a taxonomy of cases of these kinds, see Pritchard (2011a; 2012b, pt. 1).

5. Or, at least, that what differences there are in the degree of reflectively accessible rational support available to the two subjects, they are *indistinguishable* differences.

6. A distinctive element of metaphysical disjunctivism—see note 1—is the idea that there is no common metaphysical component to one's perceptual experience across pairs of good and bad cases (at least bar the trivial epistemological point that such experiences are ex hypothesi indistinguishable). It thus follows that the nature of one's perceptual experience is fundamentally very different depending on whether one is in the good case or the bad case—hence, the *disjunctivism*. Similarly, epistemological disjunctivism maintains that the rational support for one's belief is fundamentally very different (i.e., with no common component) depending on whether one is in the good case or the bad case, contra the new evil demon intuition.

7. See especially Pritchard (2012b, passim).

8. For some key defenses of this standard view about the relationship between seeing that p and knowing that p, see Dretske (1969, 78–139), Williamson (2000a, chap. 1), and Cassam (2007a; 2007b).

9. See Pritchard (2011a; 2012b, pt. 1) for a fuller version of this line of argument. Incidentally, McDowell (2002b, 277–79) appears to agree that seeing that p isn't a form of knowing that p, and for similar reasons. See also Turri (2010) for a defense of a related view, to which French (2012) responds, and Sosa (2011, chap. 4). For further critical discussion of the putative entailment from seeing that

p to knowing that p, see Ranalli (2014). For a recent critique of my response to the basis problem, see Littlejohn (2013).

10. See McKinsey (1991). For a recent set of discussions of this tension between first-person authority and content externalism, see Nuccetelli (2003). See also Pritchard (2002*a*).

11. For a more developed account of the access problem and why it is illusory, see Pritchard (2012*b*, pt. 1). See also Neta & Pritchard (2007).

12. "Undeniable" might be too strong, as a certain kind of radical metaphysical disjunctivism might well be willing to deny this claim. But recall that we are here considering only epistemological disjunctivism, and setting the status of metaphysical disjunctivism to one side (see note 1). More generally, we are aiming to defend, as best we can, an anti-skeptical proposal that does not appeal to any further contentious theses from outwith epistemology.

13. The zebra/cleverly disguised mule example is, of course, due to Dretske (1970).

14. I offer a more developed account of the distinction between favoring and discriminating epistemic support in Pritchard (2010*d*). See also Carter & Pritchard (forthcoming). For further discussion of how this distinction helps epistemological disjunctivism to avoid the distinguishability problem, see Pritchard (2012*b*, pt. 2).

15. Note that for ease of expression I have renamed the three claims that make up this skeptical paradox, compared with the formulation that was offered in chapter 2. Nothing of any consequence hangs on these changes.

16. McDowell motivates the idea that epistemological disjunctivism (our terminology rather than his) is rooted in our folk epistemic concepts by showing how the philosophical reasoning that rejects this proposal trades on a style of argument—the "highest common factor" argument—that he argues is dubious. See, especially, McDowell (1995; cf. McDowell 2002*a*). I sympathetically discuss McDowell's treatment of this point in Pritchard (2012*b*, pt. 1).

17. That we can appeal to this distinction to deal with local skeptical scenarios is important to our understanding of the skeptical problem though, since with this distinction in place the case for some varieties of anti-skepticism is severely undermined. For more on this point, see Pritchard (2010*d*).

18. For more on this point, see the taxonomy of "good" and "bad" cases, and the different ways in which they bear on the subject's rational position, as set out in Pritchard (2012*b*, pt. 1). See also Pritchard (2011*a*).

19. I think this point also explains why epistemological disjunctivism doesn't face a version of the so-called *paradox of dogmatism*. Roughly, this paradox concerns the fact that if one has sufficient rational support to know that p, then why isn't one in a position to thereby conclude that any evidence that not-p is misleading, and hence adopt a completely dogmatic stance with regard to p? One might think that epistemological disjunctivism faces an acute version of this problem, in that it allows that the rational support for one's knowledge can be factive. It seems to follow that the epistemological disjunctivist cannot appeal to the idea that one's rational support for p, while sufficient for knowledge that p, is nonetheless defeasible, which is a standard response to this puzzle. Once we spell out what is involved in being presented with evidence that not-p, however,

this puzzle, as it specifically applies to epistemological disjunctivism anyway, disappears. On the one hand, if this just means the mere presentation of a not-p possibility, then there is nothing inherently suspect about the idea that our agent can continue to cite the factive rational support she has for the target proposition, and hence regard this error possibility as excluded. Effectively, she is treating this particular evidence for not-p as misleading (though "evidence" is not quite the right word, given that the error possibility isn't rationally motivated). On the other hand, where the error possibility is rationally motivated, then our agent cannot simply continue to cite the factive rational support that she offered in support of her belief previously and must instead rationally engage with this error possibility. But in this scenario it's also the case that she is no longer in possession of factive rational support, since the presence of a rationally motivated error possibility entails that the epistemic conditions are no longer paradigmatic. Either way, the possibility of factive rational support doesn't generate the advertised dogmatic conclusion. For more on the paradox of dogmatism, see Harman (1973) and Kripke (2011). See also Sorensen (1988; 2011, §6.2).

20. For further discussion of some of the conversational constraints on appropriate knowledge claims that are relevant here, see Pritchard (2012b, pt. 3).

21. The mere presentation of a radical skeptical hypothesis thus doesn't suffice to turn one's epistemic situation into a suboptimal one (i.e., such that by epistemological disjunctivist lights factive rational support is no longer reflectively available). To argue otherwise is, I would contend, to concede far too much to the radical skeptic. For further discussion of the "good" cases in which one has reflectively accessible factive rational support for one's beliefs by epistemological disjunctivist lights, see Pritchard (2012b, pt. 1). See also Pritchard (2011a).

22. I further explore these dialectical issues as part of a recent symposium on Pritchard (2012b)—see especially Goldberg (forthcoming), but also Littlejohn (forthcoming) and Neta (forthcoming), to which Pritchard (forthcoming–b) is a response. See also Zalabardo (forthcoming).

Chapter 6. Epistemological Disjunctivism and Closure-Based Radical Skepticism

1. Note that once we combine epistemological disjunctivism with a Wittgensteinian anti-skeptical proposal, which is what we will be doing in chapter 7, then we will have a further philosophical basis on which to critique attributer contextualism, in terms of its appeal to epistemically high-standards skeptical contexts of epistemic appraisal. Insofar as these contexts of epistemic appraisal are understood as attempting—whether directly or indirectly via a rational assessment of one's hinge commitments—universal rational evaluations of one's beliefs, then they are employing epistemic standards that are, by Wittgensteinian lights, inherently and fatally problematic. I return to this point in chapter 7. See also note 3 below.

2. Henceforth, when I refer to "attributer contextualism" without qualification, I will have the standard version of this view (as encountered in chapter 2) in mind.

3. Once we combine epistemological disjunctivism with a Wittgensteinian anti-skeptical proposal, which is what we will be doing in chapter 7, then we

can motivate an even stronger point in this regard. According to the Wittgensteinian account of the structure of reasons, after all, there is something inherently dubious about the kind of epistemically high-standards contexts of epistemic appraisal employed by the skeptic in which doubt of our hinge commitments is in play. See chapter 7, §4.

4. This scenario is just a variant of a standard kind of case where one is in possession of misleading defeaters. It is an interesting question just what one's epistemic position is in such a case, according to epistemological disjunctivism. It is clear that the subject no longer knows that p, since she doesn't any longer believe that p, but that doesn't settle what her epistemic position is in this regard. My own view, articulated at length in Pritchard (2011a; 2012b, pt. 1), is that in these conditions the subject continues to see that p, but that her seeing that p can no longer be part of the rational support reflectively available to her in support of her knowledge that p (and thus she is not the market for knowledge that p on this basis even if she did happen to believe that p). McDowell seems to agree—see, e.g., McDowell (2002b, 277–78; 2003, 680–81). See also note 5.

5. McDowell agrees with this point about how it is possible to be hoodwinked by radical skepticism into reducing the scope of the rational support available to one. See, in particular, McDowell (2012), where he approvingly discusses Clarke's (1965) idea that it is possible, simply through an effort of attention on the part of the subject, for an agent to regard his otherwise normal perceptual experience as providing mere seemings rather than direct perception of objects. See also note 4.

6. I explore Neta's proposal in more detail in Pritchard (2005c), where I also consider how this view relates to Williams's inferential contextualism. We will return to consider rational support contextualism and inferential contextualism again in chapter 7—see §4—once we have a full description of our (part Wittgensteinian, part McDowellian) anti-skeptical proposal on the table.

7. See also Johnsen (2001). In addition, see the explanatory contextualism advanced by Rieber (1998), which is a form of attributer contextualism that explicitly incorporates a contrastive element. For a helpful critical discussion of the relative merits of contrastivism and the view that we are here calling rational support contextualism—albeit one that sides with the latter over the former—see Neta (2008b).

8. Schaffer (2004) in fact contrasts attributer contextualism with contrastivism, though note that he is building much more detail into his characterization of contrastivism than we are here.

9. The observant reader will spot that we are moving back and forth here between presenting contrastivism in terms of an ability to discriminate between specific objects (as in the second Schaffer quotation just offered) and in terms of being able to discriminate between one state of affairs, propositionally described, and an incompatible state of affairs, also propositionally described (as in the first Schaffer quotation). The second way of putting things is, I take it, Schaffer's considered view, but for our purposes we can gloss over this distinction here.

10. Note that part of the case that Schaffer mounts in defense of contrastivism is linguistic—see, especially, Schaffer (2008)—but I take this to be controversial, and won't be exploring it here. Our critique of the position will instead be

focused on other aspects of the contrastivist proposal. See Rickless (forthcoming) for a helpful recent critical discussion of the linguistic case for contrastivism.

11. I critically evaluate contrastivism in more detail in Pritchard (2008*a*).

12. See also Pryor (2004; 2012). In addition, see Huemer's (2001; 2007) defense of the closely related view known as *phenomenal conservatism*.

13. See McGrath (2013) for an insightful discussion of the role of defeaters with regard to the dogmatist position.

14. For some useful critical discussions of dogmatism, see Neta (2004*a*), White (2006), Wright (2007), Silins (2008), McGrath (2013), and Williams (2013). See also the essays collected in Tucker (2013), which covers both dogmatism and the related view known as phenomenal conservatism (see note 12).

15. Note that for ease of expression I have renamed the three claims that make up this skeptical paradox, compared with the formulation that was offered in chapter 2. Nothing of any consequence hangs on these changes.

16. This was the approach I took in Pritchard (2012*b*, pt. 3). As I explain in the introduction, the reason I took this approach wasn't that I was convinced by it, but rather that for the purposes of that particular book it was vital to present epistemological disjunctivism in such a way that it did not depend on further philosophical claims, epistemological or otherwise, that were independently contentious.

17. See Schaffer (2007) for a heroic attempt at defending something like the closure principle for contrastivism. See also Kvanvig (2008) and Hughes (2013).

18. But see Hughes (2013), who argues that contrastivism *can* adequately defend closure-style inferences for knowledge, but that it cannot avoid the epistemically immodest consequences of such inferences. Since this is, as we have just noted, effectively the problem that epistemological disjunctivism faces in this regard, it would follow that contrastivism fares no better than epistemological disjunctivism as an anti-skeptical strategy even if we restrict ourselves to closure$_{RK}$-based radical skepticism.

Chapter 7. Farewell to Epistemic Angst

1. Or, at least, the universality of rational evaluation thesis has to go to the extent that it applies to our commitments in general, whether (knowledge-apt) beliefs or hinge commitments. As we saw in chapter 4—see notes 9, 14, and 32—insofar as one restricts this thesis to (knowledge-apt) beliefs, then it is entirely compatible with the Wittgensteinian account of the structure of rational evaluation, at least on the nonbelief reading. This is because the thesis would now be simply inapplicable to the rational evaluations of one's hinge commitments. There is thus a sense in which the universality of rational evaluation thesis, construed in a very specific way, could potentially be squared with a Wittgensteinian epistemology.

2. One issue on which inferential and rational support contextualism arguably fares better than the biscopic proposal is with regard to so-called abominable conjunctions (see chapter 1, §1). Recall that this is a problem, due to De-Rose (1995), which concerns the oddity of simultaneously asserting both that one has knowledge of an everyday proposition and that one lacks knowledge of a

denial of a skeptical hypothesis (even though the everyday proposition is clearly logically incompatible with the skeptical hypothesis). Although this problem is directly applicable to anti-skeptical positions that deny the closure principle (in all its various guises), it also applies to any view that, like contextualist proposals, wants to treat any claim to know that one is not the victim of a skeptical hypothesis as expressing a falsehood. Contextualists of all stripes can respond to this problem by maintaining that there is no single context of epistemic appraisal relative to which the assertion of an abominable conjunction expresses a truth. The first conjunct, if asserted in isolation, may well express a truth relative to an everyday context of epistemic appraisal. But by bringing in the skeptical hypothesis at issue in the second conjunct, one thereby changes the context of epistemic appraisal, such that while the second conjunct may well now express a truth (if asserted in isolation anyway), the first conjunct no longer does. In this way, contextualists can account for why any claim to know the denial of a skeptical hypothesis expresses a falsehood without having to deny either (i) the closure (or closure$_{RK}$) principle or (ii) that everyday knowledge claims express truths. The biscopic proposal doesn't involve denying the relevant closure-style principles either, of course, but it does allow that one cannot have knowledge, including rationally grounded knowledge, of the denials of skeptical hypotheses, and so this problem still applies. Although the biscopic account cannot appeal to a shift in contexts of epistemic appraisal to explain away abominable conjunctions, it does have a diagnostic story to tell in this regard. After all, once one has become apprised of the Wittgensteinian account of the structure of rational evaluation, and in particular its epistemic implications with regard to our hinge commitments, one will no longer expect there to be an inferential route from rationally grounded knowledge of an everyday proposition to rationally grounded knowledge of the denial of a skeptical hypothesis. Accordingly, abominable conjunctions are now no longer puzzling, since they merely highlight the point that the scope of one's rational evaluations doesn't extend to one's hinge commitments.

3. For some useful recent discussions of the contrastivist defense of a closure-style principle, see Schaffer (2007), Kvanvig (2008), and Hughes (2013). Relatedly, note that contrastivists will also need to offer a diagnostic story with regard to so-called abominable conjunctions (see note 2).

4. Or at least the skeptical problematic in the guises that we have engaged with. Recall from chapter 1 (note 1) that while we have here dealt with a prominent and fundamental type of radical skepticism, there are still other varieties remaining.

5. See Boult & Pritchard (2013) and Pritchard (2014a). I have recently become aware that Putnam (2006) also uses the analogy of vertigo in the context of radical skepticism when discussing Cavell's (1979) treatment of the skeptical problem. While there are similarities between the approach I take to radical skepticism and that offered by Cavell, ultimately his stance on this topic is more concessive than mine. In particular, Cavell wants to claim that while the radical skeptical challenge is not bona fide, there is nonetheless a "truth in skepticism." For some useful recent discussions of what Cavell has in mind in this regard, see Putnam (2006) and Shieh (2006).

6. Note that in earlier work I used the phrase *epistemic angst* as a cover-all term in this regard—see, for example, Pritchard (2005b, passim; 2005e; 2008c)—such that it referred both to a general epistemological anxiety brought on by the radical skeptical problematic and to what we are here calling *epistemic vertigo*. I now use this phrase so that it applies only to the former, and not also the latter.

7. I further develop my ideas about the general notion of risk, including as regards epistemic risk specifically, in Pritchard (2014b; 2015).

8. The idea that it is the detached perspective that generates radical skepticism is a recurring motif in the literature on this topic. For some of the key texts in this regard, see Clarke (1972), Cavell (1979), Stroud (1984), and Nagel (1986, chaps. 5–6; cf. Nagel 1970). Wittgenstein (1969) and Heidegger (1962) may also belong in this list, depending on one's interpretation of them on this score. See Williams (1991) for an important, Wittgenstein-inspired, discussion of this way of thinking about radical skepticism. See Minar (1999; 2001a; 2001b) for some helpful discussions of Heidegger's treatment of radical skepticism. Incidentally, Nagel is unusual in taking the detached perspective of philosophical reflection as being the source of a range of philosophical problems. For a discussion of the connection he draws between radical skepticism and the meaning of life, for example, see Pritchard (2010a).

9. The *angst* that remains might well be best thought of as a form of *alief*, which is a possibility that we rejected earlier as an account of the propositional attitude involved in our hinge commitments (see chapter 4, note 13). At the very least, the kind of propositional attitude involved in epistemic vertigo as just described is similar to the propositional attitude involved in acrophobia, and the latter is usually classified as an alief. For further discussion of aliefs, see Gendler (2008a; 2008b), Nagel (2012), and Mandelbaum (2013).

Bibliography

Adler, J. (1994). "Testimony, Trust, Knowing," *Journal of Philosophy* 91, 264–75.
—— (2002). *Belief's Own Ethics*, Cambridge, MA: MIT Press.
Alston, W. P. (1986). "The Deontological Conception of Epistemic Justification," *Philosophical Perspectives* 2, 257–99.
—— (1988). "An Internalist Externalism," *Synthese* 74, 265–83.
Altschul, J. (2011). "Epistemic Entitlement," *Internet Encyclopedia of Philosophy*, (eds.) J. Fieser & B. Dowden, www.iep.utm.edu/ep-en/.
Annis, D. B. (1978). "A Contextualist Theory of Epistemic Justification," *American Philosophical Quarterly* 15, 213–19.
Austin, J. L. (1961). "Other Minds," in his *Philosophical Papers*, (eds.) J. O. Urmson & G. J. Warnock, 76–116, Oxford: Clarendon.
—— (1962). *Sense and Sensibilia*, Oxford: Oxford University Press.
Axtell, G. (1997). "Recent Work in Virtue Epistemology," *American Philosophical Quarterly* 34, 410–30.
Bach, K. (1985). "A Rationale for Reliabilism," *Monist* 68, 246–63.
Baldwin, T. (1990). *G. E. Moore*, London: Routledge.
—— (1993). "G. E. Moore," *A Companion to Epistemology*, (eds.) J. Dancy & E. Sosa, 283–85, Oxford: Blackwell.
Beebe, J. R. (2009). "The Abductivist Reply to Skepticism," *Philosophy and Phenomenological Research* 79, 605–36.
Beebee, H. (2011). "David Hume," *Routledge Companion to Epistemology*, (eds.) S. Bernecker & D. H. Pritchard, 730–40, London: Routledge.
Berker, S. (2008). "Luminosity Regained," *Philosophers' Imprint* 8, 1–22.
Bernecker, S. (2007). "Remembering Without Knowing," *Australasian Journal of Philosophy* 85, 137–56.
Bett, R. (2011). "Pyrrhonian Skepticism," *Routledge Companion to Epistemology*, (eds.) S. Bernecker & D. H. Pritchard, 403–13, London: Routledge.
Black, T. (2002). "A Moorean Response to Brain-in-a-Vat Scepticism," *Australasian Journal of Philosophy* 80, 148–63.
—— (2006). "Contextualism in Epistemology," *Internet Encyclopedia of Philosophy*, (eds.) J. Fieser & B. Dowden, www.iep.utm.edu/contextu/.
—— (2008). "Defending a Sensitive Neo-Moorean Invariantism," *New Waves in Epistemology*, (eds.) V. Hendricks & D. H. Pritchard, 8–27, London: Palgrave Macmillan.
—— (2011a). "Modal and Anti-luck Epistemology," *Routledge Companion to Epistemology*, (eds.) S. Bernecker & D. H. Pritchard, 187–98, London: Routledge.
—— (2011b). "Review of Perception as a Capacity for Knowledge, by John McDowell," *Notre Dame Philosophical Reviews*, http://ndpr.nd.edu/news/24767/?id=24292.
BonJour, L. (1985). *The Structure of Empirical Knowledge*, Cambridge, MA: Harvard University Press.

BonJour, L. (1999). "Foundationalism and the External World," *Philosophical Perspectives* 13, 229–49.
—— (2002). "Internalism and Externalism," *Oxford Handbook of Epistemology*, (ed.) P. Moser, 234–64, Oxford: Oxford University Press.
Boult, C., & Pritchard, D. H. (2013). "Wittgensteinian Anti-scepticism and Epistemic Vertigo," *Philosophia* 41, 27–35.
Brady, M. S., & Pritchard, D. H. (2005). "Epistemological Contextualism—Problems and Prospects," *Philosophical Quarterly* 55, 161–71.
Brandom, R. (1995). "Knowledge and the Social Articulation of Reasons," *Philosophy and Phenomenological Research* 55, 889–908.
—— (1998). "Insights and Blindspots of Reliabilism," *Monist* 81, 371–92.
Brenner, W., & Moyal-Sharrock, D. (2005). "Introduction," *Readings of Wittgenstein's* On Certainty, London: Palgrave Macmillan.
Brewer, B. (2000). *Perception and Reason*, Oxford: Oxford University Press.
Brogaard, B. (2010). "Disjunctivism," *Oxford Bibliographies: Philosophy*, (ed.) D. H. Pritchard, DOI: 10.1093/OBO/9780195396577-0033.
Brueckner, A. (1986). "Charity and Skepticism," *Pacific Philosophical Quarterly* 67, 264–68.
—— (1991). "The Omniscient Interpreter Rides Again," *Analysis* 51, 192–205.
—— (1994). "The Structure of the Skeptical Argument," *Philosophy and Phenomenological Research* 54, 827–35.
—— (2010a). "Skepticism and Closure," *A Companion to Epistemology* (2nd Edn.), (eds.) J. Dancy, E. Sosa, & M. Steup, 3–12, Oxford: Blackwell.
—— (2010b). "~K~SK," in his *Essays on Skepticism*, 367–81, Oxford: Oxford University Press.
—— (2012). "Skepticism and Content Externalism," *Stanford Encyclopedia of Philosophy*, (ed.) E. Zalta, http://plato.stanford.edu/entries/skepticism-content-externalism/.
Brueckner, A., & Fiocco, M. O. (2002). "Williamson's Anti-Luminosity Argument," *Philosophical Studies* 110, 285–93.
Burge, T. (1993). "Content Preservation," *Philosophical Review* 102, 457–88.
—— (2003). "Perceptual Entitlement," *Philosophy and Phenomenological Research* 67, 503–48.
Byrne, A. (2004). "How Hard Are the Sceptical Paradoxes?," *Noûs* 38, 299–325.
—— (Forthcoming). "McDowell and Wright on Anti-Scepticism etc.," *Contemporary Perspectives on Scepticism and Perceptual Justification*, (eds.) D. Dodd & E. Zardini, Oxford: Oxford University Press.
Byrne, A., & Logue, H. (2008). "Either/Or," *Disjunctivism: Perception, Action, Knowledge*, (eds.) A. Haddock & F. Macpherson, 57–94, Oxford: Oxford University Press.
—— (eds.) (2009a). *Disjunctivism: Contemporary Readings*, Cambridge, MA: MIT Press.
—— (2009b). "Introduction," *Disjunctivism: Contemporary Readings*, (eds.) A. Byrne & H. Logue, vii–xxix, Cambridge, MA: MIT Press.
Callanan, J. J. (2011). "Making Sense of Doubt: Strawson's Anti-Scepticism," *Theoria* 77, 261–78.
Campbell, J. (2001). "Rationality, Meaning, and the Analysis of Delusion," *Philosophy, Psychiatry & Psychology* 8, 89–100.

Carter, J. A. (2012). "Recent Work on Moore's Proof," *International Journal for the Study of Skepticism* 2, 115–44.
Carter, J. A., & Pritchard, D. H. (Forthcoming). "Perceptual Knowledge and Relevant Alternatives," *Philosophical Studies*.
Cassam, Q. (1987). "Transcendental Arguments, Transcendental Synthesis and Transcendental Idealism," *Philosophical Quarterly* 37, 355–78.
——— (2007a). *The Possibility of Knowledge*, Oxford: Oxford University Press.
——— (2007b). "Ways of Knowing," *Proceedings of the Aristotelian Society* 107, 339–58.
——— (2008). "Foreword," *Scepticism and Naturalism: Some Varieties*, by P. F. Strawson, vii–xviii, London: Routledge.
Cavell, S. (1979). *The Claim of Reason: Wittgenstein, Skepticism, Morality, and Tragedy*, Cambridge, MA: Harvard University Press.
——— (1988). *In Quest of the Ordinary: Lines of Skepticism and Romanticism*, Chicago: University of Chicago Press.
Chignell, A., & McLear, C. (2010). "Three Skeptics and the Critique: Critical Notice of Michael Forster's *Kant and Skepticism*," *Philosophical Books* 51, 228–44.
Chisholm, R. M. (1977). *Theory of Knowledge* (2nd Edn.), Englewood Cliffs, NJ: Prentice Hall.
Christensen, D. (2004). *Putting Logic in Its Place: Formal Constraints on Rational Belief*, Cambridge: Cambridge University Press.
——— (2010). "Higher-Order Evidence," *Philosophy and Phenomenological Research* 81, 215–85.
Clarke, T. (1965). "Seeing Surfaces and Physical Objects," *Philosophy in America*, (ed.) M. Black, 98–114, London: George Allen & Unwin.
——— (1972). "The Legacy of Skepticism," *Journal of Philosophy* 64, 754–69.
Cohen, S. (1984). "Justification and Truth," *Philosophical Studies* 46, 279–96.
——— (1988). "How to Be a Fallibilist," *Philosophical Perspectives* 2, 91–123.
——— (1998). "Two Kinds of Sceptical Argument," *Philosophy and Phenomenological Research* 58, 143–59.
——— (1999). "Contextualism, Skepticism, and the Structure of Reasons," *Philosophical Perspectives* 13, 57–89.
——— (2000). "Contextualism and Skepticism," *Philosophical Issues* 10, 94–107.
Coliva, A. (2010). *Moore and Wittgenstein: Scepticism, Certainty, and Common Sense*, Basingstoke, UK: Palgrave Macmillan.
——— (2012). "Moore's Proof, Liberals, and Conservatives: Is There a (Wittgensteinian) Third Way?," *Mind, Meaning, and Knowledge: Themes from the Philosophy of Crispin Wright*, (ed.) A. Coliva, 323–51, Oxford: Oxford University Press.
Collins, J. (2006). "Epistemic Closure Principles," *Internet Encyclopedia of Philosophy*, (eds.) J. Fieser & B. Dowden, www.iep.utm.edu/epis-clo/.
Comesaña, J. (2005). "Justified *versus* Warranted Perceptual Belief: A Case Against Disjunctivism," *Philosophy and Phenomenological Research* 71, 367–83.
Conant, J. (1998). "Wittgenstein on Meaning and Use," *Philosophical Investigations* 21, 222–50.
——— (2004). "Varieties of Scepticism," *Wittgenstein and Scepticism*, (ed.) D. McManus, 97–136, London: Routledge.

Conant, J. (2012). "Two Varieties of Skepticism," *Rethinking Epistemology* (vol. 2), (eds.) G. Abel & J. Conant, 1–73, Berlin: Walter De Gruyter.
Conee, E. (2007). "Disjunctivism and Anti-skepticism," *Philosophical Issues* 17, 16–36.
——— (2008). "Opposing Skepticism Disjunctively," typescript.
Conee, E., & Feldman, R. (2000). "Internalism Defended," *Epistemology: Internalism and Externalism*, (ed.) H. Kornblith, 231–60, Oxford: Blackwell.
——— (2004). *Evidentialism*, Oxford: Oxford University Press.
——— (2011). "Reply to Pritchard," *Evidentialism and Its Discontents*, (ed.) T. Dougherty, 440–44, Oxford: Oxford University Press.
Dancy, J. (2008). "On How to Act—Disjunctively," *Disjunctivism: Perception, Action, Knowledge*, (eds.) A. Haddock & F. Macpherson, 262–82, Oxford: Oxford University Press.
David, M., & Warfield, T. (2008). "Knowledge-Closure and Skepticism," *Epistemology: New Essays*, (ed.) Q. Smith, 137–88, Oxford: Oxford University Press.
Davidson, D. (1975). "Thought and Talk," *Mind and Language*, (ed.) S. Guttenplan, 7–23, Oxford: Oxford University Press.
——— (1977 [1984]). "The Method of Truth in Metaphysics," reprinted as essay 14 in his *Inquiries into Truth and Interpretation*, Oxford: Clarendon.
——— (1983 [1986]). "A Coherence Theory of Truth and Knowledge," reprinted as chapter 16 in *Truth and Interpretation: Perspectives on the Philosophy of Donald Davidson*, (ed.) E. LePore, Oxford: Blackwell.
——— (1999). "Reply to Barry Stroud," *The Philosophy of Donald Davidson*, (ed.) L. E. Hahn, 162–66, Chicago: Open Court.
Davies, M. (2004). "Epistemic Entitlement, Warrant Transmission and Easy Knowledge," *Proceedings of the Aristotelian Society* 78 (supp. vol.), 213–45.
DeRose, K. (1995). "Solving the Skeptical Problem," *Philosophical Review* 104, 1–52.
——— (1999). "Contextualism: An Explanation and Defense," *Blackwell Guide to Epistemology*, (ed.) J. Greco & E. Sosa, 187–205, Oxford: Blackwell.
DeRose, K., & Grandy, R. (1999). "Conditional Assertions and 'Biscuit' Conditionals," *Noûs* 33, 405–20.
Descartes, R. (1970 [1644]). *The Principles of Philosophy*, in his *The Philosophical Works of Descartes* (vol. 1), (eds.) E. S. Haldane & G. R. T. Ross, 219–302, Cambridge: Cambridge University Press.
Dorsch, F. (2011). "The Diversity of Disjunctivism," *European Journal of Philosophy* 19, 304–14.
Dougherty, T. (ed.) (2011). *Evidentialism and Its Discontents*, Oxford: Oxford University Press.
Douven, I. (2011). "Abduction," *Stanford Encyclopedia of Philosophy*, (ed.) E. Zalta, http://plato.stanford.edu/entries/abduction/.
Dretske, F. (1969). *Seeing and Knowing*, London: Routledge & Kegan Paul.
——— (1970). "Epistemic Operators," *Journal of Philosophy* 67, 1007–23.
——— (2005a). "The Case Against Closure," *Contemporary Debates in Epistemology*, (eds.) E. Sosa & M. Steup, 13–26, Oxford: Blackwell.
——— (2005b). "Reply to Hawthorne," *Contemporary Debates in Epistemology*, (eds.) E. Sosa & M. Steup, 43–46, Oxford: Blackwell.

Engel, M. (1992). "Personal and Doxastic Justification," *Philosophical Studies* 67, 133–51.
Feldman, R. (1999). "Contextualism and Skepticism," *Philosophical Perspectives* 1, 91–114.
——— (2001). "Skeptical Problems, Contextualist Solutions," *Philosophical Studies* 103, 61–85.
Fish, W. (2009). "Disjunctivism," *Internet Encyclopedia of Philosophy*, (eds.) J. Fieser & B. Dowden, www.iep.utm.edu/d/disjunct.htm.
Fogelin, R. (1994). *Pyrrhonian Reflections on Knowledge and Justification*, Oxford: Oxford University Press.
Foley, R. (1987). *A Theory of Epistemic Rationality*, Cambridge, MA: Harvard University Press.
Foley, R., & Fumerton, R. (1985). "Davidson's Theism?," *Philosophical Studies* 48, 83–89.
Forster, M. N. (2010). *Kant and Skepticism*, Princeton, NJ: Princeton University Press.
——— (2011). "Immanuel Kant," *Routledge Companion to Epistemology*, (eds.) S. Bernecker & D. H. Pritchard, 741–49, London: Routledge.
French, C. (2012). "Does Propositional Seeing Entail Propositional Knowledge?," *Theoria* 78, 115–27.
——— (Forthcoming). "The Formulation of Epistemological Disjunctivism," *Philosophy and Phenomenological Research*.
Fumerton, R. (1990). "Metaepistemology and Skepticism," *Doubting: Contemporary Perspectives on Skepticism*, (eds.) M. D. Roth & G. Ross, Dordrecht: Kluwer.
——— (1992). "Skepticism and Reasoning to the Best Explanation," *Philosophical Issues* 2, 149–69.
——— (2005). "The Challenge of Refuting Skepticism," *Contemporary Debates in Epistemology*, (eds.) E. Sosa & M. Steup, 85–97, Oxford: Blackwell.
Gascoigne, N. (2002). *Scepticism*, London: Acumen.
Gaukroger, S. (2011). "René Descartes," *Routledge Companion to Epistemology*, (eds.) S. Bernecker & D. H. Pritchard, 678–86, London: Routledge.
Gendler, T. S. (2008a). "Alief and Belief," *Journal of Philosophy* 105, 634–63.
——— (2008b). "Alief in Action (and Reaction)," *Mind and Language* 23, 552–85.
Gendler, T. S., & Hawthorne, J. (2005). "The Real Guide to Fake Barns: A Catalogue of Gifts for Your Epistemic Enemies," *Philosophical Studies* 124, 331–52.
Glendinning, S., & de Gaynesford, M. (1998). "John McDowell on Experience: Open to the Sceptic?," *Metaphilosophy* 29, 20–34.
Goldberg, S. (Forthcoming). "Comments on Pritchard's *Epistemological Disjunctivism*," *Journal of Philosophical Research*.
Goldman, A. (1976). "Discrimination and Perceptual Knowledge," *Journal of Philosophy* 73, 771–91.
——— (1979). "What Is Justified Belief?," *Justification and Knowledge*, (ed.) G. Pappas, 1–23, Dordrecht: Reidel.
——— (1986). *Epistemology and Cognition*, Cambridge, MA: Harvard University Press.
——— (1988). "Strong and Weak Justification," *Philosophical Perspectives 2: Epistemology*, (ed.) J. Tomberlin, 51–69, Atascadero, CA: Ridgeview.

Goldman, A. (2008). "Reliabilism," *Stanford Encyclopedia of Philosophy*, (ed.) E. Zalta, http://plato.stanford.edu/entries/reliabilism/.

Greco, J. (1999). "Agent Reliabilism," *Philosophical Perspectives* 13, 273–96.

—— (2000). *Putting Skeptics in Their Place: The Nature of Skeptical Arguments and Their Role in Philosophical Inquiry*, Cambridge: Cambridge University Press.

—— (2003). "Knowledge as Credit for True Belief," *Intellectual Virtue: Perspectives from Ethics and Epistemology*, (eds.) M. DePaul & L. Zagzebski, 111–34, Oxford: Oxford University Press.

—— (2004). "Externalism and Skepticism," *The Externalist Challenge: New Studies on Cognition and Intentionality*, (ed.) R. Shantz, 53–64, New York: de Gruyter.

—— (2007). "The Nature of Ability and the Purpose of Knowledge," *Philosophical Issues* 17, 57–69.

—— (2010). *Achieving Knowledge: A Virtue-Theoretic Account of Epistemic Normativity*, Cambridge: Cambridge University Press.

Grice, H. P. (1961). "The Causal Theory of Perception," *Proceedings of the Aristotelian Society* (suppl. vol.) 35, 121–52.

—— (1989). "Logic and Conversation," in his *Studies in the Way of Words*, 22–40, Cambridge, MA: Harvard University Press.

Haddock, A. (2011). "The Disjunctive Conception of Perceiving," *Philosophical Explorations* 14, 69–88.

Haddock, A., & Macpherson, F. (eds.) (2008*a*). *Disjunctivism: Perception, Action, Knowledge*, Oxford: Oxford University Press.

—— (2008*b*). "Introduction: Varieties of Disjunctivism," *Disjunctivism: Perception, Action, Knowledge*, (eds.) A. Haddock & F. Macpherson, 1–24, Oxford: Oxford University Press.

Haddock, A., Millar, A, & Pritchard, D. H. (eds.) (2009). *Epistemic Value*, Oxford: Oxford University Press.

Halpern, J. Y. (2008). "Intransitivity and Vagueness," *Review of Symbolic Logic* 1, 530–47.

Harman, G. (1973). *Thought*, Princeton, NJ: Princeton University Press.

Hawthorne, J. (2004). *Knowledge and Lotteries*, Oxford: Clarendon.

—— (2005). "The Case for Closure," *Contemporary Debates in Epistemology*, (eds.) E. Sosa & M. Steup, 26–43, Oxford: Blackwell.

Hawthorne, J., & Kovakovich, K. (2006). "Disjunctivism," *Proceedings of the Aristotelian Society* (suppl. vol.) 80, 145–83.

Hazlett, A. (2013). *A Critical Introduction to Skepticism*, London: Bloomsbury.

—— (2014). "Limning Structure as an Epistemic Goal," manuscript.

Heidegger, M. (1962 [1927]). *Being and Time* [*Sein und Zeit*], (tr.) J. Macquarrie & E. Robinson, Oxford: Blackwell.

Heller, M. (1999). "Relevant Alternatives and Closure," *Australasian Journal of Philosophy* 77, 196–208.

Hetherington, S. (2013). "There Can Be Lucky Knowledge," *Contemporary Debates in Epistemology* (2nd Edn.), (eds.) M. Steup & J. Turri, 164–76, Oxford: Blackwell.

Hinton, J. M. (1967*a*). "Experiences," *Philosophical Quarterly* 17, 1–13.

—— (1967b). "Visual Experiences," *Mind* 76, 217–27.
—— (1973). *Experiences: An Inquiry into Some Ambiguities*, Oxford: Clarendon.
Hornsby, J. (2008). "A Disjunctive Conception of Acting for Reasons," *Disjunctivism: Perception, Action, Knowledge*, (eds.) F. Macpherson & A. Haddock, 244–61, Oxford: Oxford University Press.
Huemer, M. (2001). *Skepticism and the Veil of Perception*, Lanham, MD: Rowman & Littlefield.
—— (2007). "Compassionate Phenomenal Conservatism," *Philosophy and Phenomenological Research* 74, 30–55.
—— (2013). "Phenomenal Conservatism," *Internet Encyclopedia of Philosophy*, (eds.) J. Fieser & B. Dowden, www.iep.utm.edu/phen-con/.
Hughes, M. (2013). "Problems for Contrastive Closure: Resolved and Regained," *Philosophical Studies* 163, 577–90.
Hume, D. (2007 [1739]). *A Treatise of Human Nature*, (ed.) D. F. Norton & M. J. Norton, Oxford: Oxford University Press.
Jenkins, C. (2007). "Entitlement and Rationality," *Synthese* 157, 25–45.
Johnsen, B. (2001). "Contextualist Swords, Skeptical Plowshares," *Philosophy and Phenomenological Research* 62, 385–406.
Kant, I. (1978 [1781/1787]). *Critique of Pure Reason*, (tr.) N. K. Smith, London: Macmillan.
Kaplan, M. (2011a). "John Langshaw Austin," *Routledge Companion to Epistemology*, (eds.) S. Bernecker & D. H. Pritchard, 798–810, London: Routledge.
—— (2011b). "Tales of the Unknown: Austin and the Argument from Ignorance," *The Philosophy of J. L. Austin*, (eds.) M. Gustafsson & E. Sørli, 51–77, Oxford: Oxford University Press.
—— (2013). "Coming to Terms with Our Human Fallibility: Christensen on the Preface," *Philosophy and Phenomenological Research* 87, 1–35.
Kelp, C. (2011). "A Problem for Contrastivist Accounts of Knowledge," *Philosophical Studies* 152, 287–92.
Kelp, C., & Pedersen, N. J. L. L. (2011). "Second-Order Knowledge," *Routledge Companion to Epistemology*, (eds.) S. Bernecker & D. H. Pritchard, 586–96, London: Routledge.
Kienzler, W. (2006). "Wittgenstein and John Henry Newman On Certainty," *Grazer Philosophische Studien* 71, 117–38.
Klein, P. (1981). *Certainty: A Refutation of Scepticism*, Minneapolis: University of Minnesota Press.
—— (1995). "Skepticism and Closure: Why the Evil Genius Argument Fails," *Philosophical Topics* 23, 213–36.
Kornblith, H. (2000). "The Contextualist Evasion of Epistemology," *Philosophical Issues* 10, 24–32.
—— (ed.) (2001). *Epistemology: Internalism and Externalism*, Oxford: Blackwell.
Kripke, S. (2011). "Two Paradoxes of Knowledge," in his *Philosophical Troubles: Collected Papers Volume 1*, 27–51, Oxford: Oxford University Press.
Kusch, M. (2010). "Kripke's Wittgenstein, *On Certainty*, and Epistemic Relativism," *The Later Wittgenstein on Language*, (ed.) D. Whiting, 213–30, Basingstoke, UK: Palgrave Macmillan.

Kvanvig, J. L. (2006). "Closure Principles," *Philosophy Compass* 1, 256–67.
——— (2008). "Contrastivism and Closure," *Social Epistemology* 22, 247–56.
Kyburg, H. E. (1961). *Probability and the Logic of Rational Belief*, Middletown, CT: Wesleyan University Press.
Lawlor, K. (2013). *Assurance: An Austinian View of Knowledge and Knowledge Claims*, Oxford: Oxford University Press.
Lehrer, K., & Cohen, S. (1983). "Justification, Truth, and Coherence," *Synthese* 55, 191–207.
Lewis, D. (1973). *Counterfactuals*, Oxford: Blackwell.
——— (1996). "Elusive Knowledge," *Australasian Journal of Philosophy* 74, 549–67.
Lipton, P. (1991). *Inference to the Best Explanation*, London: Routledge.
——— (1998). "The Epistemology of Testimony," *Studies in History and, Philosophy of Science* 29, 1–31.
Littlejohn, C. (2009). "The New Evil Demon Problem," *Internet Encyclopedia of Philosophy*, (eds.) J. Fieser & B. Dowden, www.iep.utm.edu/evil-new/.
——— (2013). "Perceptual Knowledge and the Basis Problem," manuscript.
——— (Forthcoming). "Pritchard's Reasons," *Journal of Philosophical Research*.
Longworth, G. (2012). "John Langshaw Austin," *Stanford Encyclopedia of Philosophy*, (ed.) E. Zalta, http://plato.stanford.edu/entries/austin-jl/.
Ludwig, K. (1992). "Skepticism and Interpretation," *Philosophy and Phenomenological Research* 52, 317–39.
Luper, S. (1984). "The Epistemic Predicament: Knowledge, Nozickian Tracking, and Skepticism," *Australasian Journal of Philosophy* 62, 26–50.
——— (2003). "Indiscernability Skepticism," *The Skeptics: Contemporary Essays*, (ed.) S. Luper, 183–202, Aldershot: Ashgate.
——— (2010). "The Epistemic Closure Principle," *Stanford Encyclopedia of Philosophy*, (ed.) E. Zalta, http://plato.stanford.edu/entries/closure-epistemic/.
——— (2011). "Cartesian Skepticism," *Routledge Companion to Epistemology*, (eds.) S. Bernecker & D. H. Pritchard, 414–24, London: Routledge.
Macarthur, D. (2003). "McDowell, Scepticism, and the 'Veil of Perception,'" *Australasian Journal of Philosophy* 81, 175–90.
Machuca, D. (ed.) (2011). *Pyrrhonism in Ancient, Modern and Contemporary Philosophy*, Dordrecht: Springer.
Madison, B. (2010). "Epistemic Internalism," *Philosophy Compass* 5, 840–53.
Makinson, D. C. (1965). "The Paradox of the Preface," *Analysis* 25, 205–7.
Mandelbaum, E. (2013). "Against Alief," *Philosophical Studies* 165, 197–211
Martin, M. G. F. (1997). "The Reality of Appearances," *Thought and Ontology*, (ed.) M. Sainsbury, 77–96, Milan: Franco Angeli.
——— (1998). "Setting Things Before the Mind," *Contemporary Issues in the Philosophy of Mind*, (ed.) A. O'Hear, 157–79, Cambridge: Cambridge University Press.
——— (2002). "The Transparency of Experience," *Mind and Language* 17, 376–425.
——— (2003). "Particular Thoughts and Singular Thought," *Thought and Language*, (ed.) A. O'Hear, 173–214, Cambridge: Cambridge University Press.
——— (2004). "The Limits of Self-Awareness," *Philosophical Studies* 120, 37–89.

——— (2006). "On Being Alienated," *Perceptual Experience*, (eds.) T. S. Gendler & J. Hawthorne, 354–410, Oxford: Oxford University Press.
Matheson, J., & Vitz, R. (eds.) (2014). *The Ethics of Belief*, Oxford: Oxford University Press.
McCain, K. (2012). "A Predictivist Argument Against Scepticism," *Analysis* 72, 660–65.
McDowell, J. (1982). "Criteria, Defeasibility and Knowledge," *Proceedings of the British Academy* 68, 455–79.
——— (1986). "Singular Thought and the Extent of Inner Space," *Subject, Thought and Context*, (eds.) P. Pettit & J. McDowell, 137–68, Oxford: Clarendon.
——— (1994a). "Knowledge by Hearsay," *Knowing from Words: Western and Indian Philosophical Analysis of Understanding and Testimony*, (eds.) B. K. Matilal & A. Chakrabarti, 195–224, Dordrecht: Kluwer.
——— (1994b). *Mind and World*, Cambridge, MA: Harvard University Press.
——— (1995). "Knowledge and the Internal," *Philosophy and Phenomenological Research* 55, 877–93.
——— (2002a). "Knowledge and the Internal Revisited," *Philosophy and Phenomenological Research* 64, 97–105.
——— (2002b). "Responses," *Reading McDowell: On Mind and World*, (ed.) N. H. Smith, 269–305, Routledge, London.
——— (2003). "Subjective, Intersubjective, Objective," *Philosophical and Phenomenological Research* 67, 675–81.
——— (2008). "The Disjunctive Conception of Experience as Material for a Transcendental Argument," *Disjunctivism: Perception, Action, Knowledge*, (eds.) A. Haddock & F. Macpherson, 376–89, Oxford: Oxford University Press.
——— (2009). "Wittgenstein's 'Quietism,'" *Common Knowledge* 15, 365–72.
——— (2011). *Perception as a Capacity for Knowledge*, Milwaukee, WI: Marquette University Press.
——— (2012). "Reply to Narboux," *Autour de l'Esprit et le Monde de John McDowell*, (eds.) A. Le Goff & C. Al-Saleh, 128–36, Paris: Vrin.
McGinn, M. (1989). *Sense and Certainty: A Dissolution of Scepticism*, Blackwell, Oxford.
——— (2002). "What Kind of Senselessness Is This? A Reply to Conant on Wittgenstein's Critique of Moore," manuscript.
——— (2008). "Wittgenstein on Certainty," *Oxford Handbook to Skepticism*, (ed.) J. Greco, 372–91, Oxford: Oxford University Press.
——— (2011). "Ludwig Wittgenstein," *Routledge Companion to Epistemology*, (eds.) S. Bernecker & D. H. Pritchard, 763–73, London: Routledge.
McGrath, M. (2013). "Dogmatism, Underminers and Skepticism," *Philosophy and Phenomenological Research* 86, 533–62.
McKinsey, M. (1991). "Anti-Individualism and Privileged Access," *Analysis* 51, 9–16.
Millar, A. (2005). "Travis' Sense of Occasion," *Philosophical Quarterly* 55, 337–42.
——— (2007). "What the Disjunctivist Is Right About," *Philosophy and Phenomenological Research* 74, 176–98.

Millar, A. (2008a). "Disjunctivism and Skepticism," *Oxford Companion to Skepticism*, (ed.) J. Greco, 581–604, Oxford: Oxford University Press.
—— (2008b). "Perceptual-Recognitional Abilities and Perceptual Knowledge," *Disjunctivism: Perception, Action, Knowledge*, (eds.) A. Haddock & F. Macpherson, 330–47, Oxford: Oxford University Press.
Minar, E. (1999). "The Thinking of the Thing: A Late Heideggerian Response to Skepticism," *Philosophical Topics* 27, 287–307.
—— (2001a). "Heidegger's Response to Skepticism in Being and Time," *Future Pasts: The Analytic Tradition in Twentieth Century Philosophy*, (eds.) J. Floyd & S. Shieh, 193–214, Oxford: Oxford University Press.
—— (2001b). "Heidegger, Wittgenstein, and Skepticism," *Harvard Review of Philosophy* 9, 37–45.
Moore, G. E. (1925). "A Defence of Common Sense," *Contemporary British Philosophy* (2nd series), (ed.) J. H. Muirhead, 191–224, London: Allen & Unwin.
—— (1939). "Proof of an External World," *Proceedings of the British Academy* 25, 273–300.
Moyal-Sharrock, D. (2004). *Understanding Wittgenstein's* On Certainty, London: Palgrave Macmillan.
Murphy, P. (2014). "Justified Belief from Unjustified Belief," manuscript.
Nagel, J. (2012). "Gendler on Alief," *Analysis* 72, 774–88.
Nagel, T. (1970). "The Absurd," *Journal of Philosophy*, 68, 716–27.
—— (1986). *The View from Nowhere*, Oxford: Oxford University Press.
Neta, R. (2002). "S Knows That P," *Noûs* 36, 663–89.
—— (2003). "Contextualism and the Problem of the External World," *Philosophy and Phenomenological Research* 66, 1–31.
—— (2004a). "Perceptual Evidence and the New Dogmatism," *Philosophical Studies* 119, 199–214.
—— (2004b). "Skepticism, Abductivism, and the Explanatory Gap," *Philosophical Perspectives* 14, 296–325.
—— (2007). "Fixing the Transmission: The Neo-Mooreans," *Themes from G. E. Moore: New Essays in Epistemology and Ethics*, (ed.) S. Nuccetelli & G. Seay, 62–83, Oxford: Oxford University Press.
—— (2008a). "In Defence of Disjunctivism," *Disjunctivism: Perception, Action, Knowledge*, (eds.) A. Haddock & F. Macpherson, 311–29, Oxford: Oxford University Press.
—— (2008b). "Undermining the Case for Contrastivism," *Social Epistemology* 22, 289–304.
—— (Forthcoming). "How Holy Is the Disjunctivist Grail?," *Journal of Philosophical Research*.
Neta, R., & Pritchard, D. H. (2007). "McDowell and the New Evil Genius," *Philosophy and Phenomenological Research* 74, 381–96.
Newman, J. H. (1979 [1870]). *An Essay in Aid of a Grammar of Assent*, Notre Dame, IN: University of Notre Dame Press.
Nielsen, K. (1967). "Wittgensteinian Fideism," *Philosophy* 42, 237–54.
Nietzsche, F. (1990 [1889/1895]). *Twilight of the Idols/The Anti-Christ*, (tr.) R. J. Hollingdale, London: Penguin.
Nozick, R. (1981). *Philosophical Explanations*, Oxford: Oxford University Press.

Nuccetelli, S. (ed.) (2003). *New Essays on Semantic Externalism and Self-Knowledge*, Cambridge, MA: MIT Press.
Overgaard, S. (2011). "Disjunctivism and the Urgency of Scepticism," *Philosophical Explorations* 14, 5–21.
Pappas, G. (2005). "Internalist versus Externalist Conceptions of Epistemic Justification," *Stanford Encyclopedia of Philosophy*, (ed.) E. Zalta, http://plato.stanford.edu/entries/justep-intext/.
Peacocke, C. (2003). *The Realm of Reason*, Oxford: Oxford University Press.
Pedersen, N. J. (2009). "Entitlement, Value and Rationality," *Synthese* 171, 443–57.
Phillips, D. Z. (1976). *Religion Without Explanation*, Oxford: Oxford University Press.
—— (2005). "The Case of the Missing Propositions," *Readings of Wittgenstein's* On Certainty, (eds.) D. Moyal-Sharrock & W. H. Brenner, 16–29, London: Palgrave Macmillan.
Plant, B. (2011). "Religion, Relativism, and Wittgenstein's Naturalism," *International Journal of Philosophical Studies* 19, 177–209.
Plantinga, A. (1986). "The Foundations of Theism: A Reply," *Faith and Philosophy* 3, 310–12.
Poston, T. (2008). "Internalism and Externalism in Epistemology," *Internet Encyclopedia of Philosophy*, (eds.) J. Fieser & B. Dowden, www.iep.utm.edu/int-ext/.
Pritchard, D. H. (2000a). "Closure and Context," *Australasian Journal of Philosophy* 78, 275–80.
—— (2000b). "Doubt Undogmatized: Pyrrhonian Scepticism, Epistemological Externalism, and the 'Metaepistemological' Challenge," *Principia—Revista Internacional de Epistemologia* 4, 187–214.
—— (2000c). "Is 'God Exists' a 'Hinge' Proposition of Religious Belief?," *International Journal for Philosophy of Religion* 47, 129–40.
—— (2001a). "Contextualism, Scepticism, and the Problem of Epistemic Descent," *Dialectica* 55, 327–49.
—— (2001b). "Radical Scepticism, Epistemological Externalism, and 'Hinge' Propositions," *Wittgenstein-Jahrbuch 2001/2002*, (ed.) D. Salehi, 97–122, Frankfurt, Germany: Peter Lang.
—— (2001c). "Scepticism and Dreaming," *Philosophia* 28, 373–90.
—— (2002a). "McKinsey Paradoxes, Radical Scepticism, and the Transmission of Knowledge across Known Entailments," *Synthese* 130, 279–302.
—— (2002b). "Radical Scepticism, Epistemological Externalism, and Closure," *Theoria* 68, 129–61.
—— (2002c). "Recent Work on Radical Skepticism," *American Philosophical Quarterly* 39, 215–57.
—— (2002d). "Resurrecting the Moorean Response to Scepticism," *International Journal of Philosophical Studies* 10, 283–307.
—— (2002e). "Two Forms of Epistemological Contextualism," *Grazer Philosophische Studien* 64, 19–55.
—— (2003). "McDowell on Reasons, Externalism and Scepticism," *European Journal of Philosophy* 11, 273–94.

Pritchard, D. H. (2005a). "Contextualism, Scepticism and Warranted Assertibility Manoeuvres," *Knowledge and Skepticism*, (eds.) J. Keim-Campbell, M. O'Rourke, & H. Silverstein, 85–104, Cambridge, MA: MIT Press.
―――― (2005b). *Epistemic Luck*, Oxford: Oxford University Press.
―――― (2005c). "Neo-Mooreanism, Contextualism, and the Evidential Basis of Scepticism," *Acta Analytica* 20, 3–25.
―――― (2005d). "Neo-Mooreanism *versus* Contextualism," *Grazer Philosophische Studien* 67, 20–43.
―――― (2005e). "Scepticism, Epistemic Luck and Epistemic *Angst*," *Australasian Journal of Philosophy*, 83, 185–206.
―――― (2005f). "The Structure of Sceptical Arguments," *Philosophical Quarterly* 55, 37–52.
―――― (2005g). "Wittgenstein's *On Certainty* and Contemporary Anti-Scepticism," *Investigating* On Certainty: *Essays on Wittgenstein's Last Work*, (eds.) D. Moyal-Sharrock & W. H. Brenner, 189–224, London: Palgrave Macmillan.
―――― (2007a). "Anti-Luck Epistemology," *Synthese* 158, 277–97.
―――― (2007b). "How to Be a Neo-Moorean," *Internalism and Externalism in Semantics and Epistemology*, (ed.) S. Goldberg, 68–99, Oxford: Oxford University Press.
―――― (2007c). "Knowledge, Luck, and Lotteries," *New Waves in Epistemology*, (eds.) V. F. Hendricks & D. H. Pritchard, 28–51, Aldershot: Ashgate.
―――― (2008a). "Contrastivism, Evidence, and Scepticism," *Social Epistemology* 22, 305–23.
―――― (2008b). "McDowellian Neo-Mooreanism," *Disjunctivism: Perception, Action, Knowledge*, (eds.) A. Haddock & F. Macpherson, 283–310, Oxford: Oxford University Press.
―――― (2008c). "Radical Scepticism, Epistemic Luck and Epistemic Value," *Proceedings and Addresses of the Aristotelian Society* (suppl. vol.) 82, 19–41.
―――― (2008d). "Sensitivity, Safety, and Anti-luck Epistemology," *Oxford Handbook of Scepticism*, (ed.) J. Greco, 437–55, Oxford: Oxford University Press.
―――― (2009a). "Apt Performance and Epistemic Value," *Philosophical Studies* 143, 407–16.
―――― (2009b). "Defusing Epistemic Relativism," *Synthese* 166, 397–412.
―――― (2009c). *Knowledge*, Basingstoke, UK: Palgrave Macmillan.
―――― (2009d). "Safety-Based Epistemology: Whither Now?," *Journal of Philosophical Research* 34, 33–45.
―――― (2009e). "Scepticism and the Possibility of Knowledge," *Analysis* 69, 317–25.
―――― (2009f). "Wright *Contra* McDowell on Perceptual Knowledge and Scepticism," *Synthese* 171, 467–79.
―――― (2010a). "Absurdity, Angst and the Meaning of Life," *Monist* 93, 3–16.
―――― (2010b). "Contemporary Skepticism," *Oxford Bibliographies: Philosophy*, (ed.) D. H. Pritchard, DOI: 10.1093/OBO/9780195396577-0109.
―――― (2010c). "Epistemic Relativism, Epistemic Incommensurability and Wittgensteinian Epistemology," *Blackwell Companion to Relativism*, (ed.) S. Hales, 266–85, Oxford: Blackwell.

——— (2010d). "Relevant Alternatives, Perceptual Knowledge and Discrimination," *Noûs* 44, 245–68.
——— (2011a). "Epistemological Disjunctivism and the Basis Problem," *Philosophical Issues* 21, 434–55.
——— (2011b). "Evidentialism, Internalism, Disjunctivism," *Evidentialism and Its Discontents*, (ed.) T. Dougherty, 362–92, Oxford: Oxford University Press.
——— (2011c). "What Is the Swamping Problem?," *Reasons for Belief*, (eds.) A. Reisner & A. Steglich-Petersen, 244–59, Cambridge: Cambridge University Press.
——— (2011d). "Wittgensteinian Pyrrhonism," *Pyrrhonism in Ancient, Modern, and Contemporary Philosophy*, (ed.) D. Machuca, 193–202, Dordrecht: Springer.
——— (2011e). "Wittgensteinian Quasi-Fideism," *Oxford Studies in the Philosophy of Religion* 4, 145–59.
——— (2011f). "Wittgenstein on Scepticism," *Oxford Handbook on Wittgenstein*, (eds.) O. Kuusela & M. McGinn, 521–47, Oxford: Oxford University Press.
——— (2012a). "Anti-luck Virtue Epistemology," *Journal of Philosophy* 109, 247–79.
——— (2012b). *Epistemological Disjunctivism*, Oxford: Oxford University Press.
——— (2012c). "In Defence of Modest Anti-luck Epistemology," *The Sensitivity Principle in Epistemology*, (eds.) T. Black & K. Becker, 173–92, Cambridge: Cambridge University Press.
——— (2012d). "Two Conceptions of Radical Scepticism," *Ámbitos* 28, 13–20.
——— (2012e). "Wittgenstein and the Groundlessness of Our Believing," *Synthese* 189, 255–72.
——— (2013a). "Davidson on Radical Skepticism," *Blackwell Companion to Donald Davidson*, (eds.) E. LePore & K. Ludwig, 521–33, Oxford: Blackwell.
——— (2013b). "Disagreement, Scepticism, and Track-Record Arguments," *Disagreement and Scepticism*, (ed.) D. Machuca, 150–68, London: Routledge.
——— (2013c). "There Cannot Be Lucky Knowledge," *Contemporary Debates in Epistemology* (2nd Edn.), (eds.) M. Steup & J. Turri, 152–63, Oxford: Blackwell.
——— (2014a). "Entitlement and the Groundlessness of Our Believing," *Contemporary Perspectives on Scepticism and Perceptual Justification*, (eds.) D. Dodd & E. Zardini, 190–212, Oxford: Oxford University Press.
——— (2014b). "The Modal Account of Luck," *Metaphilosophy* 45, 594–619.
——— (2014c). "Sceptical Intuitions," *Intuitions*, (eds.) D. Rowbottom & T. Booth, 213–31, Oxford: Oxford University Press.
——— (2014d). "Truth as the Fundamental Epistemic Good," *The Ethics of Belief: Individual and Social*, (eds.) J. Matheson & R. Vitz, 112–29, Oxford: Oxford University Press.
——— (2015). "Risk," manuscript.
——— (Forthcoming–a). "Anti-luck Epistemology and the Gettier Problem," *Philosophical Studies*.
——— (Forthcoming–b). "Responses to My Critics," *Journal of Philosophical Research*.

Pritchard, D. H. (Forthcoming–c). "Wittgenstein on Faith and Reason: The Influence of Newman," *God, Truth and Other Enigmas*, (ed.) M. Szatkowski, Berlin: Walter de Gruyter.
——— (Forthcoming–d). "Wittgenstein on Hinges and Radical Scepticism in *On Certainty*," *Blackwell Companion to Wittgenstein*, (eds.) H.-J. Glock & J. Hyman, Oxford: Blackwell.
Pritchard, D. H., Millar, A., & Haddock, A. (2010). *The Nature and Value of Knowledge: Three Investigations*, Oxford: Oxford University Press.
Pritchard, D. H., & Ranalli, C. (Forthcoming–a). "On Metaepistemological Scepticism," *Traditional Epistemic Internalism*, (eds.) M. Bergmann & B. Coppenger, Oxford: Oxford University Press.
——— (Forthcoming–b). "Skepticism and Disjunctivism," *Skepticism: From Antiquity to the Present*, (eds.) D. Machuca & B. Reed, London: Continuum.
——— (2013). "Rorty, Williams and Davidson: Skepticism and Metaepistemology," *Humanities* 2, 351–68.
Pryor, J. (2000). "The Skeptic and the Dogmatist," *Noûs* 34, 517–49.
——— (2001). "Highlights of Recent Epistemology," *British Journal for the Philosophy of Science* 52, 95–124.
——— (2004). "Is Moore's Argument an Example of Transmission Failure?," *Philosophical Issues* 14, 349–78.
——— (2012). "When Warrant Transmits," *Mind, Meaning, and Knowledge: Themes from the Philosophy of Crispin Wright*, (ed.) A. Coliva, 269–303, Oxford: Oxford University Press.
Putnam, H. (1981). *Reason, Truth, and History*, Cambridge: Cambridge University Press.
——— (1998). "Strawson and Skepticism," *The Philosophy of P. F. Strawson*, (ed.) L. E. Hahn, 273–87, Chicago: Open Court.
——— (1999). *The Threefold Chord*, New York: Columbia University Press.
——— (2001). "Skepticism, Stroud and the Contextuality of Knowledge," *Philosophical Explorations* 4, 2–16.
——— (2006). "Philosophy as the Education of Grown-Ups: Stanley Cavell and Skepticism," *Reading Cavell*, (eds.) A. Crary & S. Shieh, 119–30, London: Routledge.
——— (2012). "Skepticism and Occasion-Sensitive Semantics," in his *Philosophy in an Age of Science: Physics, Mathematics and Skepticism*, (eds.) M. De Caro & D. Macarthur, 514–34, Cambridge, MA: Harvard University Press.
Radford, C. (1966). "Knowledge—By Examples," *Analysis* 27, 1–11.
Ranalli, C. (2014). "Luck, Propositional Perception, and the Entailment Thesis," *Synthese* 191, 1223–47.
Ribeiro, B. (2002). "Cartesian Skepticism and the Epistemic Priority Thesis," *Southern Journal of Philosophy* 40, 573–86.
Rickless, S. C. (Forthcoming). "The Contrast-Insensitivity of Knowledge Ascriptions," *Philosophy and Phenomenological Research*.
Rieber, S. (1998). "Skepticism and Contrastive Explanation," *Noûs* 32, 189–204.
Rorty, R. (1986). "Pragmatism, Davidson and Truth," *Truth and Interpretation: Perspectives on the Philosophy of Donald Davidson*, (ed.) E. LePore, 333–55, Oxford: Blackwell.

——— (1997). "Comments on Michael Williams's *Unnatural Doubts*," *Journal of Philosophical Research* 22, 1–10.
Ruben, D. H. (2008). "Disjunctive Theories of Perception and Action," *Disjunctivism: Perception, Action, Knowledge*, (eds.) A. Haddock & F. Macpherson, 227–43, Oxford: Oxford University Press.
Russell, B. (1921). *The Analysis of Mind*, London: George Allen & Unwin.
Rysiew, P. (2011a). "Contextualism," *Routledge Companion to Epistemology*, (eds.) S. Bernecker & D. H. Pritchard, 523–35, London: Routledge.
——— (2011b). "Epistemic Contextualism," *Stanford Encyclopedia of Philosophy*, (ed.) E. Zalta, http://plato.stanford.edu/entries/contextualism-epistemology/.
Sainsbury, R. M. (1997). "Easy Possibilities," *Philosophy and Phenomenological Research* 57, 907–19.
Schaffer, J. (2004). "From Contextualism to Contrastivism," *Philosophical Studies* 119, 73–104.
——— (2005). "Contrastive Knowledge," *Oxford Studies in Epistemology*, (eds.) T. Gendler & J. Hawthorne, Oxford: Oxford University Press.
——— (2007). "Closure, Contrast, and Answer," *Philosophical Studies* 133, 233–55.
——— (2008). "The Contrast-Sensitivity of Knowledge Ascriptions," *Social Epistemology* 22, 235–45.
Schiffer, S. (1996). "Contextualist Solutions to Skepticism," *Proceedings of the Aristotelian Society* (new series) 96, 317–33.
Schönbaumsfeld, G. (2013). "McDowellian Neo-Mooreanism?," *International Journal for the Study of Skepticism* 3, 201–17.
Shah, N. (2003). "How Truth Governs Belief," *Philosophical Review* 112, 447–83.
Shah, N., & Velleman, D. (2005). "Doxastic Deliberation," *Philosophical Review* 114, 497–534.
Shieh, S. (2006). "The Truth in Skepticism," *Reading Cavell*, (eds.) A. Crary & S. Shieh, 131–65, London: Routledge.
Sider, T. (2011). *Writing the Book of the World*, Oxford: Oxford University Press.
Silins, N. (2008). "Basic Justification and the Moorean Response to the Skeptic," *Oxford Studies in Epistemology* 2, 108–40.
Sinnott-Armstrong, W. (2006). *Moral Skepticisms*, New York: Oxford University Press.
Snowdon, P. (1980–81). "Perception, Vision and Causation," *Proceedings of the Aristotelian Society* (new series) 81, 175–92.
——— (1990–91). "The Objects of Perceptual Experience," *Proceedings of the Aristotelian Society* (suppl. vol.) 64, 121–50.
——— (2005). "The Formulation of Disjunctivism: A Response to Fish," *Proceedings of the Aristotelian Society* 105, 129–41.
——— (2008). "Hinton and the Origins of Disjunctivism," *Disjunctivism: Perception, Action, Knowledge*, (eds.) A. Haddock & F. Macpherson, 35–56, Oxford: Oxford University Press.
Sorensen, R. (1988). *Blindspots*, Oxford: Clarendon.
——— (2002). "Formal Problems in Epistemology," *The Handbook of Epistemology*, P. Moser (ed.), 539–68, Oxford: Oxford University Press.

Sorensen, R. (2011). "Epistemic Paradoxes," *Stanford Encyclopedia of Philosophy*, (ed.) E. Zalta, http://plato.stanford.edu/entries/epistemic-paradoxes/.
Sosa, E. (1988). "Beyond Skepticism, to the Best of Our Knowledge," *Mind* 97, 153–89.
———— (1991). *Knowledge in Perspective: Selected Essays in Epistemology*, Cambridge: Cambridge University Press.
———— (1998). "P. F. Strawson's Epistemological Naturalism," *The Philosophy of P. F. Strawson*, (ed.) L. E. Hahn, 361–69, Chicago: Open Court.
———— (1999). "How to Defeat Opposition to Moore," *Philosophical Perspectives* 13, 141–54.
———— (2000). "Skepticism and Contextualism," *Philosophical Issues* 10, 1–18.
———— (2003). *Epistemic Justification: Internalism vs. Externalism, Foundations vs. Virtues*, Oxford: Blackwell.
———— (2007). *A Virtue Epistemology: Apt Belief and Reflective Knowledge*, Oxford: Oxford University Press.
———— (2009). *Reflective Knowledge: Apt Belief and Reflective Knowledge*, Oxford: Clarendon.
———— (2011). *Knowing Full Well*, Princeton, NJ: Princeton University Press.
Soteriou, M. (2009). "The Disjunctive Theory of Perception," *Stanford Encyclopedia of Philosophy*, (ed.) E. Zalta, http://plato.stanford.edu/entries/perception-disjunctive/.
Stalnaker, R. (1968). "A Theory of Conditionals," *Studies in Logical Theory*, (ed.) N. Rescher, 98–112, Oxford: Blackwell.
Stanley, J. (2005). *Knowledge and Practical Interests*, Oxford: Clarendon.
Stern, R. (2003). "On Strawson's Naturalistic Turn," *Strawson and Kant*, (ed.) H.-J. Glock, 219–34, Oxford: Oxford University Press.
Steup, M. (1999). "A Defense of Internalism," *The Theory of Knowledge: Classical and Contemporary Readings* (3rd Edn.), (ed.) L. Pojman, 310–21, Belmont, CA: Wadsworth.
———— (2009). "Are Mental States Luminous?," *Williamson on Knowledge*, (eds.) P. Greenough & D. H. Pritchard, 217–36, Oxford: Oxford University Press.
Stevenson, L. (2002). "Six Levels of Mentality," *Philosophical Explorations* 5, 105–24.
Stine, G. (1976). "Skepticism, Relevant Alternatives, and Deductive Closure," *Philosophical Studies* 29, 249–61.
Strawson, P. F. (1959) *Individuals: An Essay in Descriptive Metaphysics*, London: Methuen.
———— (1974). "Causation in Perception," in his *Freedom and Resentment*, 73–93, London: Methuen.
———— (1985). *Skepticism and Naturalism: Some Varieties*, New York: Columbia University Press.
———— (1998a). "Reply to Hilary Putnam," *The Philosophy of P. F. Strawson*, (ed.) L. E. Hahn, 288–92, Chicago: Open Court.
———— (1998b). "Reply to Ernest Sosa," *The Philosophy of P. F. Strawson*, (ed.) L. E. Hahn, 370–72, Chicago: Open Court.
Stroll, A. (1994). *Moore and Wittgenstein on Certainty*, Oxford: Oxford University Press.

——— (2005). "Why *On Certainty* Matters," *Investigating* On Certainty*: Essays on Wittgenstein's Last Work*, (eds.) D. Moyal-Sharrock & W. H. Brenner, 33–46, London: Palgrave Macmillan.
Stroud, B. (1984). *The Significance of Philosophical Scepticism*, Oxford: Clarendon.
——— (1994). "Scepticism, 'Externalism,' and the Goal of Epistemology," *Proceedings of the Aristotelian Society* (suppl. vol.) 68, 290–307.
——— (1999). "Radical Interpretation and Philosophical Scepticism," *The Philosophy of Donald Davidson*, (ed.) L. E. Hahn, 131–61, Chicago: Open Court.
——— (2002). "Sense-Experience and the Grounding of Thought," *Reading McDowell: On Mind and World*, (ed.) N. H. Smith, 79–91, London: Routledge.
Sturgeon, S. (2006). "Reflective Disjunctivism," *Proceedings of the Aristotelian Society* (suppl. vol.) 80, 185–216.
Tanesini, A. (2004). *Wittgenstein: A Feminist Interpretation*, London: Polity.
Tennant, N. (2009). "Cognitive Phenomenology, Semantic Qualia," *Williamson on Knowledge*, (eds.) P. Greenough & D. H. Pritchard, 237–56, Oxford: Oxford University Press.
Thomas, A. (Forthcoming). "McDowell on Transcendental Arguments, Scepticism and 'Error Theory,'" *International Journal for the Study of Skepticism*.
Travis, C. (1989). *The Uses of Sense: Wittgenstein's Philosophy of Language*, Oxford: Oxford University Press.
——— (1997). "Pragmatics," *A Companion to the Philosophy of Language*, (eds.) B. Hale & C. J. G. Wright, 87–107, Oxford: Blackwell.
——— (2001). *Unshadowed Thought: Representation in Thought and Language*, Cambridge, MA: Harvard University Press.
——— (2004). "The Silence of the Senses," *Mind* 113, 57–94.
——— (2005a). "The Face of Perception," *Hilary Putnam*, (ed.) Y. Ben-Menahem, 53–82, Cambridge: Cambridge University Press.
——— (2005b). "A Sense of Occasion," *Philosophical Quarterly* 55, 286–314.
——— (2006). *Thought's Footing: A Theme in Wittgenstein's Philosophical Investigations*, Oxford: Oxford University Press.
——— (2008). *Occasion-Sensitivity: Selected Essays*, Oxford: Oxford University Press.
Treanor, N. (2013). "The Measure of Knowledge," *Noûs* 47, 577–601.
——— (2014). "Trivial Truths and the Aim of Inquiry," *Philosophy and Phenomenological Research* 89, 552–59.
Tucker, C. (ed.) (2013). *Seemings and Justification: New Essays on Dogmatism and Phenomenal Conservatism*, Oxford: Oxford University Press.
Turri, J. (2010). "Does Perceiving Entail Knowing?," *Theoria* 76, 197–206.
Unger, P. (1968). "An Analysis of Factual Knowledge," *Journal of Philosophy* 65, 157–70.
Vermazen, B. (1983). "The Intelligibility of Massive Error," *Philosophical Quarterly* 33, 69–74.
Vogel, J. (1990). "Cartesian Skepticism and Inference to the Best Explanation," *Journal of Philosophy* 87, 658–66.
——— (1997). "Skepticism and Foundationalism: A Reply to Michael Williams," *Journal of Philosophical Research* 22, 11–28.
——— (2004). "Skeptical Arguments," *Philosophical Issues* 14, 426–55.

Vogel, J. (2005). "The Refutation of Skepticism," *Contemporary Debates in Epistemology*, (eds.) E. Sosa & M. Steup, 72–84, Oxford: Blackwell.
Wedgwood, R. (2002). "The Aim of Belief," *Philosophical Perspectives* 16, 268–97.
Weiner, M. (2005). "Must We Know What We Say?," *Philosophical Review* 114, 227–51.
—— (2007). "Norms of Assertion," *Philosophy Compass* 2, 187–95.
—— (2011). "Assertion," *Oxford Bibliographies: Philosophy*, (ed.) D. H. Pritchard, DOI: 10.1093/OBO/9780195396577-0148.
White, R. (2006). "Problems for Dogmatism," *Philosophical Studies* 131, 525–57.
Williams, M. (1977). *Groundless Belief: An Essay on the Possibility of Epistemology*, Princeton, NJ: Princeton University Press.
—— (1988a). "Epistemological Realism and the Basis of Scepticism," *Mind* 97, 415–39.
—— (1988b). "Scepticism and Charity," *Ratio* 1, 176–94.
—— (1991). *Unnatural Doubts: Epistemological Realism and the Basis of Scepticism*, Oxford: Blackwell.
—— (1993). "The Unreality of Knowledge," *Canadian Journal of Philosophy* 23, 265–93.
—— (1997). "Still Unnatural: A Reply to Vogel and Rorty," *Journal of Philosophical Research* 22, 29–39.
—— (2001a). "Contextualism, Externalism and Epistemic Standards," *Philosophical Studies* 103, 1–23.
—— (2001b). *Problems of Knowledge: A Critical Introduction to Epistemology*, Oxford: Oxford University Press.
—— (2004a). "Context, Meaning, and Truth," *Philosophical Studies* 117, 107–30.
—— (2004b). "Knowledge, Reflection and Sceptical Hypotheses," *Erkenntnis* 61, 315–43.
—— (2004c). "Scepticism and the Context of Philosophy," *Philosophical Issues* 14, 456–75.
—— (2004d). "Wittgenstein's Refutation of Idealism," *Wittgenstein and Scepticism*, (ed.) D. McManus, 76–96, London: Routledge.
—— (2006). "Science and Sensibility: McDowell and Sellars on Perceptual Experience," *European Journal of Philosophy* 14, 302–25.
—— (2007). "Why (Wittgensteinian) Contextualism Is Not Relativism," *Episteme* 4, 93–114.
—— (2010). "Self-Profile: Michael Williams," *A Companion to Epistemology* (2nd Edn.), (eds.) J. Dancy, E. Sosa, & M. Steup, 194–99, Oxford, Blackwell.
—— (2012). "Wright Against the Sceptics," *Mind, Meaning, and Knowledge: Themes from the Philosophy of Crispin Wright*, (ed.) A. Coliva, 352–76, Oxford: Oxford University Press.
—— (2013). "Skepticism, Evidence and Entitlement," *Philosophy and Phenomenological Research* 87, 36–71.
Williamson, T. (1995). "Is Knowledge a State of Mind?," *Mind* 104, 533–65.
—— (1996a). "Cognitive Homelessness," *Journal of Philosophy* 93, 554–73.
—— (1996b). "Knowing and Asserting," *Philosophical Review* 105, 489–523.

——— (2000a). *Knowledge and Its Limits*, Oxford: Oxford University Press.
——— (2000b). "Scepticism and Evidence," *Philosophy and Phenomenological Research* 60, 613–28.
——— (2009). "Replies to My Critics," *Williamson on Knowledge*, (eds.) P. Greenough & D. H. Pritchard, 279–384, Oxford: Oxford University Press.
Wittgenstein, L. (1953). *Philosophical Investigations*, (eds.) G. E. M. Anscombe & R. Rhees, (tr.) G. E. M. Anscombe, Oxford: Blackwell.
——— (1966). *Wittgenstein's Lectures and Conversations on Aesthetics, Psychology and Religious Belief*, (ed.) C. Barrett, Oxford: Basil Blackwell.
——— (1969). *On Certainty*, (eds.) G. E. M. Anscombe & G. H. von Wright, (tr.) D. Paul & G. E. M. Anscombe, Oxford: Blackwell.
Wright, C. J. G. (1985). "Facts and Certainty," *Proceedings of the British Academy* 71, 429–72.
——— (1991). "Scepticism and Dreaming: Imploding the Demon," *Mind* 397, 87–115.
——— (1996). "Human Nature?," *European Journal of Philosophy* 4, 235–53.
——— (2000). "Cogency and Question-Begging: Some Reflections on McKinsey's Paradox and Putnam's Proof," *Philosophical Issues* 10, 140–63.
——— (2002). "(Anti-)Skeptics Simple and Subtle: G. E. Moore and John McDowell," *Philosophy and Phenomenological Research* 65, 330–48.
——— (2003a). "Some Reflections on the Acquisition of Warrant by Inference," *New Essays on Semantic Externalism and Self-Knowledge*, (ed.) S. Nuccetelli, 57–78, Cambridge, MA: MIT Press.
——— (2003b). "Wittgensteinian Certainties," *Wittgenstein and Scepticism*, (ed.) D. McManus, 22–55, London: Routledge.
——— (2004a). "Hinge Propositions and the Serenity Prayer," *Knowledge and Belief*, (eds.) W. Loffler & P. Weingartner, 287–306, Vienna: Holder-Pickler-Tempsky.
——— (2004b). "Scepticism, Certainty, Moore and Wittgenstein," *Wittgenstein's Lasting Significance*, (eds.) M. Kolbel & B. Weiss, 228–48, London: Routledge.
——— (2004c). "Warrant for Nothing (and Foundations for Free)?," *Proceedings of the Aristotelian Society* (supp. vol.) 78, 167–212.
——— (2007). "The Perils of Dogmatism," *Themes from G. E. Moore: New Essays in Epistemology and Ethics*, (eds.) S. Nuccetelli & G. Seay, 25–48, Oxford: Oxford University Press.
——— (2008a). "Comment on John McDowell's 'The Disjunctive Conception of Experience as Material for a Transcendental Argument,'" *Disjunctivism: Perception, Action and Knowledge*, (eds.) A. Haddock & F. Macpherson, 390–404, Oxford: Oxford University Press.
——— (2008b). "Internal-External: Doxastic Norms and the Defusing of Skeptical Paradox," *Journal of Philosophy* 105, 501–17.
Yalçin, Ü. (1992). "Sceptical Arguments from Underdetermination," *Philosophical Studies* 68, 1–34.
Zagzebski, L. (1996). *Virtues of the Mind: An Inquiry into the Nature of Virtue and the Ethical Foundations of Knowledge*, Cambridge: Cambridge University Press.

Zalabardo, J. (2012). "Wright on Moore," *Mind, Meaning, and Knowledge: Themes from the Philosophy of Crispin Wright*, (ed.) A. Coliva, 304–22, Oxford: Oxford University Press.
——— (Forthcoming). "Epistemic Disjunctivism and the Evidential Problem," *Analysis*.

Index

Abductivism, 25–28, 193, 194
Accessibilism, 192, 209
Adler, J., 193
Aliefs, 204, 205, 215
Altschul, J., 200
Annis, D. B., 206
Attributer contextualism, 36–46, 103, 144–52, 164, 179, 195, 196, 199, 205, 206, 211, 212
Austin, J. L., 68–69, 149, 199, 202
Axtell, G. 200

Bach, K., 198
Baldwin, T., 199
Beebe, J. R., 194
Beebee, H., 190
Bett, R., 190
Black, T., 193, 195
BonJour, L., 192, 194
Boult, C., 214
Brady, M. S., 195
Brogaard, B., 209
Brueckner, A., 190, 192, 194, 208
Burge, T., 200
Byrne, A., 194, 207, 209

Campbell, J., 205
Carter, J. A., 193, 199, 210
Cassam, Q., 192, 207, 209
Cavell, S., 9, 189, 214, 215
Charity, principle of, 199
Chignel, A., 190
Chisholm, R. M., 190, 192, 209
Christensen, D. 197
Clarke, T., vii, 212, 215
Closure principle, 3–6, 11–28, 29–32, 33, 36, 38–50, 53–60, 63, 72–81, 84, 86–88, 89, 91–94, 98–103, 111, 114–16, 118–19, 123, 143, 144, 152, 155, 157–59, 161–66, 169–84, 191, 192, 193, 194, 195, 196, 197, 200, 204, 206, 208, 213, 214
Cohen, S., 194, 195, 198
Coliva, A., 200, 201, 202, 203, 205
Collins, J., 192, 204
Conant, J., 189, 190, 202, 203
Conee, E., 192

Contrastivism, 153–57, 164–65, 182–83, 212, 213

David, M., 191
Davidson, D., 110, 112–13, 199, 208
Davies, M., 193, 200
DeRose, K., 14, 42, 76, 191, 195, 200
Descartes, R., 9, 189, 204
Dogmatism, 157–60, 163, 165, 183–84, 201, 213
Dogmatism, paradox of, 210, 211
Dorsch, F., 209
Douven, I,. 193
Dretske, F., 192, 209, 210

Engel, M., 198
Entitlement, 77–84, 88, 89, 92, 158, 192, 200, 201, 207, 208
Epistemic priority, 103–5, 116–18, 181–82, 206
Epistemic relativism, 109–10, 199, 200, 204, 206, 207
Epsitemic vertigo, 6–7, 184–88, 214, 215
Epistemological disjunctivism, 2–5, 121–66, 175–84, 196, 208, 209, 210, 211, 212, 213

Favoring/discriminating epistemic support, 132, 136–43, 155–63, 182–83, 210
Feldman, R., 192, 196
Fish, W., 209
Fogelin, R., 190
Foley, R., 208
Forster, M. N., 190
French, C., 209
Fumerton, R., 194, 208

Gascoigne, N., 190
Gaukroger, S., 190
Gendler, T. S., 205, 215
Goldberg, S., 211
Goldman, A., 193, 200
Greco, J., 182
Grice, H. P., 191

Haddock, A., 199, 209
Harman, G., 211

Hawthorne, J., 191, 192, 204, 209
Hazlett, A., 190, 203
Heidegger, M., 10, 215
Heller, M., 195
Hinge commitments, 4–7, 66, 69, 71–81, 85–88, 89–119, 158, 173–76, 180–83, 187, 189, 199, 202, 204, 205, 206, 207, 211, 212, 213, 214, 215
Hinton, J. M., 209
Huemer, M., 213
Hughes, M., 213, 214
Hume, D., 110–11, 189, 190

Inferential contextualism, 103–10, 116, 181–82, 205, 206, 207, 212, 213

Jenkins, C., 200
Johnsen, B., 212

Kant, I., 1, 93, 167, 189, 190
Kaplan, M., 197, 199
Kelp, C., 204
Klein, P., 193
Kornblith, H., 196
Kovakovich, K., 209
Kripke, S., 211
Kusch, M., 200
Kvanvig, J. L., 192, 213, 214
Kyburg, H. E., 197

Lawlor, K., 199
Lehrer, K., 198
Lewis, D., 195
Lipton, P., 193
Littlejohn, C., 198, 210, 211
Logue, H., 209
Longworth, G., 199
Lottery puzzle, 197
Ludwig, K., 208
Luper, S., 190, 192

Macpherson, F., 209
Machuca, D., 190
Makinson, D. C., 197
Martin, M. G. F., 209
Matheson, J., 203
McDowell, J., 1, 118–19, 121, 123, 190, 209, 210, 212
McGinn, M., 201, 202
McGrath, M., 213
McKinsey, M., 129, 210

McLear, C., 190
Mandelbaum, E., 205, 215
Mentalism, 192
Metaphysical disjunctivism, 208, 209, 210
Millar, A., 189, 199, 202, 209
Minar, E., 215
Moore, G. E., 21, 63–70, 85–86, 153, 193, 199, 201–2
Mooreanism/neo–Mooreanism, 1–2, 4, 21, 24, 33, 39–40, 42, 73–77, 89, 107, 153, 158, 174, 193, 195, 202
Moyal-Sharrock, D., 201, 203

Nagel, J., 205
Nagel, T., 215
Neta, R., 147–48, 194, 196, 201, 209, 210, 211, 212, 213
Newman, J. H., 61, 207
New evil demon, 55–56, 59, 124–25, 133–34, 142, 159, 172, 198, 209
Nielsen, K., 207
Nozick, R., 192, 199
Nuccetelli, S., 210

Overriding/undercutting anti-skeptical strategies, 4–5, 16–28, 32–46, 58–60, 63, 67–70, 75–76, 79, 87–88, 103, 111–12, 113, 134–36, 142, 144, 151–52, 157, 172, 178–80, 185–86, 192, 194

Pappas, G., 192
Peacocke, C., 200
Pedersen, N. J., 200, 204
Phillips, D. Z., 201, 207
Plant, B., 207
Poston, T., 192
Preface paradox, 197
Pritchard, D. H., 3, 189, 190, 192, 193, 194, 195, 196, 197, 199, 200, 201, 203, 204, 205, 206, 207, 208, 209, 210, 211, 212, 213, 214, 215
Process reliabilism, 20, 193, 200
Pryor, J., 157, 192, 200, 201, 213
Putnam, H., 190, 202, 207, 214

Radford, C., 201
Ranalli, C., 204, 205, 208, 210
Rational support contextualism, 144–52, 163–64, 179–81, 196, 199, 212, 213
Ribeiro, B., 206
Rickless, S., C. 213

Rieber, S., 212
Rorty, R., 205, 208
Russell, B., 199
Rysiew, P., 195, 196

Schaffer, J., 153, 196, 212, 213, 214
Schiffer, S., 192, 196
Shah, N., 203
Shieh, S., 214
Sider, T., 203
Silins, N., 213
Snowdon, P., 209
Sorensen, R., 197, 211
Sosa, E., 190, 193, 196, 200, 201, 204, 207, 209
Soteriou, M., 209
Stanley, J., 196
Steup, M., 192
Stevenson, L., 201, 205
Strawson, P. F., 110–12, 203, 207, 208, 209
Stroll, A., 201
Stroud. B., 69, 149, 191, 199, 204, 208, 215
Sturgeon, S., 209

Tanesini, A., 203
Transmission principle, 193, 200
Travis, C., 199, 202
Treanor, N., 203
Tucker, C., 213
Turri, J., 209

Underdetermination principle, 3–6, 29–60, 63, 105, 113–19, 123, 132–37, 141–43, 144–52, 157–58, 161–63, 166, 170–72, 176–82, 194, 196, 198, 206, 207, 208

Velleman, D., 203
Vermazen, B., 208
Virtue epistemology, 77, 200
Vitz, R., 203
Vogel, J., 193, 194, 205

Warfield, T., 191
Wedgwood, R., 203
White, R., 213
Williams, M., 103–10, 112, 116–18, 190, 192, 195, 199, 200, 201, 202, 203, 204, 205, 206, 207, 208, 212, 213, 215
Williamson, T., 191, 201, 209
Wittgenstein, L., 1–6, 9, 61, 63–74, 77, 84–88, 89–98, 100–103, 105–6, 108–19, 123, 149, 166, 167, 173–78, 180–85, 187, 189, 192, 199, 200, 201, 202, 203, 204, 205, 206, 207, 208, 211, 212, 213, 214, 215
Wright, C. J. G., 79, 81–84, 191, 192, 193, 200, 201, 203, 204, 208, 213

Yalçin, Ü., 194

Zalabardo, J., 200, 211

GPSR Authorized Representative: Easy Access System Europe - Mustamäe tee
50, 10621 Tallinn, Estonia, gpsr.requests@easproject.com

www.ingramcontent.com/pod-product-compliance
Lightning Source LLC
Chambersburg PA
CBHW030618230426
43661CB00053B/2046